RICE UNIVERSITY

SEMICENTENNIAL PUBLICATIONS

Literary Views
CRITICAL AND HISTORICAL ESSAYS

EDITOR

Charles CARROLL CAMDEN

CONTRIBUTORS

HARRY LEVIN

ARTHUR E. BARKER

FREDSON BOWERS

BERTRAND H. BRONSON

FREDERICK A. POTTLE

LIONEL TRILLING

PERRY MILLER

LOUIS B. WRIGHT

NORTHROP FRYE

WILLARD THORP

RENÉ WELLEK

Literary

Views

CRITICAL AND HISTORICAL ESSAYS

Access. No. 95910

PUBLISHED FOR

WILLIAM MARSH RICE UNIVERSITY

BY

THE UNIVERSITY OF CHICAGO PRESS

Library of Congress Catalog Card Number: 64-13715

THE UNIVERSITY OF CHICAGO PRESS, CHICAGO & LONDON
The University of Toronto Press, Toronto 5, Canada

Introduction

T HE ESSAYS included in this volume were originally presented as lectures sponsored by the Department of English at Rice University during the year of its semicentennial celebration, 1962–1963. The purpose of the editor was to bring together a series of essays which would illustrate various ways of looking at literature, and at the same time would give the literary public an opportunity of examining the work of some of the best-known scholars, critics, and essayists of our time. Scholarship has its own fashions, and though its styles do not change rapidly, nevertheless they do change. With scholarship, indeed, it is obvious that many modes of literary analysis may and do continue side by side.

As would be expected in a volume devoted essentially to value judgments, there is something less than unanimity among the various contributors to this volume. Superficially the essays may seem to have some links. Both Mr. Frye and Mr. Wright speak of culture and anarchy; but one is relating Matthew Arnold's work to nineteenth-century concepts of spiritual authority, while the other is simply utilizing the words of Arnold's title to describe a situation on the American frontiers. Again, one might suppose that when Mr. Frye mentions William Morris's *News from Nowhere* he has in mind some of the thoughts which prompted Mr. Trilling to discuss Dostoevsky's *Notes from Underground*. But of course Mr. Frye is writing of the source of spiritual authority in Morris, while Mr. Trilling is using Dostoevsky's book as an illustration of the point that in our own time it seems possible to derive some form of gratification from "unpleasure."

Mr. Barker approves of Mr. Levin's refusal to follow the simplifications of cultural historians who emphasize the cyclical periodicity of history; and he also endorses Mr. Levin's suggestion that the response to humanist and Christian-humanist rhetoric varied greatly, and that there was all the difference in the world between this response in major writers and that in their lesser fellows. But Mr. Barker disparages Mr. Wellek's argument that Sidney's *Defence* is typical of the self-contradiction of the English Renaissance because it is derivative of Italian aesthetics and merely the "casually ironic apology made by a minor poet." Mr. Wellek, in his turn, seems somewhat surprised at Mr. Trilling's support of F. R. Leavis in the Snow controversy, though happy at his rejection of Leavis's "unexampled ferocity." And Mr. Thorp takes exception to Mr. Frye's concept of the archetypal method of critical analysis. On the other hand Mr. Thorp uses Mr. Miller's introduction to an edition of Thoreau's notebook as an example of how Freudian notions can successfully be brought to bear on literary problems as Mr. Miller found in the notebook evidence to explain Thoreau's pride in his chastity, his attitude toward women, and his reclusiveness. Mr. Wright's essay links both with Mr. Miller's essay on the Transcendentalists, who turned to nature from the mechanism which they considered a corrupting influence in America, and with Frye's essay on spiritual authority emphasizing that we must look to the universities for our higher loyalties; for Mr. Wright firmly believes that the battle between the humanistic tradition and our crassly materialistic and expedient society still continues on our own frontier.

The use of mythology in literary analysis is exemplified in Mr. Levin's essay, even though he does not use his particular myth to derive the structure of any one poem. He shows that the idea of a golden age is related to that of utopia or the good place, the Elysian Fields, the Big Rock Candy Mountain, and is therefore primitive in origin. He indicates that the golden age is an age of peace, plenty, leisure, and eternal spring, usually set in Greece but translated by Virgil to Italy. Mr. Levin traces this concept through the Middle Ages (Chaucer's *Former Age*, and *The Romance of the Rose*) to Torquato Tasso, and relates it to the sixteenth-century pastoral and the golden new world of America. Montaigne is treated extensively and leads easily into reference to Shakespeare. Mr. Levin concludes his essay with Sidney's affirmation that the golden age is the age that poets create from the baser metals of the world of nature.

Using Sidney as a point of departure, Mr. Barker goes on to consider divergent views of the Renaissance and especially of Renaissance poetry. He notes the tensions between classical, medieval, Hebraic, and scientific concepts, and emphasizes his belief that philosophically, ethically, and culturally speaking, the Renaissance was not marked by an organic rebirth but rather by the pangs of these confused tensions. He argues that the tensions, confusions, and bumblings which characterized the last years of Elizabeth's reign can hardly have produced the mood of buoyant optimism which is frequently said to have brought about the burst of literary genius. Nor can the Christian-humanist ethical ideal, even when supported by medieval or Protestant systematic philosophy, scarcely be said to be characteristic of an age which was skeptical on one side, rigidly dogmatic in the middle, and Neo-Platonically idealistic or mystical on the other side.

At the beginning of his essay, Mr. Bowers underscores the point that although Shakespeare's plays are in poetic form, when dramatic structure is neglected for matters of poetic style we no longer have dramatic criticism. His thesis is that many times Shakespeare believes that he is unable to trust to the normal trial-and-error dramatic method by which an audience arrives at a generally accepted collective judgment. At such times the dramatist wants to guide the audience to a particular point of view and an exact response. Whenever it is clear that Shakespeare has used an extraordinary dramatic device to manipulate the point of view of his audience, then the critic must realize that something important is at stake and should look closely into these circumstances.

Mr. Bronson shows the complexities of analyzing folk songs by using "Barbara Allen" as an example, which he considers the best-known of our ballads. He points out that the idea of love as a destructive power is as old as the records of Western civilization, but he surmises that "Barbara Allen" probably dates from the mid-seventeenth century. Mr. Bronson is especially concerned with the variants of both words and tune. He has found four groupings of the song which differ in mode, tune, and scale. In his lecture Mr. Bronson illustrated these variations by playing on a small recorder, and it is to be regretted that we can supply no record which would make the lay reader cognizant of the haunting melodies in the Dorian and Aeolian modes.

Mr. Pottle's revaluation of Boswell is based upon additions to the Boswell canon acquired in recent years by the Yale library. As is well known, these consist chiefly of private journals formerly in Malahide Castle and in Fettercairn House. Mr. Pottle demonstrates that Boswell's journalistic writings are essentially dramatic—not only because of the dialogue structure and the preparations of character which resemble stage directions, but also because Boswell gave "each moment its own proper emotional tone." It is part of Mr. Pottle's thesis that Boswell has not received a fair and just treatment. Although Boswell's *Johnson* would probably be included as one of the ten greatest prose works in English, we are reluctant to include Boswell in a list of the ten greatest prose writers because we seem unsure just how much of the biography is Boswell and how much Johnson. We think of an artist as rearranging experience but think of Boswell as recording events as they happened and in much the same language as that used by the speakers. Yet Boswell did not make on-the-spot recordings of the conversations.

Changing concepts of pleasure in the nineteenth century are the specific concern of Mr. Trilling. With Wordsworth, "the grand elementary principle of pleasure" constitutes "the naked and native dignity of man." His pleasure always moved toward joy, but he was not preoccupied with creature-pleasures as was Keats. In Wordsworth the concept is austerely abstract; in Keats it is voluptuously illicit, even though he seemed to recognize that the erotic life tended toward self-negation—"turning to Poison as the bee-mouth sips." Keats also felt (*Sleep and Poetry*) that though a young poet should write of the pleasures of the senses, in later years he should write of matters more fitting to the gravity of maturity, avoiding distressing scenes since poetry should soothe the cares of life and lift the thoughts. Wordsworth, too, wished to protect the reader and believed that the metrical language of poetry would mitigate the unpleasantness of certain situations. Mr. Trilling finds Keats's ideas somewhat embarrassing and seems to turn with sympathy to Dostoevsky, who more nearly represents the modern (or Trilling's) view of pleasure in saying that gratification can be derived from unpleasure. According to Mr. Trilling, we have devalued the pleasure principle and are not seeking "peace," or "bliss," or another Eden. He sees more spirituality in modern literature and believes that we are developing "an ideal of the experience of those psychic energies which are linked with unpleasure and which are directed toward self-definition and self-affirmation"—Lear's "Who . . . can tell me who I am? . . . I would learn that."

Mr. Miller calls Transcendentalism a "parochial disturbance" of the 1830's and 1840's in New England, but he finds that many of its principles, such as Emerson's "self-reliance," belong to the whole country. Transcendentalism was a movement of protest, especially against the mechanization of America. It may have found its roots in the Romantic movement in Europe (since its followers were devoted to Wordsworth and to the Germans), but it was uniquely American because America lacked an eighteenth century; it had no French Revolution and therefore no unrepentant revolutionaries. The followers of Transcendentalism did not go to Nature as a solace from betrayals but as a source of resistance against the mechanism which was corrupting American civilization; and they therefore "stand for the moral innocence which they identify with Nature."

In discussing culture and anarchy on the frontier, Mr. Wright calls attention to the concern which the early settlers had for education. As early as 1619 ten thousand acres were set aside in Virginia for a university, and a collection of £1,500 was undertaken to support it. In later centuries education was encouraged because it could contribute to the material advancement of the individual. A good bit of Puritanism is simply bourgeois; and the "prudential morality" of colonial America, with its stress upon thrift, diligence, and sobriety, can be traced to middle-class ethics of the sixteenth and seventeenth centuries. It was this morality and philosophy which was epitomized by Ben Franklin in his *Way to Wealth* and other writings. Mr. Wright concludes with a plea for leadership in our own battle of culture with the anarchy of our materialistic society, arguing that only the humanities can provide the leadership necessary to save us from the cheap and tawdry wares of Madison Avenue.

To analyze the state of spiritual authority in the nineteenth century, Mr. Frye begins with illustrations from writers of previous centuries. Milton found spiritual authority in the revelation from God as found in the Gospel. The eighteenth century nurtured the conception of Bolingbroke and Rousseau that spiritual authority is to be found in natural society, since man is a child of nature rather than of God. Burke, on the other hand, found spiritual authority in "a sense of belonging to a social organism whose health is preserved by maintaining a balance of power among the different organs." Samuel Butler seems to find the source of spiritual authority in the aristocracy, as does Carlyle. These deeply conservative writers find that this social organism is linked with the "ideal aristocracy" implied in the word "gentleman." But with William Morris, who was something of a revolutionary, spiritual authority is isolated from society and is confined to a small group repudiating society and repudiated by it. Newman, however, believed that spiritual authority is established in the church, while Arnold found it in "right reason" to which we are led by culture. It is Mr. Frye's belief that the ultimate source of spiritual authority lies in religion and in the churches which guard and interpret its tradition. But in a society like ours, dominated by science and technology, the churches have only a small role in personifying that spiritual authority which society will accept. Mr. Frye concludes with the stirring argument that since real society can only be the world revealed to us through the study of the arts and sciences (that is, the total body of human achievement), we should look to the universities. "Of this world the universities are the social embodiment, and they represent what seems to me today the only visible direction in which our higher loyalties and obligations can go."

If this volume has a theme, it is indicated in the purpose of the editor to bring together essays showing many approaches to literary analysis. Mr. Thorp's essay, then, would lie at the center, since it is specifically concerned with changing styles in literary scholarship and criticism. Mr. Thorp finds that in various periods a variety of methods have been used by literary scholars: philological, historical, appreciative, Freudian, symbolical, mythical, archetypal, Jungian, and the new-critical. He believes that it is good that we have moved from mere appreciation to a technical criticism, but finds two somewhat simliar dangers. One is the tendency of a critic to use one method and exclude all others. The second is the tendency to conclude that if a poem has a symbolic structure there is little need to pay further attention to it. If the right button is pushed, the analysis falls into one's lap.

Perhaps the idea of this volume is made more explicit as Mr. Wellek considers the criticism of F. R. Leavis. He finds that Mr. Leavis is rather limited in his critical likes and dislikes. In poetry Leavis praises Donne, Pope, Wordsworth, Keats, Hopkins, the later Yeats, and T. S. Eliot. Similarly, he approves of the novels of George Eliot, Henry James, Conrad, Lawrence, Hawthorne, and Mark Twain. Mr. Leavis has no use for literary history or scholarship. Mr. Wellek seems quite fair in his appraisal of Leavis, who has attacked Wellek at several points. In essence, Mr. Leavis believes that a poet always has an important social function and should relate his work to the moral bases of society. In summary, Mr. Wellek finds that Mr. Leavis is rather ambiguous and vague in his statement of his critical principles. He shows that Leavis is provincial and insular in his neglect of all literature not English or American. But Mr. Wellek believes that Leavis will find a place in the history of English criticism near that of the "sweeter tempered" Matthew Arnold.

Contents

THE GOLDEN AGE AND THE RENAISSANCE   1
    Harry Levin

AN APOLOGY FOR THE STUDY OF RENAISSANCE POETRY   15
    Arthur E. Barker

SHAKESPEARE'S ART: THE POINT OF VIEW   45
    Fredson Bowers

"ALL THIS FOR A SONG?"   59
    Bertrand H. Bronson

BOSWELL REVALUED   79
    Frederick A. Pottle

THE FATE OF PLEASURE: WORDSWORTH TO DOSTOEVSKY   93
    Lionel Trilling

NEW ENGLAND'S TRANSCENDENTALISM: NATIVE OR IMPORTED?   115
    Perry Miller

CULTURE AND ANARCHY ON THE FRONTIER   131
    Louis B. Wright

THE PROBLEM OF SPIRITUAL AUTHORITY IN THE
NINETEENTH CENTURY   145
    Northrop Frye

THE LITERARY SCHOLAR AS CHAMELEON   159
    Willard Thorp

THE LITERARY CRITICISM OF FRANK RAYMOND LEAVIS   175
    René Wellek

HARRY LEVIN

The Golden Age and the Renaissance

THE READER who turns from his morning paper to literature may
well feel more comfortable with the past than with the present; but,
if he reads very widely or deeply, he knows that any given period of
the past, so long as it was the present, had its discomforts—and probably also had its yearnings for more distant periods. We cannot look
back to an age which did not look back: to time immemorial, to its
primordial forebears, creatures of mythology if not of history. Childhood, as modern storytellers like to remind us, is a sort of golden age,
insofar as it recapitulates the infantile fantasies of the race, its fabulous
memories of once upon a time. What we conjure up is really timeless:
a giant race before the flood, a garden existence before the Fall,
archetypal situations to which man longs to return after so many centuries of more or less painful experience. The Judeo-Christian tradition moves from Paradise Lost to Paradise Regained, from Eden to
Canaan, the land flowing with milk and honey, and hence from retro-
spect to prophecy; it looks forward from Belshazzar's dream and the
monster with head of gold, arms of silver, belly of brass, and feet of
clay, to the second Isaiah and his vision of the lion recumbent with the
lamb or the swords beaten into plowshares, and toward the Apoca-
lypse with its city of gold, the New Jerusalem. And when these visions shift from the past to the future, they harbor terrors as well as
hopes; Antichrist must battle with the Messiah, and Doomsday precede the kingdom of God on earth. However, our main concern is
not millennial but primitivistic; an interest in golden days should lead
us not to ends but to beginnings.

Primitivism was well defined by its closest student, the late Arthur
Lovejoy, as "the discontent of the civilized with civilization." As
those carefully chosen words imply, its positive charge is activated by

HARRY LEVIN is Irving Babbitt Professor of Comparative Literature and Chairman of the Department at Harvard University.

a negative recoil; not only is its praise of the past, its *laus temporis acti*, an implicit criticism of nowadays; but its love of what it fancies to be primitive is essentially a sophisticated—not to say a sentimental—state of mind. "Happy is that man who, far from affairs . . ."

Beatus ille qui procul negotiis. . . .

And, having drawn a sharp alternative between *negotium* and *otium*, business and leisure, Horace continues with a townsman's nostalgic description of the countryside which week-enders and exurbanites have been echoing ever since. The way of life the poet especially envies is the leisure he imagines the shepherd to enjoy, fondly imagining—if we may judge from the vast body of poetry devoted to this subject—that shepherds spend more of their efforts in chasing shepherdesses than sheep. Such nostalgia, like that of the queen playing milkmaid, takes many forms. Some of them have been suggestively analyzed by William Empson in *Some Versions of Pastoral;* a fascinating series of articles by Renato Poggioli promises a more definitive treatment, *The Oaten Flute*. Now the pastoral, as Alexander Pope succinctly described it, is "an image of the Golden Age." It is hard to detach this temporal image from a spatial one. "Utopia," our name for the model of all model kingdoms, means nowhere. Its namer, Sir Thomas More, intended a pun in Greek on "Eutopia," the good place—that happy island, that ideal commonwealth which never existed on land or sea. In much the same way, we may allude to "Uchronia" or "Euchronia" to signify either nowhile or the good time.

You can see how the concept of the good old days is logically related to that of a great good place: a view of then or there from now or here. The landscape varies according to the various cultures that envision it. It shades off imperceptibly into an afterlife: the Elysian Fields or the Fortunate Islands. It springs up again and again in folklore; compare the Land of Cockaigne with the Big Rock Candy Mountain, two similar though quite independent notions of the poor man's heaven. Invariably it projects a collective wishdream of the happiest possible community, of the good life far away and long ago. The denizens of the Golden Age, as Erasmus wrote in his elaborate treatise on simplicity, *The Praise of Folly*, were simple people who lived according to nature and instinct. The Greek tradition, which goes back to the very oldest writers, represents them living in peace and plenty under the reign of Chronos. Then, when Zeus and the gods of Olympus overthrew the Titans, came the Silver Age; and strife and care accumulated through the Age of Brass—the next generation—into the Age of Iron, until Astrea, the maiden goddess of justice, left the earth to dwell in the zodiac under the sign of Virgo. This is where we come in, acutely conscious of the long-range contrast between iron and gold, between an uncomfortable present and a mythical past. The myth, in its classical form, has been richly documented by Professors Lovejoy and Boas, with their *History of Primitivism and Related Ideas*. Since only the first volume of that fine work has ever appeared, alas, we shall be on our own as soon as we depart from antiquity. But first I must mention two or three Latin texts, since we must fix the theme in mind to appreciate the variations later played upon it.

The canonical account—I suppose I may term it the *locus classicus*—occurs near the beginning of that most fruitful of literary sources, Ovid's mythological compendium, *The Metamorphoses*.

> The Golden Age was first, which uncompelled,
> And without rule, in faith and truth excelled. . . .

So it begins in the early sevententh-century translation of George Sandys. Ovid puts "uncompelled" more affirmatively ("sua sponte"), as opposed to "without rule" ("sine lege"), and goes on to stress the absence of warfare as well as law—somewhat negativistically, since this implies their presence at the moment the poet is writing. The key word seems to be *nondum*: not yet were men constrained to face the evils of civilization so-called.

> To visit other worlds no wounded pine
> Did yet from hills to faithless seas decline.

Here the pine becomes by synecdoche a mast and thence a ship, and it seems to have been victimized in the process. There is as yet no navigation, and consequently no trade. There is no agriculture; the earth yields its crop—mostly acorns, the fruit of Jove's tree, the oak—spontaneously, *sua sponte*. No plow wounds the soil—and that pejorative verb becomes a stock expression which we encounter repeatedly. Similarly, the ilex or holm-oak exudes or sweats honey; and, of course, the rivers flow with milk. As for the weather, it was eternal spring: "ver erat aeternum." The Age of Silver would bring in the other seasons and crucially winter, just as in the biblical story, where that is the price paid for the expulsion from Eden after the Fall; "the season's difference," for Shakespeare, is "the penalty of Adam."

The Brazen Age is worse, and the Iron Age is worst. In recounting how the land was subdivided, and how the soil was originally shared before it was parceled out, the poet harks back rather more positively to the primeval stage. His phrase, "communemque prius," corresponds to words which are used in most English versions, "all things in common," and which may be traced to a Wycliffite sermon propounding a kind of Christian socialism. Another verbal twist figures in this connection: the statement that there was no distinction between *meum* and *tuum,* in phraseology to recur in the Vulgate, no demarcation between mine and thine, no invidious sense of property. Even more of a desecration is mining; to delve in the earth was to flout a taboo against forbidden knowledge, to pry too audaciously into nature's secrets: "Curst steel, more cursèd gold she now forth brought." This is not mere obscurantism; it is the curse of a pastoral against an industrial society. More than that, it seems to involve a special paradox: the fact that the root of all evil is also the touchstone of value, that the gold standard has a different significance in economic than in ethical terms. In the Renaissance the founder of metallurgical science, George Agricola, would feel it incumbent upon him to answer such objections from the poets. The contradiction has been most tersely expressed by Boethius, in one of the poems interspersed through his *Consolation of Philosophy,* where he speaks of metals as "precious perils"—the English is Chaucer's literal translation. We catch an echo in Milton's "precious bane." At all events, Astrea takes her departure from the sky, and Ovid moves on to the flood.

If this is the normative account, it is his contemporary, Virgil, who gives two significant twists to the theme. In the first place, in *The Aeneid* he transfers the setting from Greece to Italy, identifying Chronos with Saturn, the prehistoric king of Latium. Secondly and more significantly, it is Virgil who conflates the pastoral with the Golden Age. Whereas the Hellenistic pastorals of his master Theocritus were set in Sicily, Virgil transferred the scene to the now remoter Arcadia—the rugged hinterland of the Peloponnesus, a land of springs and of flocks presided over by Pan, and fertile in acorns. We have not heard the last of those unpretentious nuts. The conflation takes place in Virgil's famous *Fourth Eclogue,* dedicated to the new consul Pollio and based upon the oracles of the Cumaean Sybil. Thus it deals not with *prior aetas* but with *ultima,* not with the earlier age but with a later, the latest, the last; it looks from the present toward the immediate future, and the Golden Age is seen to be on its way back: "The Maid returns and brings back Saturn's reign." So reads an English version contemporaneous with Sandys's Ovid. The masts return to the forest, the plows fall into disuse, and there is the typical efflorescence of honey from the oak, et cetera. There will be another Trojan War; Apollo and Pan will revive their respective activities. The identity of the child, whose imminent birth is saluted, has been much argued over by scholars; but the devout have seen in it a prediction of the birth of Christ forty years afterward; and Jesus, as pastor or shepherd of the Christian flock, can be connected with the pastoral mode. Indeed his symbol, the lamb, coalesces with pictures of the Golden Age, whose innocents are characterized in Chaucer's "Former Age" as "the lambish peple, voyd of alle vyce."

Virgil was hailing the principate of Augustus; the imperial epoch that followed was to be known as the Silver Age. Perhaps its characteristic spokesman was Seneca; and we are not surprised to find him illustrating his Stoic philosophy with concrete glimpses of pristine frugality; in his *Ninetieth Epistle* he appeals to stark nature as his authority against hypercivilized corruption, and to humanistic wisdom as against scientific ingenuity. Although we have many other allusions from the Romans, there is an outstanding gap between Rome and the Renaissance. The continuity from classical through medieval culture, as it has been retraced by Ernst Robert Curtius in his monumental study, *European Literature and the Latin Middle Ages,* has tended to fall back upon certain great commonplaces or *topoi* from Homer through Dante; and it is a striking fact that our particular consideration has no place among them. Between the last of the ancients, as Boethius has been called, and the first of the moderns, as we might call Jean de Meung, there is virtually no reference to the Golden Age. Dante—the great exception that proves the rule—was well aware of the *topos* and could explain its neglect by orthodox Christian poets. As a Greco-Roman myth it is a false adumbration of the Judeo-Christian Eden; and Dante makes his simile explicit in stating that the earliest age was as beautiful as gold ("Lo secol primo quant' oro fu bello"); yet when he reaches the top of the purgatorial mount and enters the terrestrial paradise, he cannot help recalling the old dream of the pagan poets.

The motif was taken up by Jean de Meung in his forward-looking sequel to the medieval allegory, *The Romance of the Rose,* and brought to bear on its preoccupation with courtly love and marital problems: the mutual incompatibility of *amour* and *seignourie* or mastery. Even Ovid, among the classics, had hardly begun to exploit that angle. Yet it is recurrent among the poems of the Medici circle, which typified the mood of the Italian Renaissance. Lorenzo de' Medici himself recounts at some length how the psychology of the lover reproduces all the phenomena of the Golden Age in his subjective response to his lady. His favorite poet, Politian, invokes the same phenomena for the more traditional purpose of praising rustic life, so far removed from commerce and as yet uncorrupted by the cruel thirst for gold. Since his stanzas were written for a tournament at Fiesole, before the villa to which the merchant prince retreated from his commercial city of Florence, they reflect the irony of pastoralism. The idyl was acted out at the court of Ferrara in 1573, with the pastoral play or "sylvan fable" by Torquato Tasso, *Aminta*. In Tasso's romantic epic, *Jerusalem Delivered*, the amorous episode of Armida's palace is compared with the pleasures of the Golden Age. In *Aminta*, the title character is a shepherd who woos the shepherdess Dafne and wins her after a series of misunderstandings and counter-accusations, but is long put off by her professions of chastity, *onestate*. At the end of the first act, a chorus voices his impatience for him in what is probably the most purple of the passages before us: "O bella età de l'oro."

> O happy Golden Age,

—it runs in Samuel Daniel's translation—

> Not for that rivers ran
> With streams of milk, and honey dropped from trees. . . .

And all the traditional characteristics are enumerated in the negative. The age was not golden because of its voluntary fruits, its eternally flowering spring, or its lack of ships and wars,

> But only for that name,
> The idle name of wind,
> That idol of deceit, that empty sound
> Call'd Honor, which became
> The tyrant of the mind,
> And so torments our nature without ground,
> Was not yet vainly found.

Nondum, not yet—and here the erotic motive comes to the fore. Opinions differ concerning the sexual ethics of the Golden Age. John Donne agrees with this libertine view that our sires practiced promiscuity, or "plurality of loves." On the other hand, Juvenal refers to their stable marriages as a basis for attacking the mores of his day, so deficient in shame or *pudicitia*. Tasso's lyric is not so much a protest against the hard laws of *Onor* or respectability as it is a paean in praise of

> golden laws like these,
> Which nature wrote: *That's lawful which doth please.*

Further stanzas contrast the pursuit of pleasure through the cult of free love with the repressive morality that would veil such sensual delights, ending with a paraphrase of Catullus, the perennial lover's appeal for haste to his coy mistress:

> Let's love; the sun doth set and rise again
> But whenas our short light
> Comes once to set, it makes eternal night.

Now the hedonistic doctrine of the Golden Age is summed up by Tasso in the single law: "S'ei piace, ei lice." If it pleases, it's permitted. This runs counter to the moral code of the Middle Ages, when Dante condemned Semiramis to hell because she made lust permissible in her law ("che libito fe' licito in sua legge"). A latterday moralist, Matthew Arnold, criticized the whole of modern culture for its principle of "doing as one likes." Tasso's rival dramatist, Giovanni Battista Guarini, sought to outdo him in a tragicomedy entitled *The Faithful Shepherd*, which is more than twice as long as *Aminta* and several times as complex. It imitates the chorus about the Golden Age so slavishly that it uses the same rimes; yet, when it arrives at a moral, it plays safe. Guarini's law is "Piaccia se lice." It is pleasing, if it's permitted. This is a much more cautious, conventional—if not syco-phantic—sentiment, as contrasted with the bold individualism of Tasso's line. But Tasso had an unhappy career, which would be dram-atized by Goethe as a parable of misunderstood genius. Therein Tasso learns that the Golden Age is merely a poetic fantasy. When he tries to say, "What's pleasing is permitted" ("Erlaubt ist, was gefällt"), he is corrected with, "What's proper is permitted" ("Erlaubt ist, was sich ziemt"), and we are back in the domain of orthodoxy again.

We might well expect the somewhat puritanical Spenser to take the more respectable position when he evokes the bucolic innocence of the antique age in *The Faerie Queene*:

> Then loyal love had royal regiment,
> And each unto his lust did make a law,
> From all forbidden things his liking to withdraw.

But the bolder minds of the Renaissance celebrated the pleasure prin-ciple. It was central to the ethos of More's Utopians, who regulated their lives by the prescript of nature. And when Rabelais sketched out his ideal community in his First Book, he designated it as the Abbey of Free Will—L'Abbaie de Thélème—and set above its gate the inscription: "Fais ce que voudras." This jovial monk, turned humanitarian doctor, conceived his monastery as a magnificent chateau where the inhibitions of poverty, chastity, and obedience were re-leased by affluence, marriage, and liberty. Other French writers, notably the poets of the Pléiade, were fond of appealing to the Golden Age in discussing contemporary topics such as the religious wars or the voyages of discovery. There the myth was reinforced by history and given an immense geographic expansion. The exploration of the western hemisphere opened up a golden world where the natives sub-sisted as epicureans, owning all things in common, not bothering to distinguish between mine and thine, and presumably doing whatever came naturally. You will find such comparisons spelled out by Peter Martyr writing about Columbus, by Amerigo Vespucci on South America, by Richard Hakluyt on Virginia, and by many other early chroniclers of the New World. All of them seem to have been struck by the fact that, though gold was plentiful and indeed the main attraction for Europeans, it possessed little value for the Indians.

Such is the argument of Montaigne's whimsical and searching essay, "Of the Cannibals." It poses a reflexive question—who's a barbarian? who's a civilized person? or else, as Melville would ask, who ain't a cannibal?—by drawing a full-length portrait of the noble savage as observed by a family servant who had spent ten years in America. That happy condition of man, Montaigne is convinced, actually surpasses the fictions about the Golden Age, and a first-hand acquaintance with savages would have jolted the preconceived ideas of such philosophers as Plato. And Montaigne itemizes in his turn:

It is a nation, would I answer Plato, that hath no kind of traffic, no knowledge of letters, no intelligence of numbers, no name of magistrate nor of public superiority; no use of service, of riches, or of poverty; no contracts, no successions, no partitions, no occupation but idle; no respect of kindred but common; no apparell but natural; no manuring of lands, no use of wine, corn, or metal.

As Montaigne specifies and speculates, he makes it clear in his equilibrating way that he is less concerned with the virtues of savagery than with the vices of self-styled civilization. Hence, after the visiting cannibal has been told about France, he is less impressed with its king than with its extremes of wealth and poverty. The train of speculation ends with a shrug—"But, after all, they wear no trousers"—suggesting, at first glance, that such informants ought not to be taken very seriously. However, Montaigne's expression for trousers is *haut-de-chausses*; the comparative nakedness of the Amerindians is juxtaposed to the ridiculous foppery of the breeches and hose then worn by French courtiers; and the question lingers, who has the last laugh. The ambiguity, as usual with Montaigne, is double-edged.

Montaigne points the way for his avid reader Shakespeare, who was always fascinated by "golden times" and who versified an entire page of the essay as he had read it in the resplendent Elizabethan translation of John Florio. It becomes a speech in the second act of *The Tempest*, a play inspired by the misadventures of certain Anglo-American voyagers; and, like the monologue on order in *Troilus and Cressida* or the tale of the belly and the members in *Coriolanus*, the speech sets forth an ideal from which the dramatic reality deviates. You will remember that Gonzalo, the merry old councillor, makes an attempt to cheer up the shipwrecked King of Naples by playing the childish game of "If I were king." He pretends that the island is his commonwealth, which he would govern by a system contrary to the practices of Europe in all respects, and with such success as to excel the Golden Age.

> All things in common nature should produce
> Without sweat or endeavour. Treason, felony,
> Sword, pike, knife, gun, or need of any engine
> Would I not have; but nature should bring forth,
> Of it own kind, all foison, all abundance,
> To feed my innocent people.

The enumeration of merits evinced and of defects avoided follows Montaigne specifically: no traffic nor magistrate, no letters nor contracts, no riches nor poverty, no wine, corn, nor metal—in fact, no sovereignty. The cynical courtiers, Sebastian and Antonio, who keep interrupting with their banter and who are even then hatching a plot which completely violates these ideals and subverts Shakespeare's norms, call attention to the inconsistency here:

> No sovereignty.
>   Yet he would be king on't.

That is the crux of the problem of anarchy: someone must take office. Responsibility presupposes authority; authority imposes responsibility. Miranda's "brave new world" turns out, ironically, to be the same old one.

Prospero, the former Duke of Milan, has preferred his books to the responsibilities of ruling. Therefore he has been dethroned and exiled to this enchanted isle; he has gone, perforce, back to nature. His single slave is Caliban, the animal-like indigene; and though that name is borrowed, slightly twisted, from Montaigne's essay on the cannibals, Caliban seems to be a much cruder creature than Montaigne's exemplary primitive; for this child of nature is without nurture—education —and Shakespeare emphasizes the critical difference. Still Caliban can teach Prospero something about "the qualities of the isle": where the fresh water or nourishing herbs can be found. His master compounds that lore with his own book-knowledge to form his fully pondered art, which has the symbolic guise of natural magic. Thereby he learns how to become a good ruler and returns to his duchy for the happy ending. The same lesson of exile and return, of society refreshed by recourse to the norms of nature, and of art as a mediator between them shapes the pattern of other Shakespearean plays. One thinks of *The Winter's Tale*, with its sheep-shearing festival, and above all of *As You Like It*, where Shakespeare's very title seems to restate Tasso's law, and the banished Duke in the Forest of Arden with his merry men is reported to "live like the old Robin Hood of England" and to "fleet the time carelessly as they did in the golden world." Nor is it surprising, when Englishmen pine for the Golden Age, that what should stand out about it for them is not its gold but its greenery. One could cite many English witnesses during the sixteenth and seventeenth centuries who, in invoking the Golden Age or more often a golden world, couple the allure of greenwoods or gardens together with their fears of enclosure, industry, and urbanization.

Spenser's *Faerie Queene* is full of nostalgia for "the goodly usage of those antique times." Heroic romance has a pastoral interlude when Sir Calidore courts the chaste Pastorella, aided in his pursuit of the Blatant Beast by a wild man who is much gentler and kinder than Caliban. Spenser's friend, the Cambridge scholar Gabriel Harvey, took him to task in a letter:

You suppose the first age was the Golden Age. It is nothing so. Bodin defendeth the Golden Age to flourish now, and our first grandfathers to have rubbed through in the Iron and Brazen Age at the beginning, when all things were rude and unperfect in comparison with the exquisite fineness and delicacy that we have grown to in these days.

Jean Bodin, the French jurisconsult, had attacked the myth of the Golden Age in his *Method for the Easy Comprehension of History*. In the light of subsequent development, he argued that what had really subsisted then was an iron age of lawlessness and disorder. Furthermore, he challenged a closely related misconception: the effort to interpret the elements of Daniel's prophecy—gold, silver, brass, and clay—in terms of four successive monarchies, and thereby to predict the end of the world with the coming of a Fifth Monarchy. Would-be prophets were watching and waiting for the millennium, while moralists were lamenting that nature was in decay and that culture was decadent. But, out of that battle of the ancients and moderns, the modernists were bound to emerge triumphant, because they had the advantage of being alive. Harvey's sentiment of living in a golden age was felt by many other subjects of Queen Elizabeth. As the Virgin Queen she was identified with Astrea, so that poets could attest that she was bringing back the regime of justice. George Peele wrote a masque on this conceit, and Sir John Davies a sequence of acrostics. Since Elizabeth was likewise addressed as England's Eliza, Michael Drayton paid his compliment in *The Muses' Elysium*, where Eliza's England has all the standard features of the Golden Age— except that significantly, given its northern climate, the weather is not an eternal spring but an eternal summer. Yet in his ode on the Queen's namooalto, Virginia, Drayton reminds Hakluyt that the winters there are short. Virginia is "Earth's only paradise," and there

the Golden Age
Still nature's laws doth give.

Reports from the pioneering colonists are sprinkled with reminiscences of the Golden Age: the unclad beauty of the aborigines, their amiable habit of disregarding their abundant gold. "Come boys, Virginia longs till we share the rest of her maidenhead," roars the sea captain in the comedy by Jonson, Chapman, and Marston, *Eastward Ho!* He illustrates her plenitude by explaining that the chamberpots there are made of pure gold—a perversion of the whimsy put forward by Thomas More to show how much the Utopians scorned the substance. This Virginian voyage gets no farther than the Isle of Dogs, a garbage dump in the Thames, where it runs aground in disillusionment. Yet George Chapman could afford to be more idealistic in a masque which welcomes the milk-and-honey age; while his sometime collaborator, Ben Jonson, composed many masques for the Stuart court, located in such never-never lands as Arcady and peopled by such characters as old Saturn. Nonetheless, in his realistic comedies, the acquisition of gold is the principal target of Jonson's satire. The seamy underworld of *The Alchemist* is the antipodes of the Golden Age; it is a gilded age, whose currency is fools' gold. The arch-speculator Sir Epicure Mammon talks "all in gold," but it is all talk: "If his dream last, he'll turn the age to gold." So they say, but the dream is harshly interrupted. The ebbing of general confidence, the elegiac feeling that a great age has been passing away is registered in Jonson's unfinished pastoral, *The Sad Shepherd*, with its rearguard action against the Puritans and its lament for the happier days of Robin Hood. When the Stuarts came back to their insecure throne after the Puritan interregnum, Abraham Cowley greeted them in an "Ode upon His Majesty's Restoration and Return," a pair of events which he describes as the advent of "this golden age." Another ode of Cowley's, "In Commemoration of the Time We Live in, under the Reign of our Gracious King Charles II," ends by complimenting the sovereign on having attained and applied the philosophers' stone:

> Our Charles, blest alchemist (though strange,
> Believe it, future times), did change
> The Iron Age of old
> Into an Age of Gold.

But future times, after the Glorious Revolution of 1688, had little reason to believe it. It was later than Cowley thought, though he was bard of the Royal Society, and had opined in his youthful "Dream of Elysium" that it is usually later than poets think.

The seventeenth century thought of itself as "this iron age." The utilitarian Francis Bacon gloried in it; in his speech to Parliament pointing out that iron is really more useful and valuable than gold, he correctly anticipated the future of Britain in industrialism, shipping, and steel. The person who considered himself divinely appointed to restore the Golden Age in this iron age was that most absurd and touching of heroes, Don Quixote, whose generous project was as fore-doomed to failure as the institution of chivalry was doomed by the invention of gunpowder. His eulogy of the Golden Age is a set piece which Spanish schoolboys memorize. On his second sally into the outer world, he is bashed in the head through a characteristic encounter; he is then offered the modest hospitality of a group of goatherds; and he insists that his squire, Sancho Panza, sit and eat with them, because chivalry has a democratizing effect. As the meal concludes, he takes up a handful of acorns for dessert, and a quirk of association inspires him to a discourse:

Happy time and fortunate ages were those whereon our ancestors bestowed the title of golden, not because gold—so much prized in this our iron age—was got in that happy time without any labors, but because those which lived in that time knew not those two words, *thine* and *mine*. In that holy age all things were in common. . . .

And the rest is eloquent but familiar, though Cervantes makes us aware that we are in Spain when he mentions cork trees, and his mention of shepherdesses prepares us for the episode of the unhappy Marcela. Possibly the saddest rebuff of the many received by the knight is that the only case of retributive justice he meets is that of the highwayman Roque Guinart, while the squire has equivocal success in his ambition to rule an island. The realism of Cervantes, hard-won through the actuality of warfare and imprisonment and balanced against the artificiality of the pastorals he had tried to write, definitively measures the distance between those visions we have been considering and the situations on which they comment.

The period of Cervantes and Lope de Vega and so many other great Spanish writers is hallowed in the history of literature as the golden century, *el siglo de oro*. But that is a retrospective designation, conferred in the 1830's by a romantic exile, Francisco Martinez de la Rosa. What may be the best of times for some can for others be the worst of times. From our century it is easy enough to look back at the Renaissance as one of the greatest epochs in art and thought. A number of its greatest minds, in spite of their misgiving and self-criticism, were by no means unaware of its greatness. The humanist Ficino eulogized the city of Florence for harboring talents which Plato would have termed golden. Erasmus hailed the accession of the Medici pope, Leo X, who would metamorphose the iron age to gold through his revival of learning. Vasari, the historian of painting, coined the metaphor of renascence for the rebirth of the classic arts, the restoration of ancient culture. Rabelais, in his letter from Gargantua to Pantagruel, symbolized the transition from the Middle Ages to the Renaissance by welcoming the restitution of letters along with the new gains in printing, education, science, technology, and man's control over his physical environment. These are testimonials that we should recall when some of our neo-medievalists seek to neutralize the historical impact of the Renaissance.

In his *Advancement of Learning* Bacon spoke of his own time as a third visitation: the first two visitations were those of Greece and Rome. By the time that Voltaire addressed himself to the problems of historiography, he was ready to discern four ages: Greece, Rome, the Renaissance, and the century of Louis XIV—which was continued into the eighteenth century by whom but Voltaire himself? In *Candide* he made his own approach to our golden paradox: the aureate kingdom of Eldorado could never be rediscovered. In his ironic poem "The Worldling" he revels in the comforts and conveniences of modernity. Let him who will regret the good old days, Voltaire exclaims: "O le bon temps que ce siècle de fer!" It is pleasant enough to live in this iron age; and Paris has become an earthly paradise, what with its boulevards and cafés, its luxury articles and sparkling wines, its operas by Rameau and paintings by Poussin. Meanwhile Voltaire's philosophical rival, Jean-Jacques Rousseau, was reverting to the myth in its naïve form. In his *Second Discourse on the Origins of Inequality* he charged that it was not gold and silver but corn and iron—that is to say, agriculture and metallurgy—which had civilized men and ruined humanity. He blamed it all upon the first man who had enclosed his piece of property and labeled it "mine." In his appendix, Rousseau is forced to admit that he himself has become too civilized to eat acorns; he is skeptical of, rather than hostile to, reforming institutions.

The reversal of the usual sequence, proceeding from iron to gold as mankind has proceeded from past to present—in other words, the theory of progress enunciated by the Renaissance—has been an increasing commitment for later centuries. The socialist Saint-Simon, in a manifesto, declared: "The Golden Age is not behind us, but in front of us. It is the perfection of social order. Our fathers have not seen it; our children will arrive there one day, and it is for us to clear the way for them." The American reformer Edward Bellamy, after outlining his New England Utopia in *Looking Backward,* concluded with a postscript looking forward: ". . . the Golden Age lies before us and not behind us, and is not far away." That most progressive of poets, Shelley, was moved by the Greek Revolution to believe that the cycle had come full circle; and in his visionary chorus he foresaw another Hellas arising, as Virgil had foreseen it nearly two millenniums before:

> The world's great age begins anew,
> The golden years return.

When Shelley's friend Thomas Love Peacock wrote his *Four Ages of Poetry*, he used the old progression or retrogression to frame an argument which several other critics have formulated more solemnly: that poets truly belong to the childhood of the race and that civilization has made their role technologically obsolescent. Shelley's answer, his *Defence of Poetry*, in affirming the place of the literary imagination in the modern world, was a reaffirmation of what the Renaissance poet Sir Philip Sidney had urged in his *Defence of Poesie:* that literature itself was the truest alchemy, that fiction was a means of improving upon the baser metals of actuality, that nature had created a brazen world which the poets re-created in gold.

ARTHUR E. BARKER

An Apology for the Study
of Renaissance Poetry

To JUDGE from the variety and energy of recent publication it has been my privilege to survey a couple of times of late for Rice's stellar luminary in the constellation of learned literary quarterlies,[1] the critically historical study of Renaissance English poetry seems just now to be at once experiencing a somewhat unpropitious conjunction of influences in the academic universe and exhibiting illuminating manifestations of a renaissance of its own. If this is so, it is entirely appropriate to what such studies work with, for the Renaissance itself was at once confusedly star-crossed and marked by pregnant manifestations of a process of new or re-birth. This sort of situation was what the newly and highly articulate English poetry of the sixteenth and seventeenth centuries was, in general, about, and consequently must be what current critically historical activity is principally about.

I

To the involved specialist, no less than to the detached non-specialist, this activity presents a variety of apparently contradictory (often heatedly incoherent) approaches and evaluations, ranging from the antiquarianism of bibliographical and biographical labors on major and just now many minor poets, through varieties of more or less humanistic and homiletic ethical interpretation and of medievalized, rationalized, or scientifically modernized intellectual literary history, to the reconstruction and reappraisal of Renaissance techniques of communication, academically rhetorical or journalistic or homiletic or imaginatively poetic, and through efforts to render intelligible yet a newer Laokoön by way of analogies with the history of art or the

ARTHUR E. BARKER is Professor of English at the University of Illinois.

[1] *Studies in English Literature*, I (1961), No. 1, 121–157; III (1963), 119 150.

musicology of the Renaissance, conceived of as a definitive historical period, to the ultimate transcendental dogmatisms of modern, unhistorical aesthetic criticism. This range involves much active difference of opinion about an infinite variety of basic questions—for instance, to instance a few at preoccupied random, as to whether the early sixteenth-century humanism of such as More or Erasmus is to be regarded as having had a directly significant influence on later sixteenth- and seventeenth-century poetry or rather as having been radically modified by counter-renaissances, skeptical or scientific, or counter-reformations, mystical or sectarian, and whether, if it had a direct influence, this is to be regarded as principally rhetorical, or through its formulation of a still admirable Christian-humanist ethic, or through its translation into the vernacular chiefly of classical literary irony; or again, as to whether Spenser's *Faerie Queene* is to be interpreted as a self-consistent ethical and even philosophical poem, or as a darkly verbalized Neo-Platonic conceit; or again, as to the relation, rhetorical, poetic, metaphysical, psychotic, between the cynically satiric Jack Donne and the convertedly devotional Dean Donne; or again, as to the relation to the main English poetic tradition and to Continental fashions (High Renaissance, Mannerist, Baroque) of such poetic fashions as the mythological, the Petrarchan, the malcontent complaint, the complimentary epistle, the bucolic or Horatian horticultural meditation, the confessional religious devotion, and with this as to the significance of minor poets, representing one or another of these fashions, in the clarification of the main tradition and its tensions, as for instance in the relation between the secular or seductive love-tradition in many sonneteers and cavaliers and the liturgical or mystical tradition in poets like Herbert or Crashaw; or again, as to whether the values of Shakespeare's plays are or are not by implication essentially Christian, or humanistic, or skeptical, or confused, or as to the degree of ironic humor involved in the response to pagan myth in such poems as *Venus and Adonis;* or again, as to whether Milton's *Mask* (*Comus*) is to be interpreted as a poetical statement of integrated Christian-humanist ethics, or as an expression of Neo-Platonic idealism, or as an urbane entertainment with a sharp political bearing, or whether *Paradise Lost* is to be regarded as a conclusive epic expression of the integratedly humane and religious aspirations of the age, or as a metaphorical structure expressing the transcendent and time-repudiating absolutes of more or less Christianized Orphic myth, or as the frustrated and self-frustrating record of all the paralyzing conflicts the late-Renaissance seventeenth century was heir to. Despite this variety of method and appraisal—which of course can here be only inadequately summarized within the marked limits of my understanding and space, it is remarkable that there seems, as yet, no very great difference of opinion as to which are the major English Renaissance poets about whom we should disagree. Though some journalistic critics (apparently imitating current methods of denigrating Brand X) are inclined to reverse the critical absurdity of the thirties by now announcing that Donne's star is falling as they focus their attention on Milton's superior flame, and though both evoke and deserve constant reappraisal, it must surely be a markedly limited, probably impercipiently uncritical, historically uninformed, and essentially unimaginative and doctrinaire approach that cannot responsively appreciate both. Indeed, the majority of the major poets is underlined by the historically important and efficient editing of a number of hitherto virtually unheard-of minors—Alabaster, George Daniel, John Collop—though what is chiefly striking about them is their inability to make out of their materials forcefully unified poems and sequences such as, say, Donne makes, and hence their invitation to us to inquire more particularly into what Donne has done where Alabaster cracks up. Again, there have been of late no really major evidential discoveries demanding revisions of judicial opinion—the time for such discoveries perhaps now being past, so that the hope of discovery somewhat lugubriously leads but to the grave. One continues to hope there remain undiscovered Renaissance pigsties or tennis-boxes that may afford, say, documentary evidence as to the process of the composition and revision of *The Faerie Queene* or the complete manuscript material for *Paradise Lost.* Another secondary manuscript of Donne's poems has been found (by a student of Miss Gardner), and this of course induces further examination of the complex problem of the text and its transmission and should reinforce curiosity as to the special character of the audience his poems are evidently very consciously and efficiently aimed at. An, as I think, ironic portrait of Jack Donne from Dean Donne's study, rediscovered not long since, perhaps ought to induce us to consider what John saw when he looked in Renaissance London for the New Jerusalem. The question of Milton's system of spelling still awaits definitive investigation through the newly developed bibliographical techniques that have been applied to Shakespeare: some important reports are coming in, and the Hinman machine and the immensely unique collection of copies of Milton's works at Illinois await patient investigators. The learned journals record the increasingly lively amount of investigation, made possible by happily increasing research funds, into biographical and textual detail for every poet, as also into the sociological background of Renaissance English poetry, where at the moment perhaps the most significant findings have to do with the by-no-means small Latin and less Greek of the grammar schools and with the humanistic influences that operated—as instructors' programs and students' book lists have recently been made to demonstrate—through the college tutorial systems of Oxford and Cambridge despite half-medieval and, as always, outdated university requirements. A little research indicates that similar findings are badly needed as to the instructional programs of the law schools of the Inns of Court, where so many Renaissance English poets, however sophisticatedly reckless they may seem as law-student young-men-about-town, got their sense of the continuity of medieval English common law (and common criminality and litigiousness) in a humanistic context. Such findings bring us a vitally detailed understanding of the disciplines of mind Renaissance poetry emerged from and of the varied basic material—classical, patristic, medieval, Continental—it worked in, though they may also focus our attention on the question how major poetic minds responded to these disciplines, what they did poetically with these basic materials, how they manipulated and modified them, and to what enduring purpose (which is our ultimate business).

It is perhaps hence—through methodological disagreements and differences of opinion, the accumulation by research of much material and of about as much major material as we can expect, and a healthy critical determination to come to grips with the main matter—that the most lively activity in Renaissance English studies nowadays principally concerns itself with poetic technique and through that with poetic purpose—with the relation of Renaissance English poetry to humanistic rhetoric (traditional or Ramistic) and to homiletic (Augustinian or otherwise), with the dimensions of communication in which it differs from rhetoric and homiletic: with its organizing principles, with its manipulation of figures and tropes, images, metaphors, conceits, with its metaphoric allusiveness, ironic or symbolic, with the complex web of reference, classical, biblical, patristic, medieval, available to the Renaissance mind, especially just now with its response to Orphic myth or Christian mystery, controlled and given point (if the critic's mind leans to the formal) through its manipulation of medieval forms, or neoclassical literary genres, crossed with what it supposed to be the scriptural genres, or with the self-administered rhetoric of Counter-Reformation meditational routines, to produce dynamically empowered and precisely guided poetic missives. This preoccupation with technique and texture has tended to render unglamorous what used to be our dominant approach to the Renaissance, through the history of ideas, and the response to Renaissance poetry tends to be lifted out of history altogether by some extremely aesthetic interpreters who seem to reflect the undifferentiated and syncretic enthusiasm of Renaissance Neo-Platonism—and whose approach we may, remembering that seventeenth-century enthusiast and anti-Baconian Henry Reynolds, term "mythomystic," since this approach seems chiefly intent on seeing, shadowed forth in sixteenth- and seventeenth-century poetry, its own metaphorical or figural image and tries thereby to escape the limitations of merely deadly history by passing through the poetic mirror to identification with the absolute. Yet it is in investigations of the techniques, and so of the function, of Renaissance poetry that one can chiefly see the signs of a renaissance in Renaissance literary studies. Happily the debate between orthodox historians of ideas and such critics as they tended to regard (in Prynne's phrase) as "new wandering-blazing stars and firebrands, styling themselves new lights," has now sufficiently subsided and passed into history so that we can take our dividends from it while regarding it as something of a tempest in a well-wrought teapot. The effect of the historical investigation of poetic techniques that still operate on our sensibilities is to increase our awareness of the ways in which Renaissance poets use, manipulate, and modify ideas in their poetic process of communication. But the interpretative process remains nowadays, if stimulating, confusing; and a graduate student must still carefully inquire to what historical or critical sect his examiners belong. (I think sadly of the Illinois student who asked me recently whether a course I proposed for the next semester would be historical or critical. To which I could only confusedly reply that I hoped it would prove either critically historical or historically critical, and not too confusing. He, wisely, did not, by the by, register for it.)

II

It seems possible that this critical variety and the current preoccupation with poetic partly result from our response as literary historians to the radical reappraisals the concept of the Renaissance in general has undergone during the past thirty years or so at the hands of many distinguished philosophical, sociological, and economic historians, from our somewhat too submissive response to, our uneasy reactions against, and our independent efforts to escape from, the apparent implications of their findings. These findings render it impossible to operate on the old theory that Renaissance literature marks a decisive and general cultural break with the past, a brave new departure induced by and inducing a revival of the human spirit and the freeing of reason and imagination from the obscurantist trammels of the Middle Ages, chiefly through a rediscovery of classical and human learning and a purification of religion which together produced an efflorescence of idealistic Christian-humanist philosophy and ethics, issuing from and contributing to the dynamic development of national political societies and cultures in an economically expansive Europe—in the terms, that is to say, that used to be derived in English from John Addington Symonds (and from Jacob Burckhardt read in the light of Symonds), variously enlivened by the liberal rationalism of James Anthony Froude, the Hellenism of Matthew Arnold, and the romantic Victorian aestheticism of Algernon Swinburne and George Saintsbury. The cultural historians, in prosecuting investigations which have been largely motivated by their efforts to illuminate the crises of our day by explaining their origins, have simply destroyed this cheerfully liberating conception of the Renaissance and its literature, in detail and piecemeal. Our approaches to Renaissance English poetry tend to correspond with one or another of the period's tensions as seen by the historians, the two extreme literary approaches apparently both involving an acceptance of the historians' conclusion that the Renaissance was not a period of organic rebirth of any sort but an uneasy transitional period of sharp conflicts between the medieval and the modern, so that its most characteristic literature seems either the expression of a realistically skeptical and cynical (if ironic) libertinism or of a transcendental and absolutely idealistic (if metaphorical) withdrawal, both impinging on the English mind through highly sophisticated and admired Italian and French models, and both cutting across or modifying the Medieval-Renaissance continuities (Thomistic or Augustinian) we were initially invited to contemplate. Even if we could resolve this extreme poetic polarity, there will never, in consequence of the cultural historians' findings, again be, I think (and, I think, happily), a simply orthodox and dominating approach to Renaissance poetry, such as there perhaps was in the later nineteenth and earlier twentieth centuries—however unhappy that may make the doctoral candidate and his examiners. But unfortunately, the effect of culturally historical reappraisal seems to have been chiefly to induce intra-disciplinary rivalries and differences of opinion and an apparent confusion of approaches and sometimes frenetic methods, which may suggest to our colleagues in other disciplines or periods (and to administrators) that our material is confused, is of no great immediate educational use, is perhaps immoral or concerned with quite out-of-this-worldly transcendentals, and that we have no clear notion as to our educational aims or confidence in what we and our fellows are doing. (If this seems an exaggeratedly sensational poetic picture, there are the statistics of registration which, in most of the North American universities I have had associations with of late years, clearly confirm the general complaint of specialists that undergraduates are increasingly reluctant to elect courses in the Renaissance while graduates much prefer to work in the more relevant and less confused nineteenth or twentieth or even eighteenth centuries.)

Though this may be an aspect of a qualitative (in addition to the quantitative) crisis in North American education in general, the somewhat manic enthusiasm of some approaches to Renaissance English poetry may be specially symptomatic of the relatively depressed condition of critical literary studies in general. In response to the process by which education has responded to the immediate needs of internationalized North American culture by turning departments of literature, foreign and domestic, into "service departments," the Renaissance finds it difficult to make its claim in terms either of historically antiquarian or immediately sociological significance. When it tries for either or both, it seems either to reduce itself to the representation of unresolved conflicts or to the eulogizing of some (at that time) relatively unimportant sect, religious or political (like, say, the English Levellers). Anglo-Saxon and medieval studies appear to be capable of taking advantage of both, having at once the dignified status of pure antiquarianism (and so being imposable in considerable quantities on the doctoral candidate on the ground of their basic historical importance) and also the support of a renewedly idealistic response to medieval religion (even when their professors are quite unsectarian) and of the rapidly developed sociological and descriptive linguistics (for whose techniques they provide a respectable and definitive proving ground). Later periods and areas can support their aesthetic activities, and in some measure relate them to present reality, by claiming to be investigating historically or sociologically or at least psychologically their direct relevance to our immediate background. Even the eighteenth century can validate itself by appealing to a renewed interest in all that lies behind, say, Jeffersonianism. There has been a decided renaissance in Romantic and Victorian studies and the equivalent American studies in the past ten years or so because so much of our thinking involves adjustments in nineteenth-century assumptions and so much of our common aesthetic then originated. And of course the study of contemporary English-speaking literature (which, from occupying no place at all, has quite rightly come to occupy a very prominent academic place since my official undergraduate literary experience was stopped dead, depressingly, with Swinburne) is energized by its immediately relevant anatomies of various more-or-less socio-aesthetic evangels. But the Renaissance seems to have lost whatever unified character and relevance it had as a period. Its boundaries have been pushed back into the Middle Ages to such an extent, or alternatively its foreshadowings of the

modern in its sectarian conflicts have been to such an extent high-
lighted, that it seems unintelligible save as a transitional period chiefly
marked by the tensions between classical, medieval, Hebraic, scientific, and so on. Hence the period tends to be broken down into the
fifteenth, the earlier and later sixteenth, the earlier and later seventeenth centuries, or into High Renaissance, Mannerist, Baroque, and
so forth, by "comparative" aesthetics, just now finding it a principal
field of activity permitting large periodic aesthetic generalizations to
be made to relate the various arts while overlooking national or sectarian preoccupations or the merely diurnal realities of immediate
experience. Its principal figures—and this is the case with its theo-
logians, political theorists, and so on, as well as with its poets—are
chiefly regarded as mirroring and illustrating such tensions, conflicts,
transitions; and one of the most noticeable effects of this in recent
critical comment is a pervasive air of condescension, even of apologetic condescension far this side an earlier tendency to idolatry, in
the handling even of major authors and the confusions through which
the critic more perceptively sees—not, of course, that one would desire
again the uncritical partisan adulations of, say, Macaulay. In general,
though with of course obviously distinguished exceptions, the effect
has been to induce in Renaissance studies the extremes of a simplified,
often confusedly nostalgic and plaintive or sectarian, sociological his-
tory-of-ideas approach with a heavily moralizing emphasis (in anything but the High Renaissance manner), and of a mythomystic aestheticism which would make Renaissance poetry relevant to us by a
Neo-Platonic isolation of its Orphic voice and vision from the historical and ideological confusions it is said to have transcendentally
escaped from (despite its almost unwavering concern with what men
thought and did about that which lay before them in daily life). One
of these extremes unhappily suggests the uselessness to us, save as a
warning, of the Renaissance ideas whose conflicts we inherit. How
futile, unpractical, and academically unprofitable, it can too easily be
felt, are the recently rehearsed Erasmian-humanist complaints about
war, and how inadequate in the face of reality their moralistic educational procedures! The other extreme unhappily suggests that Renaissance poetry had then and has now no immediate relevance save
for those who would withdraw through mythomystic vision to a
transcendentally detached and self-contained verbal universe, where
the word exalts itself above all the ills that flesh is heir to and all the
confusions and frustrations of time the Renaissance has passed on to us.
How very fortunately few and how peculiarly fitted must be, among
the academic stocks and stones and trees, the visionary audience capable of repudiating time and experience in favor of the illumination

of the space-word continuum which we have of late been being urged to believe is the Miltonic reward for a lucky fall! Whatever may be said of the academic merits of these approaches—as to solid substance or imaginative perception, neither is likely to sell the Renaissance effectively in present circumstances. One tends to the pedantic, the other to the gnostic. They meet, and compromise, in carrying the seeds of their own defeatist frustration in their own typical assertions. One underlines the luxury of disillusioned academic antiquarianism, the other of the withdrawn aestheticism of refined souls.

Less disillusioned and less withdrawn approaches, if less ponderous or flashing, lie behind the critical renaissance in Renaissance literary studies that is certainly now going on, and which may have the effect of making them more academically significant (and administratively impressive). These suggest that critically historical re-examination and redefinition of Renaissance English poetic theory and practice may help us toward a redefinition and reassertion of our function in terms of the function of poetry for the English Renaissance. They suggest that English Renaissance poetry was not for its period and need not be for ours merely the echo or the escape cultural historians of the period have led us to believe it was.

III

It may soon prove profitable, as some recent discourses in review suggest, to attempt a thorough reappraisal of the literary significance of reappraisals of the period of the Renaissance by cultural historians and to ask what the implications of these reappraisals, if any, really are for critically historical literary studies.[2] Current reappraising ac-

[2] Three literary contributions to two recent surveying collections afford much comfort: those by B. Weinberg and H. Levin in *The Renaissance: A Reconsideration of the Theories and Interpretations of the Age,* ed. T. Helton (Madison, 1961), lectures occasioned by the Voigt and Burckhardt centenaries, and by D. Bush in *Seventeenth-Century Science and the Arts,* ed. H. H. Rhys (Princeton, 1961). The editor of the first seems to find it interestingly difficult to fit the two literary lectures (especially Levin's) into the pattern he finds in the others (by Mattingly, Kristeller, Rosenthal, Rosen) of cyclical return, after protest, to a revised and extended Burckhardtianism, a pattern perhaps also illustrated by H. Baron's centenary essay on Burckhardt in *Renaissance News,* XIII (1960), 207–222, and an essay by W. A. Ferguson in *Studies in the Renaissance,* VII (1960), 7–26. The two literary lectures do not fit because they are protests against the whole cycle and its assumptions, and are based on literary principles unrecognized by the other lecturers. Levin's review of the English Renaissance literary scene (dramatic and non-dramatic) declines the simplifications of the cultural historians' cyclical periodization of history (shared by them with Burckhardt) and even the effort to decipher aesthetic periods in terms of stages of Renaissance style. What is suggested instead is a datum which involves variety of response to humanist and Christian-humanist rhetoric, the *mimesis* recalled (though not specified) by a passing

tivity has been mostly in the hands of cultural historians who do not ask such blunt critical questions since their unexamined literary assumptions are relatively simple-minded and on the whole Victorian; and, until very recently and despite Miss Tuve's recommendations of the forties, most generalized literary comments on the English poetic renaissance have accepted the findings of the cultural historians (when they have been abreast of them) or have had a nervously defensive air, or have not got much beyond the titular (and, it must be admitted, as yet not very firmly answered) question, *The English Renaissance: Fact or Fiction?*

Of course it is impossible here to do anything like justice to the findings of so many eminent cultural historians, but the general conclusions to which they have invited us in their reconsiderations of the Renaissance would seem to be something like the following. As to philosophy, Professor Kristeller and others seem to tell us that the period of the Renaissance exhibits no distinctive philosophy of its

---

allusion to Auerbach and Northern realism, the capacity of the Elizabethans for muddling through very much alive while modifying extremes by indigenous insular responses to Continental influences, the collocations of an elagiac nostalgia with a vigorous impulse to satirize the immediate present, and the contrast between derivative and pedestrian writers of lesser magnitude and major authors. Despite differences of opinion and emphasis, Weinberg's Continental review of critical responses and methods, Wölfflinian, new-critical, or better, seems relatable to Levin's through its suspicion of the fragmentation of the Renaissance into renaissances, a suspicion arising less from a pro-Burckhardtian, unified-cultural-phenomena reaction against fragmenting revisionism than from a sense of (however misguided) general critical effort to provide literary history, in its own right, with some intelligible rationale, not interwoven with and obscured by varieties of other cultural phenomena to corroborate some general theory of "the Renaissance" but depending chiefly on specifically literary techniques and principles. If (as perhaps in the case of Italian criticism) this in its turn suggests an aesthetic and possibly even mythomystic detachment of literature from immediate experience, Bush's lecture seems at once to confirm Weinberg's sense of the promise of the critical future and to underline the experiential perspective of literary history. In a series chiefly concerned with the usual dislocation and modification of the seventeenth-century arts under the impact of the new science, his review of the dislocation of the orderly Elizabethan world-picture ends by focusing attention not on the dramatic modifications which are still the preoccupation of most historians (like Marie Boas) but on the continuity of literary response to and representation of the harsh and ironic drama of human experience (to whose significance the new science contributed only somewhat new and subordinate materials). Though there appears to be a delightful difference of opinion as to whether Ulysses on degree is to be taken at face or double-faced value, and though the languages of current criticism remain highly diversified, the relations between these lectures seem worth contemplating. As to cultural reappraisal, W. K. Ferguson's *The Renaissance in Historical Thought* (Boston, 1948) remains the comprehensively authoritative survey, though there have been many subsequent essays on aspects of this tired subject, several varieties of which are represented in *The Renaissance: Medieval or Modern?* ed. K. H. Dannenfeldt (Boston, 1959).

own, but rather a ferment of philosophies.[3] Even Ficino's Neo-
Platonism, though invigorating, is eclectic in principle and method,
and induces the fantastic syncretism of Pico della Mirandola—occult
and gnostic in its response to absolutes, and, though for many literary
historians the inspiration for Spenser's Gloriana, or Donne's "Shee,"
or Milton's masquing Lady, really the eye of the period's philosophical hurricane, so that critical efforts to isolate one philosophy as the
main strand in any great Renaissance poem, or in any poem beyond
a minor doctrinaire philosophical level, have the effect of throwing
into relief other strands other critics will insist on as main strands,
depending on their allegiance or inclination. Though the historian of
philosophy will not allow systematic theology to be properly philosophical, we might add that to the complex, so that the Renaissance
is thus a period of conflict between Thomism, Nominalism, various
forms of Reformation or Counter-Reformation Augustianism, Platonism, Neo-Platonism, Gnosticism, Aristotelianism, Averroistic Aristotelianism, and so forth; and poems, from this point of view, are either
versified contributions to confused philosophic debate or unsystem-
atically confuse two or more philosophies with one another. As to the
humanism which used to be thought the chief mark of the Renaissance, the findings of the philosophical and political historian combine
to reduce its importance, to the satisfaction of several varieties of
aestheticians. The historian of philosophy tells us—what is certainly
true—that humanism had no abstract systematic philosophy of its own.
From his point of view, its concerns were only with "classical learning and literary elegance," and so purely instrumental, and might serve
any philosophy, as a humanist might be an adherent of any one (or
more) of the various Renaissance philosophies. Humanism, we are
told, had its origins in the medieval Italian profession of elementary
schoolteaching letter-writing, in late medieval Italian educational de-
velopments which took over around 1300 from the dying Carolingian
French-classical educational tradition, and in the Italian response to
the rediscovered continuous Byzantine tradition of classical Greek
studies. Again we have the suggestion of reinvigoration; and it is
admitted that these origins do not explain the rapid development and
extension of humanism in the period. But we are to remember, that
humanism was concerned only with *studia humanitatis* and principally
with the teaching and exercise of rhetoric. And we find from the

---

[3] Of the several relevant studies by K. O. Kristeller, the text here and in the
paragraphs following derives chiefly from the Wisconsin lecture (see above), and
an essay in *Studies in the Renaissance*, IX (1962), 7–30; but I am also attempting to
recall the principal argument of a lecture given in October 1962 for the Division
of the Humanities of the University of Illinois and as yet, I think, unpublished.
For a quoted phrase below, see the Wisconsin lecture, pp. 39–40.

political and social historian that humanism, with most of the decorative arts, developed with the courts of petty princedoms, secular or ecclesiastical, and of nation states, to whose proceedings it gave a tone but on which it had—as humanist complaints testify—no influence. Humanists acted as literary or Latin secretaries, wrote formal letters, delivered elaborate encomia before arriving and departing ambassadors, in whose trains they might serve, dedicated edifying or elegant translations to their princely and other patrons, engaged (especially in Italy) in intellectually entertaining disputations before them, versified, and taught in the new schools and colleges or tutored royal and noble children who would, as Ascham complained, become sophisticatedly Italianate and unhumanistic as soon as they became teen-agers. But all this, the political and social historians tell us, was a sort of cultural smoke-screen, the real decisions being unhumanistically and inelegantly made in the pre-Virginia back rooms. The rhetorical Renaissance Humanist could hope only for a moderately successful and uninfluential secretarial or tutorial post, or to be some king's Polonius, or to be an unpractical Machiavel who had lost his job or a saintly martyr who had lost his head.

This view of Renaissance humanism, as it is rather disdainfully developed by philosophical, political, and social historians, may be somewhat less just as a historical appraisal of Renaissance humanism than as an expression of their opinion of their own contemporary humanist colleagues. Yet a good many recent interpreters of Renaissance poetry are evidently inclined to go along with it and with the belief of the distinguished historian of non-dramatic sixteenth-century English literature that humanism, with its neoclassical preoccupation with absolute standards of classic style and its mechanical educational methods, could not possibly have contributed anything of importance to the creative outburst of Elizabethan poetry.[4] The implication of all this is that, whether humanism is characteristic of the Renaissance or not, it gives the period no distinctive and significant character because, as Bacon said, it was concerned only with words and was essentially trivial. And in this connection, it is of less literary use than at first sight it may seem to recall Ascham's pre-Baconian observation: "Ye know not what hurt ye do to learning that care not for words but for matter, and so make a divorce between the tongue and the heart"; or even to point out further that (as the philosophical historian himself tells us, though the significance of the sequence appears to have suffered progressive reduction or a tendency to reversal of emphasis in successive essays) *studia humanitatis* extended from

[4] C. S. Lewis, *English Literature in the Sixteenth Century Excluding Drama* (Oxford, 1954), pp. 18–32.

grammar, through logic and rhetoric (and the versifying that was a branch of rhetoric) to moral philosophy. Whatever limiting defini- tions may be found in classical or medieval roots, *litterae humaniores* in the Renaissance meant a rhetoric which was the instrument of moral philosophy, and which, in the north at any rate, had through Augustine a close relation to homiletics. And moral philosophy cov- ered a multitude, indeed *the* multitude, of human activities. It may be only too true, as the political and social historians skeptically tell us, that humanistic moral philosophy—humanists being human, and human nature being what political and social history tells us it is—had no striking effect on the course of events. Professor Mattingly bluntly observes that "the moral rectitude of a people and the political power of their state would seem to have only the most tenuous connection."[5] Yet this conclusion may reflect something more significant as to the tired ethos of current political and social history than as to the ethos and effect of Renaissance humanism. Did so many underpaid but hardworking schoolteachers really have so little effect? Or is it that the effect of humanism is incalculable in the terms cultural historians now use? And as to philosophy, while moral philosophy may no longer be a legitimate division of that exaltedly detached discipline, Renaissance humanism, at any rate in the north, consistently thought of itself—and up until yesterday consistently continued to think of itself—as persuading through rhetoric to the humane life indicated by moral philosophy. To limit humanism by a definition which re- duces *studia humanitatis* to merely elegant literary instrumentality is to ignore its historical principles and its ethical dynamic, and suggests a systematically abstracting and unhistorically categorical perversity. Furthermore, whatever may be true of Italian humanism—and I can- not see that the philosophical historian has made out an adequate case for his delimited definition even of it—northern humanism cannot be characterized simply in terms of its renewed response to classical or pagan *literae humaniores*. To the historian of philosophy, systematic theology may seem unmetaphysical and matters of religion, unac- countably, entirely otherworldly, unintelligent, and inhumane. But northern humanism involves also a renewed response to the Christian *litterae humaniores* of the church Fathers, especially Augustine, as we were persuaded earlier, and to the *studia humanitatis*, including the moral philosophy and even the literary techniques, of Scripture.

Yet the philosophical and sociological historian will only go on to say—what again is perfectly true—that there is no distinctive and effec- tive Renaissance moral philosophy. The Christian-humanist ethical

[5] G. Mattingly, in his Wisconsin lecture (see above), p. 17.

ideal which is still attractive to many literary historians and critics can hardly be said, even when it is supported by medieval or Protestant systematic theology, to have been characteristic of an age so skeptical on the one hand, so rigidly dogmatic at the center, and so Neo-Platonically idealistic (if not mystical) on the other. The Christian-humanist synthesis, integrating the orders of nature and of grace, through the purifying of spiritual religion and the operation of the God-given reason on the best classical models, unifying into an ideal seven the three Christian and the four cardinal classical virtues, was certainly the Erasmian ideal inherited by northern humanism as a bulwark against theological antinomianism on the one hand and skepticism and scientism on the other, which we ought perhaps to strive to shore up. But it was, we now see, if not more than half medieval, at least somewhat more than half defensive to begin with, and the forces it ineffectively attempted to stem seem, historically, to have got out of hand (if they have not always been out of hand) before it was firmly constructed. "Oft have we known that seven-fold fence to fail. . . ." Our attention thus seems inescapably focused even by the literature of the period on the ironic existential instability of the hyphen on which the Christian-humanist synthesis depends, so that we become only too well aware of the tensions between its two terms, which the historian of philosophy underlines whenever he turns to moral philosophy. The period of the Renaissance was, it seems, chiefly characterized by the tensions extending through the extremes of one term toward mysticism and Puritan rigorism and of the other to naturalism and libertinism. Within the terms themselves there are on the one hand all the varieties of medieval, Reformation, and Counter-Reformation Christian ethics, and on the other all those represented by the miscellaneous revived schools of classical ethics, from the Neo-Platonic through the Aristotelian and Stoic to the Epicurean and Pyrrhonist.

It would thus seem that, philosophically, ethically, and culturally speaking, it must be admitted that the period of the Renaissance was marked not by an organic rebirth but by the pangs of confused tensions. And as to literary activity, there are the tensions between academic, humanist rhetoricians and university wits who became giddy, fantastic poets, all compact—as Shakespeare snidely makes his unimaginative, orderly-minded, disdainful Duke Theseus say—with lunatics and lovers. Moreover, whatever the contribution of humanism or Christian humanism to poetry—and it was significant, the cultural historian now leaves us unable to fall back on the old optimistic notion that Renaissance English poetry was the dynamic expression of the creative spirit of an expansive age. So far as I know, no economic historians have as yet said of the northern Renaissance what some have argued as to the Italian Renaissance—that it was not, as we used to suppose, the product of a period of social and economic expansiveness but rather of a short-lived and deceptive recovery in the declining rhythm of the disastrous period of depression that extended from the late Middle Ages into early modern times and aroused desperately energetic enterprises of various sorts, including explorations and the administrative reorganization of states (and universities).[6] But we know enough, if only from the continuing literature of complaint, of the economic distress and the class conflicts that went along with the population explosion and commercial enterprise in the undeveloped countries of the Renaissance north. And as to the dynamic relation of the national literatures to the political idealism and patriotic enthusiasm accompanying the administrative reorganizations induced by this situation, and whatever glow of admiration Sir John Neale may retain for England's first Eliza, we have J. B. Black's revised concentrations on the tensions of the last years of her reign when the great Elizabethan poets began to be heard in the theaters and through the presses, and even nearer to our business and bosoms, the sobering observation of Professor Mattingly in the conclusion of his authoritatively and unromantically realistic account of the English fumbling, Spanish mismanagement, and meteorological luck leading to the defeat of the Armada, that it is not easy to see how all this can have produced the mood of buoyant optimism which is sometimes said to have produced the explosion of literary genius in the later years of Elizabeth's reign, there being no link in England between the Armada campaign and any literary work such as we can find in Spain between Cervantes's incarceration because of the confusion of his collector's accounts and the writing of *Don Quixote*.[7] The completion in 1589 and publication in 1590 of the first three books of Spenser's *Faerie Queene* seem unaccountably to have been overlooked here, though of course not every student of Spenser would regard these simply as expressions of the buoyant optimism of Calidore-Raleigh or of Colin Clout before he came disconsolately home again. Yet it is certainly difficult to explain the post-Armada poetic outburst as the product simply of euphoric patriotism.

[6] See R. S. Lopez, in the volume edited by Dannenfeldt (above), pp. 58–60; and for a review of recent economic opinion, with reservations as to the depressed view, W. K. Ferguson in *Studies in the Renaissance*, VII (1960), 7–26.

[7] Sir John E. Neale, *England's Elizabeth: A Lecture Delivered at the Folger Shakespeare Library on November 17, 1958* . . . (Washington, 1958), to cite one brief appraisal out of many large; J. B. Black, *The Reign of Elizabeth* (2d ed.; Oxford, 1959), especially the revised chapters xi to xiii; G. Mattingly, *The Armada* (Cambridge, Mass., 1959), p. 398.

IV

Indeed, all that the authoritative philosophical and sociological historians have been telling us in their reappraisals of the period is matter of historical fact, and we must accept their reports willingly and with interest since their fields of investigation have, in the commonwealth of knowledge, important contiguous relations with our own. But we may yet inquire bluntly what those relations really are and what the findings of the historians really signify as to the literary Renaissance and, for my immediate colleagues and myself, as to the explosion of English Renaissance poetic genius.

In this connection there would seem to be several considerations, both historical and literary, that would reward closer attention than the cultural historians have yet given them. Among these, one is suggested by the curious fixation on Italy exhibited by all such reappraising historians and inherited by them from the nineteenth-century Burckhardtian and Symondsean hypothesis as to the Renaissance they are sedulously attempting to undermine yet as continually seem to reflect in their cyclical periodizations of history.[8] It is still a characteristically apologetic habit of English-speaking (and, for some reason or other, especially American English-speaking) literary critics to suppose that any poetic force or finesse the unsophisticated Renaissance English may display must have been picked up from sophisticated Italy, if only by way of idealistic or libertine France. This is a self-consciously apologetic misapprehension fostered by an Ultima-Thule or frontier mentality. The North was of course well aware of the sophistication of Renaissance Italy, but it regarded its sophistication and its seductive Neo-Platonism with hard-headed detachment, and

[8] Kristeller does observe in passing in his Wisconsin lecture (see above), p. 28, that the extent of Italian influence in other countries in which the Renaissance assumed different features presents a problem; but this perception, whose elaboration is to be hoped for as a result of the massively important investigation of the distribution of manuscripts, patristic as well as classical, does not seem to modify the isolation of neoclassical elegance as humanism's generic mark everywhere, despite the broad characterization of *studia humanitatis* elsewhere, pp. 34–35. D. J. Geanakopolos can devote a section of his study of the Greek revival in Italy (*Greek Scholars in Venice* [Cambridge, Mass., 1962]) to Erasmus's relations with Aldus with no reference whatever to Erasmus's earlier visit to England; though it is heartening to find Denys Hay's *The Italian Renaissance* concluding with explicitly tentative comments on the reception of the Renaissance in the North because no northern survey has yet possessed sufficient knowledge of the Italian with sufficient sense of the significant differences between Italian and northern social structures. An interesting sidelight is provided by Mattingly's turning back in his Wisconsin lecture (see above), p. 22, to Motley's account of the Dutch Republic with reference to the failure of the Italian states to co-operate for self-preservation—though Mattingly's essentially Machiavellian and un-northern explanation of this failure still stands.

its humanistic and poetically satiric characterizations of Italianate English, Macaronis, and seductively self-deceiving Astrophils depend on a thoroughly northern tradition. We are going to rediscover that tradition (which students of Anglo-Saxon, Middle English, and especially of Chaucer have been faithfully preserving for us) when we throw off the Italianate fixation of the philosophical and cultural historians and become fully aware of what as yet remains the all but lost northern fifteenth century of the great conciliar efforts. The character of that northern century and its significance as the immediate background or beginning of the northern Renaissance remains as yet obscure partly because of a peculiar combination of sectarian Protestant and Counter-Reformation with neoclassically humanist defensive instincts. But the distorting effects of sectarian concentration on relatively late and variously compromising peripheral figures in this century have already been sufficiently offset by the work of such English historians as E. F. Jacob or such American historians as Louise Ropes Loomis or such Continental historians as the unusually perceptive historian of the Council of Trent and its background, Hubert Jedin; and we shall shortly be able to discern more clearly not only the continuity of English prose (since the fifteenth century lasted rather longer in England than it did elsewhere) but also the continuity of English poetry through, for instance, those Skeltonics we have been unable to appreciate, historically or critically, because, until recently, we have been looking in the wrong places for the explanation of their nature and function. Of course we shall not find that the northern fifteenth century, with its disputatious academic conflicts between realism and nominalism, had a distinctive systematic philosophy or even theology. But what we shall find is that this metaphysical and theological collapse induced in the North the fifteenth-century Gersonian effort to reform education, which the historian of philosophy quite overlooks when he turns at 1300 from France to Italy, and that this effort to reform provides the immediate background for the literate Christian-humanism that the young Erasmus was stimulated by when he visited England, and found a lively, if untutored, interest in Greek—perhaps partly the consequence of uneasy northern sympathy with Greek orthodoxy in its difference of opinion with Rome. The northern and especially the English literary renaissance, out of which Renaissance English poetry comes, is, despite one politically or ecclesiastically caused hiatus after another, continuous with this movement and its response to philosophical and institutional collapse.

Another consideration is suggested by the subliterary (and often, I must confess it seems to me, unimaginative) approach of the cultural historians to the period of the literary Renaissance. It need not greatly trouble us (so long as we do not accept their untrained opinions as authoritative) that, with so many Renaissance humanists, they are inclined to regard versifying as a subordinate branch of rhetoric, as an instrument for educating children or whiling away the empty hours of old men in chimney corners, or as documentary cultural evidence rather less significant than the reports of Venetian ambassadors, the criminal and court records, the rent rolls, which are the principal preoccupations of historians nowadays and have induced one of them to speak of the "laundry-bill" approach to history, or, as I, remembering Catherine Moreland, would prefer to call it, the "washing-bill" method. No historian, not even a literary historian, can command too much factual detail; but Baconian inductive historical method seems to expect the geological weight of mere detail to produce fossilized sense; and as to the Renaissance its effect has so far been simply to produce an impression of multiple fragmentation. A few years ago, my distinguished compatriot, the authoritative historian of the idea of the Renaissance in history, W. A. Ferguson, called for an effort of synthesis which would relate the various fragments of the cultural historians and, by the way, shed at least some light on the background and origin of the creative Renaissance arts; but such a desire for the universalizing synthesis of so many confused human activities has a somewhat syncretic Neo-Platonic air, which is precisely the opposite of philosophical categorization, though Professor Kristeller has just invited us to "try to coordinate and integrate" the various opinions as to the "problem of the Renaissance" (and especially its delimited humanism) in some historical theory having the objective validity of a scientific hypothesis—an invitation suggesting the reduction of his own rich historical detail to some highly abstract generalization.[9] Professor Ferguson, under the influence chiefly of economic historical findings, later suggested that we should regard the Renaissance as extending from about 1300 to 1600 (dates with which most historians would be content) and as chiefly marked by the decay of late medieval commercial practices and the steady emergence of capitalist enterprise and methods. Though he would not argue that genius can be explained in these terms, yet he would apparently (and certainly in some measure rightly) see the arts and humanistic literature as taking advantage—as is, after all, typical of them—of the patronizing support of emergent capitalism in this long and tense period of economic transition. But, whatever may be the truth of the long-term economic facts of boom or bust, or however dialectically economic their impli-

[9] Ferguson in *Journal of the History of Ideas*, XII (1951), 483–495; Kristeller in *Studies in the Renaissance*, IX (1962), 9, 21–22; and for the economic view, n. 6 above.

cations, this is to extend the period of Renaissance to unintelligible cultural proportions; and, while we ought certainly to insist on the literary continuity of this period in England, it leaves the English poetic renaissance of the sixteenth and seventeenth centuries as a kind of dumb-show commercial performed when the transitional economic drama had ended.

It is perhaps time to consider what, historically speaking, has happened to the concept of Renaissance in the hands of cultural historians in the past century or so; and, tentatively and simple-mindedly, one might conclude thus. The concept originated, in the northern fifteenth and sixteenth centuries, in the midst of philosophical, ideological, religious, social, and institutional collapse, as a description of a rebirth of the hortatory arts, and in particular the literary arts and the art of poetry. Because the humanistic literary arts and the poetry of the Renaissance were much concerned with moral philosophy and every human activity, the concept was transferred to other human activities, largely through the idealism of humanists and their educational efforts. It thus began to be applied to the philosophical, political, social conditions of its period. Cultural historians of the late eighteenth and nineteenth centuries attempted to explain this literary renaissance in terms of philosophical, political, and social renaissances. The sum of what our cultural historians have succeeded in demonstrating as to literature by their cyclical reconsiderations is that, whatever the relations between literary activity and activity in these areas, there were no philosophical, political, social, or economic renaissances that adequately explain the northern literary renaissance of the late sixteenth and seventeenth centuries. We may thank them heartily for this thoroughly negative evidence as to the misleading explanations of the literary renaissance provided by their nineteenth-century colleagues, and go on more intelligently with our own business, with which the merely cultural historians are obviously incapable of dealing, that is, with the appraisal and explanation of *the* English Renaissance—the literary and poetical renaissance of the late sixteenth and seventeenth centuries. As to the indubitable historicity of that renaissance as a fact, we have the conclusive evidence of our own washing-bills, of the Short-Title Catalogue, Wing, and the Stationers' Register.

As to the relation of this fact to the commercial development of the technology of printing and paper-making, it proves, as we investigate the origins of that development in the fifteenth-century North, no more sensible to say that the literary renaissance depended on the advantage of printing than that printing developed in response to the demands of the literary renaissance. Why do cultural historians nowadays so perversely insist on putting the cart before the horse and driver and on subordinating the human spirit to the instruments it demands and gets? If anything needs explaining in cultural history, it is not the failure of nerve that rendered the humanities of the later Middle Ages, as in our day, incapable of and uneasy about presenting the claims of the best values men can conceive, but what induces that failure of nerve, the unconscionable length of time it takes administrators and scientific technologists to implement the perceptions of possibilities, including the spatial and the international, formulated and given popular currency by writers from Plato to the author of *Tom Swift*.

And as to the character of this fact, the historical literary Renaissance in England, it was sixteenth-century political propaganda as revived by nineteenth-century cultural history that produced the literarily speaking unhistorical notion that the great Elizabethan explosion of literary genius was produced by euphoric post-Armada buoyancy. This notion depends on a very simple-minded reading (if any reading at all) of poems like *The Faerie Queene*, in which George may be on his way to sainthood but through a process of hard experience, amid the terrors and dangers of a by no means golden fairyland, and of falling, despairing, recovering, trying again, tripping, and trying yet again, that may be more intelligently read—like Virgil's advice to Augustus-Æneas—as a warning to Elizabeth, her courtiers and her people, that if they continue so to fumble and be found wanting, they may not be quite as providentially lucky when the next armada crisis comes. Remembering that Spenser was an efficient civil servant in that disputed Elizabethan wasteland Ireland, that Donne was a lord keeper's secretary and an ecclesiastical administrator who had devoted his studies chiefly to the points sadly in controversy between the churches, and that Milton went blind as Latin secretary to the confused Commonwealth and Protectorate Council of State, we might observe that what the philosophical and sociological historians have been telling us in their reappraisals of the period is simply what the great poets knew about it at first hand, from their experience of unwashed public linen and the rising cost of their own laundry.

The literary renaissance did not originate in the confused tensions the reappraising historians have been telling us about, though it was certainly induced by them. Great poetry does not arise from the possession of some abstract systematic philosophy, or some Miranda-like belief in a brave new world, or some expectation of plenty. The poetry of Scripture emerged from no such situation, nor the Platonic mimesis of Socratic discourse (Gilbert Murray speaks of the Greek failure of nerve), nor the Ciceronian dialogues, nor Ovid's poetry, nor the writings of Augustine; and, though there were many ineffective and idealistic humanists, and some similar poets, there were many Renaissance humanists and poets who recognized the historical situations behind such writings and the similarities in their own. What is remarkable about the great poets of the Renaissance is that they were so sensitively aware of all the tensions—religious, philosophical, ethical, political, social, economic—the historians might have saved themselves a good deal of trouble over by learning about from poetry. The literary and poetic renaissance was a response to these tensions. The tensions provide it with its materials and are the subjects of its commentary. But this renascent poetry is not to be explained or appraised simply in terms of its material or subject of comment. Many of us have made the apologetic mistake of accepting the data of the cultural historian as providing the terms in which we must evaluate, explain, and sell the material of our discipline. That is a self-defeating effort, because our poets did not accept these inadequate terms but used them subordinately for their purposes while attacking their inadequacy. They did so, in the terms appropriate to the poetry of a literary renaissance, because the times, with the confused inadequacy even of moral philosophy, needed such poetry's satiric, homiletic, and re-energizing comment, and because men of genius were at hand capable of responding to the demand by modifying the techniques of rhetorical humanism and renewing the literary tradition through a regenerative combining of the spirits and techniques of the biblical, classical Greek, classical Roman, patristic, medieval, and even Italianate literary traditions, in a language whose continuity was dynamically renewed thereby in a new poetry. The nature and function of that literary renaissance have to be sought in appropriate literary terms which may, on the whole, be meaningless to the disdainfully unimaginative philosophical and sociological historian and may remain so for many, but were clearly not meaningless in the period of the literary renaissance and need not remain so in ours—where they are still used in everyday speech and where the techniques they represent are daily used by old and new modes of communication.

V

The historian may say he cannot imagine what significance such Renaissance literary terms have for us, but what they meant and how they are appliable to our times—through education, the disciplined accumulation of factual material, critical reappraisal, and the sustaining and re-energizing of the tongue the English renaissance spake and the faith and morals it, however confusedly, held—is what the renaissance in Renaissance literary studies is clarifying through its various investigations and critical differences of opinion. Most historical critics, appraising in these varied ways and working in their classrooms to teach the young and the new generation of teachers of the young, would be too intelligently and modestly preoccupied (or uneasy) to offer the kind of simple-minded apology attempted here; yet they are all in their degree and according to their abilities aware of what we know and have seen of the disciplined and purposeful efficiency of education on the other side of the wall—where young teenagers can speak fluent English and skilfully misinterpret Renaissance English poems of complaint for the dialectically materialistic purpose they have been imbued with, and aware that this demands of North American education and especially of the humanities an equally determined and purposeful effort to sustain and make operative whatever is most admirable in the culture whose modern form originated for us in the sixteenth and seventeenth centuries. It is easy to be simple-minded about such matters; but it is useful now and then for some simple-minded person without the perception of the angels to dare to tread a simple path. Our present situation is essentially comparable to the Renaissance situation—partly because, if we extend the period as completely as we should, we shall find we are still living in it, but more because our tensions and our risks are comparable to those of the sixteenth and seventeenth centuries, and chiefly because we need and are getting the kind of vigorous reinvestigation and discussion, comparable to what went on among rhetoricians and poets of various degrees of giftedness during the Renaissance, of modes of communication, their defects, abuses, and how they might be rendered more effectively human than they were in the later Middle Ages or are now in the hiddenly persuading hands of news-leaking politicians, journalists, or advertising agencies, or in the abstract pomposities of philosophers, moralists, reformers, and many academics.

What the study of Renaissance English poetry may contribute to this, and what historical criticism is in process of demonstrating, may be indicated by considering (though here all too briefly) some of the principles developed by Sir Philip Sidney in his pre-Armada *Defence of Poesie* written in reply to typically moralistic attacks on fantastically seductive poetry by humanist philosophers and historians, whose title in the apparently unauthorized of its two first printings in 1595 (in those post-Armada years) the title of this chapter modestly echoes. Philosophic or aesthetically oriented literary historians—like J. E. Spingarn or René Wellek or David Daiches or M. H. Abrams, whose perceptive attention is, however, focused on the nineteenth century and Coleridge[10]—condescendingly describe this defence as typical of Renaissance English self-contradiction (since, they think, it naïvely echoes Italian Neo-Platonism and neo-Aristotelianism in regarding the poet at once as in some sense Orphic and a seer and as an imitative artist whose operations should be controlled by consciously ordering literary principles) or as a nervously self-defensive and hence casually ironic apology by a minor poet who cannot escape from the stultifying moralism he dislikes. But, as everybody knows (and as Kenneth Muir has recently reminded us with brevity and point),[11] Sidney was a charming, sophisticated, cultivated, intelligent, humanistically well-educated, actively responsible courtier and soldier of influential family, who had seen in 1572 in Paris the Saint Bartholomew's Day massacre of Protestants (almost as bloody as the ideological massacres of our day), was deeply concerned with the secular and religious conflicts of Elizabethan England and Europe, hoped and worked at least for a union of Protestants if not for a union of Christendom that would include both his Roman Catholic recusant and French Huguenot friends, and was to die, honorably if somewhat recklessly, in the ideological and economic wars in the Netherlands. It is not wise to be condescending as to the principles of such a man, who would have appreciated the ironic Shavian definition of a gentleman as one who never unintentionally gives offense. If it is looked at in the light of current efforts to reappraise Renaissance English poetry, this seminal defense may be seen to have been sharply conscious of all the paralyzing tensions of the time, and, though it never mentions England's Eliza, it may prove more than consistent with

[10] J. E. Spingarn, *Literary Criticism in the Renaissance* (New York, 1899, etc.), pp. 268–274; R. Wellek, *A History of Modern Criticism* (New Haven, 1955), I, 17; D. Daiches, *Critical Approaches to Literature* (Englewood Cliffs, 1956), pp. 50–72; M. H. Abrams, *The Mirror and the Lamp* (New York, 1953), pp. 14–15, 323. Daiches's concluding comment (pp. 71–72) is typical of current responses to Sidney's theory in seeing moralizing as providing an escape from a Platonic dilemma which is perhaps more in the eye of the beholder than in his author's; cf. W. K. Wimsatt, Jr., and C. Brooks, *Literary Criticism: A Short History* (New York, 1957), p. 170. The commentary by C. S. Lewis (*English Literature in the Sixteenth Century*, pp. 343–347) remains the most perceptive, as in its insistence that the ethical is the aesthetic for Sidney, despite vagueness as to Sidney's controlling beliefs. R. L. Montgomery, Jr., uses the *Defence* effectively, though without subjecting it to significant reappraisal, in his reinterpretation of Sidney's poetry in *Symmetry and Sense* (Austin, 1961); and it has of course a collateral place in the definitive edition of the poems by W. A. Ringler, Jr. (Oxford, 1962).

[11] K. Muir, *Sir Philip Sidney* ("*Writers and Their Work*," *No. 120* [London, 1960]), though p. 11 does little more than reproduce the usual moralized view of the *Defence*.

Sidney's political theory, as this is in process of being clarified,[12] and with his ecclesiastical and religious opinions, which yet demand the clarifying study that might much illuminate the premises behind his recently and perceptively re-examined poetic practice. Further, what we know of its pre-publication circulation in manuscript and may discern of its echoed influence would seem to indicate, more clearly than has been recognized, that it helped much to teach perceptive and frustrated public servants like Spenser, Donne, Milton what their poetry might do, and how, and what it should aim at, beyond what could be taught them by humanist educators, historians, and moral philosophers. For, says Sidney, in caricatures in the Erasmian satiric tradition turned against unimaginative humanism itself, philosophers with their sullen gravity and contempt of ordinary outward things, sophistically speaking against subtilty, and casting largess as they go of definitions, divisions, distinctions, and scornful interrogatives, can deal only with the inhumanly abstract, while the historian, loaded with old mouse-eaten records, authorizing himself for the most part upon other histories built upon the notable foundation of hearsay, curious of antiquities and inquisitive of novelties, a wonder to young folk and a tyrant in table-talk as the purveyor of hard-headed, old-aged experience, is tied to the mere empirical particularity of what Henry James was to call "clumsy life at its stupid work." Neither, says Sidney, going beyond Aristotle, can be of any use to us unless they become poetical by, one gathers, imaginatively applying their abstractions to the human situation or imaginatively clarifying the constant significance of human experience. Poetry, for Sidney, is a realistic, imaginative, and significant "making" or fiction (usually though not always employing the ordering and braking effect of verse) which does both. It is usual to say that this notion incoherently reflects the interminable disputes as to what poetry imitates or mirrors, existential nature and the rational Aristotelian universals or the transcendent reality of the Platonic ideas, of Italian academic theorists as these are reviewed by Spingarn and more recently by Bernard Weinberg and Baxter Hathaway (for whom Sidney appears to remain an untutored northern provincial).[13] It seems possible that Sidney was

12 The most recent examination is by E. W. Talbert, in the well-documented fourth chapter of *The Problem of Order: Elizabethan Political Commonplaces and an Example of Shakespeare's Art* (Chapel Hill, 1962).

13 Spingarn, cited above; B. Weinberg, *A History of Literary Criticism in the Italian Renaissance* (Chicago, 1961); B. Hathaway, *The Age of Criticism: The Late Renaissance in Italy* (Ithaca, 1962). Sidney of course makes no appearance in Weinberg's volumes. For evidence of Hathaway's apparent assumption that Sidney was quite incapable of recognizing and attempting to resolve, from a different point of view, the theoretical cruxes of Italian criticism as Hathaway himself sees them in impressive philosophical detail, see especially pp. 326–327.

only too acutely aware of the increasingly pedantic futility of these disputes and that—thinking he had in the northern tradition a superior datum ignored by humanist Counter-Reformation Italians nervous of heresy—he was saying, with that Veronese admirer of the English Queen Mab who so much resembles him, a plague o' both your merely philosophical houses. What he says is that poetry is an imitation, *mimesis* in Aristotle's word, a representing, counterfeiting, or figuring forth, which seems from the context and illustrations to mean that it represents an action, or rather the process involved in an action, though by a making of something like but not the same—"counterfeiting" still having in Sidney's day rather more of its root than of our pejorative meaning, and that it does so in order to indicate or reveal something significant for us in the process that would not otherwise be so fully perceived. The context suggests that Sidney knew the Italian disputes and also, as I think, knew well his Aristotle and Plato through his northern Greek; but ironically, and surely not inadvertently, his definition of poetry (or proposition) does not tell us precisely what poetry imitates: we have to find that out for ourselves from reading his full defence responsively. As a northerner, he is less interested in and less certain of his power to say what poetry is than what it does. He is even willing to admit for that purpose that fiction is lies, for "the poet never maketh any circles about your imagination, to conjure you to believe for true what he writeth," nor anything anybody, himself or any character, may morally or philosophically say in the process of the action; it is an honest admission, for it is a wise man who is certain that his telling or his acting is not partially deceptive. Some realistic Italians, like Castelvetro, had argued that poetry was a matter not only of illusion but of counterfeiting delusion; but they had done so to prove that its sensational function was to produce wonder in vulgar minds. Sidney excludes no man and no form of poetry, even ballads, from his defence; and his defence itself illustrates the function he thinks poetry should perform. The defence is a rhetorically ordered, formally humanist forensic oration, over which (as K. O. Myrick made us see some years ago) plays the *sprezzatura*, the gracefully ironic, self-aware art of the courtier that conceals art; and through this (to go a little further than Myrick) the oration becomes itself a paradoxical fiction, a praise of lying, in which the speaker adopts (what Daiches and company have allowed themselves to be taken in by) the persona or mask of one who does not know clearly what he is talking about, in order to induce us to figure it out. Unlike most modern critics, Renaissance poets do not much care what their audiences think of them, so long as they can induce a response. I cannot here illustrate (anymore than I can imitate) Sidney's provocative irony; but what he thus figures forth is the process poetry induces, the process whereby it induces it, and the process it is imitating and counterfeiting. What is induced, Sidney thinks, is a healthily psychological process, an exercise of the whole mind whereby poetry enables men to the good actions of the whole man, a thoroughly humanistic end which, he sees from the times, merely morally philosophic humanistic rhetoric fails to achieve. For, he says in the theological terms of the time, "our erected wit maketh us to know what perfection is, and yet our infected will keepeth us from reaching unto it." Poetry energizes the will so that a man's reach may more nearly equal his grasp; but it does so by irradiating the mind in all its rational powers which, in Sidney's still half-medieval psychology include, with the intellect and will, the memory and imagination. Sidney would accept the English Christian-Stoic suspicion of the imagination or fantasy (recently well documented)[14] as the faculty most influenced by the corrupt senses and perhaps itself the seat of original sin; but for him good poetry exercises the imagination, with the other faculties, illuminates the grounds of wisdom that, in philosophy and history, "lie dark before the imaginative and judging power," and so enables the whole mind to respond healthily to the stimuli of experience coming through the senses and to act well through them. This is of course for Sidney a therapeutic process; but Sidney would, no more than I, presume to contradict anyone who thinks himself not in need of the therapy of healthy exercise. By such his argument is usually reduced to an offensively elementary moralistic level by the omission (as by Daiches) of the third term of the statement in which he says poetry gives us models of virtues and vices: he says, "notable images of virtues and vices and what else." From the context and illustrations it appears (to imitate the philosophical jargon of our own day) that the "whatelseness" poetry images is the human situation in which virtue and vice operate and conflict, with whatever else it is that the healthy human mind can discern as operating in that conflict, in classical, medieval, or Renaissance times. Mythomystic interpreters represent Sidney, because he enjoyed ballads and bards and thought Orphic poetry drew "wild untamed wits to an admiration of knowledge" in primitive times, as an inconsistent defender of the mythopoeic transcendentals for which they value Renaissance poetry. This may (though I doubt it) be an adequate approach to songs of innocence, Byzantium, or sonnets to Orpheus; but mythomysticism seems much inclined to hear the echo of its own Orphic voice and to seek its enthusiastic image out of time, by unhis-

[14] W. Rossky, "Imagination in the English Renaissance: Psychology and Poetic," *Studies in the Renaissance,* V (1958), 49–73.

torically reading the mythical metaphoric structure of such poems as, say, *Paradise Lost*, not only out of time but out of the context of their carefully organized poetic structures, that have a beginning, a middle, and an end, designed to evoke a healthy response even to all the woe we cannot escape from. Sidney's heart responds to ballads as to a trumpet that calls to war or calls the people in the wilderness to hear a proclamation of law. His poetic world is golden and not, like nature's, brazen; but in being so it suggests the realities "of that first accursed fall of Adam," and it induces the reader to imitate the poet's effort, through which he "doth grow in effect into another nature." (The preposition "into" is significantly lacking in the unauthorized 1595 edition; but, unlike most interpreters, I quote from the authorized version.) That other nature is, as Sidney implies elsewhere, human nature as it ought to be and might be but in this world is never likely quite to be; but it is the process of effort in time that matters. Of course, for Sidney, this other nature has the support, he thinks, of his superior northern datum. The proximate source for this is in the writings in which his Huguenot friends were attempting, in line with a French tradition that goes back into the conciliar fifteenth century, to modify the rigidities of Protestant and Counter-Reformation dogmatism by philosophical Augustinian and classically humanist discourse. Sidney believed with them, though more ironically and poetically, that nature remains the art of God[15] and that history, to use Burke's phrase, is the known march of His ordinary providence. Sidney seems to be implying that good poetry or fiction is not fantastic or transcendental but, through a conscious and disciplined art making good use of the providential gifts of nature and knowing what it does and to what purpose, represents this creative process, with its corrective ironies and its sustaining energy, as it proceeds, he thinks, in time and our experience. I do not of course argue for the truth of the premise provided by Sidney's superior northern datum—or even that I myself clearly understand it and its implications. That is not the business of a merely critical literary historian. But I would argue that, historically speaking, to dismiss this premise as unintelligent and aesthetically irrelevant and to reduce it to the level of mere customary or conventional morality—with Mr. Daiches and other such commentators on Sidnean Renaissance–English literary theory—is to display a failure of objective historical grasp, a lack of what the eighteenth century called "sympathetic imagination" and what the sixteenth and seventeenth

---

[15] A theme whose increasing importance in criticism is reflected, among many others, in D. Bush's revisions for *English Literature in the Earlier Seventeenth Century* (2d ed., rev.; Oxford, 1962); see *Journal of English and Germanic Philology*, LXII (1963), No. 3.

still called "charity," and an uncritical twentieth-centric presumption
as to the rightness of one's own skeptical opinions. Historically speaking, Sidney's defence has, in fact, a sharply direct, if ironic, bearing
on the increasing religious tensions of the pre- and post-Armada
years: that is perhaps why it remained unpublished but in circulation
till 1595, because of the implications as to the extremes of both
Protestant rigorism and Protestant enthusiasm in its observation (remembering the epistles) that poetry should not be "scourged out of
the church of God," its insistence on the power of what Tremellius
called "the poetical parts" of Scripture, and its constantly implied
analogy between the psychology of religious and of poetic experience. It is only an analogy, not the identity some enthusiasts then as
now would make it; for poetry is a human art and Sidney will have
no nonsense as to any fantastic divine afflatus. But his ironic defence
becomes in the end an exhortation to poets and readers not to abuse
such a natural gift, but to possess themselves of the *energeia* illustrated
by a poetry vitally conceived, consciously organized and controlled
by art, and sensitively applied to the human situation.

   Recent studies of Renaissance English poetry, especially in their
concern with poetic and the function of poetry, would seem to be
finding that their justification and the justification of their material
lie where Sidney apologetically asserted the justification of poetry
lay: in the full exercise of the mind in all its powers afforded by the
historically critical study of such poetry. Since Renaissance English
poetry at its best is always the product of the immediate human realities of its times, and since it aims at impinging on these realities by
affecting through its art what men will and do, and since it habitually
considers time and what men do in terms of the universal verities it
normally ascribes to a directing and ordering Providence and finds
mirrored (however distortingly) in history and experience, it is inevitable that some appraisers should regard it as a merely historical
mirror of the nature of Renaissance times, others as a simple sugar-
coating of morality and principles, and others as chiefly communicat-
ing a transcendent vision. Many minor poets in the period wrote verse
limited to one of these functions, as many minor critics today prefer
one or another of these simplifications. But the major poets of the
period thought of their poetry, though fictional, as inducing a total
exercise of mind, directed to sound human ends, and conducive to a
healthy response to the human situation; and they did not think that
uninspired, unimaginative, insensitive history and moral philosophy
or any other human science could induce such an exercise. It would
seem a mistake for literary humanists today to underestimate the significance of the historical fact that Renaissance English poetry repre-

sented the fullest dimensions of Renaissance *litterae humaniores*, to imitate the historians and philosophers in being content to reflect its functions only partially, while leaving the principle of preparative exercise to teachers of PE—by whom student muscles are developed through various fictional situations, including those provided by the vaulting-horse on which are practiced, in the space age, what are essentially the cavalry exercises Sidney begins his apology by comparing with more necessary literary activities. The current renaissance of critically historical Renaissance literary studies, despite the disadvantages they face, illustrates the development of an intelligently and objectively appraising, humanely sensitive, high principled, and informedly disciplined historical imagination. Since the spatial and international imagination involves the same exercise of mind as the historical, this is a development that should pay dividends beyond the academic.

FREDSON BOWERS

Shakespeare's Art: The Point of View

Shakespeare's plays were plays, first and foremost. Present-day critics, in their search for new areas of exploration, do these plays a disservice by treating them as poems—often as if they were extended lyric poems. Whether a play is in verse or in prose, it is primarily a play and must conform to the laws of the drama, not to criteria that have been set as appropriate for other literary genres. When dramatic structure is neglected for, say, an interest in style, criticism ceases to be dramatic criticism.

Moreover, a concern for dramatic structure acts as a check on another troublesome habit of present-day Shakespearean criticism: the reconstruction of a play—its people and the significance of its action—either in terms of some preconceived aesthetic theory or in terms of the critic's own ingenious sensibility. Both can be peculiarly misleading. The constant awareness that drama imposes certain rules on literature written in its form serves as a check upon mythic theory, or upon quite personal sensibility, forcibly imposed from without on Shakespeare. Any critical method that is external and not inductive runs contrary to the truth that can be sought in Shakespeare from the evidence of his plays as drama. Basically, most laws of drama that are not concerned with simple stagecraft have as their object the manipulation of the audience's point of view. By its nature the drama is perhaps the most highly developed objective literary form in existence, and thus the control of the point of view is a crucial matter. The dramatist must use action as his chief means of working out his story in terms of character. For instance, he can seldom slip into narration, except at the peril of losing the interest of his audience. Even such narrative as may be required to transmit vital facts about the antecedent action—what is technically known as the exposition—cannot be

FREDSON BOWERS is Professor of English and Chairman of the Department at the University of Virginia.

managed in the playwright's own person but must come from the mouth of one or more characters. Yet the audience cannot always be immediately certain that the account these characters give is an accurate one. When dramatic persons are not mere sticks, or automatons, they participate in the nature of all humanity, the chief characteristic of which is to be fallible. Their information may not be wholly accurate; or if it is, their personal reactions may color the interpretation in a manner that should lead an audience to view the account with some caution.

Indeed, when the interpretation of fact is involved, an audience learns to be especially wary of accepting the statement of any dramatic character as infallible truth. When in the opening scene of Shakespeare's *Antony and Cleopatra* Philo and Demetrius discuss Antony's visible subjection to Cleopatra, it is important to recognize that they are Romans. Two Egyptians, like Charmion and Iras, take the opposite position. Which is the audience to believe, or should it believe neither as representing the whole truth?

The peculiar condition of the dramatic form is that the playwright must work exclusively through the words and actions of a series of fallible characters. He can never speak in his own person, else he is breaking the form. Since characters fail if they are simple authorial mouthpieces, and the play is likely to fail with them, the major dramatic problem is to convey to the audience, within the rules of the game, what the dramatist wants it to believe. Moreover, these ideas (in other words, the dramatist's point of view) must be conveyed in such a manner that the audience is unaware that it is being manipulated and directed into certain channels of belief. Today in the experimental theater a dramatist may quite deliberately refuse to impose any point of view upon the play so that the audience is a free agent and can react in whatever unpredictable and various ways it chooses. That indeed may become the very point of the play—the deliberate withdrawal of any attempt at dramatic control over the audience's reactions to, or interpretations of, the events it is watching on the stage.

The Shakespearean drama does not have a twentieth-century soul in this respect. Ordinarily, like every other Elizabethan dramatist, Shakespeare was concerned to control for his own ends the reactions of his audience. He does so, of course, in respect to the audience for which he wrote, and he usually took particular care to control their view of character and of action. Thus if we follow the various ways by which he manipulated his audience in order to maintain his control, we can come upon some useful critical insights, for we shall have clear-cut evidence about Shakespeare's conscious intentions. Surely, before a critic proceeds to unconscious intentions (important as they may be), he had better settle first what the author was consciously trying to impress upon his audience. Such information will offer a factual basis, and for this reason the dramatist's art is singularly important to construe.

The concept of the "touchstone character" is familiar as applying to persons like Enobarbus in *Antony and Cleopatra*, or Horatio in *Hamlet*, whose important function is to act as an intermediary and translator between the audience and the events of the play. For one reason or another, generally because of a belief in the soundness of their judgment, the audience comes to trust the reactions of such persons and to take its cue from them. Hamlet's praise of Horatio's stoic incorruptibility just before the play-within-a-play (III. ii. 59–79) assists this projection, just as the military bluntness and saltiness of his humor inspire a confidence in Enobarbus as an objective judge of events and persons who is superior to Demetrius and Philo or to Charmion and Iras.

In *Much Ado About Nothing* Don Pedro in some considerable part serves the same purpose, qualifying by virtue of his high rank and the deference he receives as a humane ruler. This being so, his approval of Claudio's public rejection of Hero at the altar should indicate to the modern critic that this exposure is not to be taken as a discreditable action that is intended to besmirch Claudio as a character.[1] That the Duke could be mistaken in believing the circumstantial evidence against Hero is a powerful factor in the audience's acceptance of Claudio's corresponding belief as something other than the reaction of a young cad.

It is a part of Shakespeare's art, and his treatment of point of view, that his most lifelike touchstone characters may be mistaken, as was Don Pedro, at some crucial point in the action, and that the audience is able to see the mistake and to disengage itself from following the touchstone character into error. As just remarked, in *Much Ado* the noble Pedro's error parallels that of Claudio and therefore takes the sting out of the younger man's faulty judgment. But the manipulation of the audience here is elementary compared to that in *Antony and Cleopatra* and in *Hamlet*.

[1] Modern critics also forget (*a*) that Claudio (according to his belief) was risking the settlement of his title and the honorable reputation of his family line on a bastard if he pursued the marriage; and (*b*) if he broke off the marriage without publicly exposing Hero, he would not only ruin his own reputation as an honorable man but also put himself in the position of being an accomplice before the fact to the same deception that Hero would inevitably practice on some other innocent young man. Thus neither Claudio nor Pedro sees anything but disaster in the concealment of Hero's assumed perfidy, and the exposure of her wantonness takes on the aspect of a public duty.

Shakespeare reduces Antony to the lowest depth of fortune before beginning the contrary process of raising him to a generous death and to a height of humanity not previously exhibited. Antony's control over his reason, or judgment, progressively forsakes him under Cleopatra's influence. The different stages are marked by what seems to be the opposite process in Enobarbus, the breaking of his emotional attachment to Antony by the increasing alarm his judgment takes at Antony's irrational behavior. The audience cannot help feeling that Enobarbus's view of Antony's political and moral degeneration is accurate and that unthinking loyalty to such self-destructiveness might indeed be quixotic.

Enobarbus's rational view of Antony's emotional plunge demands, and receives, his desertion according to a defensible code of values. Then occurs a truly amazing dramatic peripeteia, or reversal of the scale of values. Antony in defeat, at the lowest ebb of his fortunes, is personally a greater man than in his triumph; the Roman rationalization that led to Enobarbus's desertion is seen to be an inadequate guide to conduct,[2] like Octavius Caesar and his code set against a larger-souled principle in Antony. Antony the political figure is ruined, but Antony the individual holds to a scale of values that surpasses material success. In this manner he upholds the great human conquest of Fate that has always represented mankind's justification of its rationale of existence. The audience, thus, gladly forsakes the man for the master, the commentator for the true reality; and the contrast—indeed, the actual transfer of the audience's sympathies—is an important technical device in the restoration of Antony to a nobility he has progressively forsaken during the course of the play.

In a less spectacular manner something of the same sort happens in *Hamlet*. When Horatio warns Hamlet to obey the augury represented by the pain about his heart, and to decline the offered fencing match, his lack of understanding of the real issues involved serves to highlight the extraordinary importance of Hamlet's reply that penetrates to the heart of the matter: "Not a whit, we defy augury; there's a special providence in the fall of the sparrow. If it be now, 'tis not to come; if it be not to come, it will be now; if it be not now, yet it will come: the readiness is all" (V. ii. 230–234).

It can be argued that this is a crucial decision for Hamlet; and that he makes it from a self-knowledge that he had not previously pos-

[2] A shrewd audience might receive an early warning that Enobarbus was no longer entirely trustworthy as a touchstone if it recognizes that in the scene that first determines his decision—Cleopatra's reception of Thyreus-Thidias, and her acquiescence, "Mine honor was not yielded, / But conquer'd merely"—he was as deceived as was Caesar's messenger about Cleopatra's real intentions.

sessed.[3] In short, it represents the healing of the breach between man's will and God's that had opened up in the closet-scene slaying of Polonius in mistake for the King. After this reconciliation, Hamlet can go on to his death-in-victory; and flights of angels can sing him to his rest. He has reversed his previous tragic error and has conquered his fate by reconciliation with divine purpose. This crucial decision in what is technically "the moment of final suspense" in the play is emphasized by Hamlet's rejection of Horatio's limited understanding. The contrast shows all the more the exaltation of perception that has come to him by its being set against the ordinary prudence of Horatio's advice.

The touchstone character is perhaps the most significant of a large variety of dramatic devices in which a playwright can use one character to illuminate another by word of mouth, or by the example of parallelism and contrast. Nevertheless, nothing approaches plot as a means of enforcing the dramatist's point of view. The plot of a play is that series of interconnecting incidents, or actions, by means of which the main story is presented. Plot in Aristotle's phrase is "the structure of the incidents" [*Poetics* vi. 9]. To Aristotle, "Tragedy is an imitation, not of man, but of an action and of life, and life consists in action, and its end is a mode of action, not a quality . . . character determines men's qualities, but it is by their actions that they are happy or the reverse. Dramatic action, therefore, is not with a view to the representation of character: character, comes in as subsidiary to the actions. Hence the incidents of the plot are the end of a tragedy; and the end is the chief thing of all" (vi. 9–10).

If plot is indeed the end of a tragedy, then we must look to the dramatist to utilize action in contrived episodes to lead the audience to the correct understanding of his theme, or purpose, in the full plot. The working-out of the plot has various incidents that serve as stations on the way. Of all these, that incident in the plot that one calls the climax, or crisis, is the most significant, for in it will reside the main action or decision that in a comedy will eventually lead the ending to come out well for the chief persons, and in a tragedy to come out ill. Since such a turning point must automatically be a significant action— else the play will be trivial, or quite meaningless—it behooves a critic to isolate this episode from the surrounding incidents of the plot. Once this crisis incident can be identified, the major significance of the plot may be determined and an important part of the total meaning of the play thereby assessed.

---

[3] The interpretation is found in Bowers, "The Moment of Final Suspense in *Hamlet*: 'We Defy Augury,'" *Shakespeare: 1564–1964: A Collection of Modern Essays by Various Hands* (Providence, R.I.: Brown University Press, 1964).

Long ago Aristotle evolved the doctrine of the tragic flaw in a man of moderate virtue as the central means by which the catharsis, or emotional response of the audience to the tragic outcome, could be controlled. Whether Shakespeare knew Aristotle is not perhaps demonstrable. But the point is unimportant, because Aristotle was merely codifying the dramatic practice he had observed, and such a psychological requirement in the manipulation of the audience is universal. Indeed, the Renaissance drama of Shakespeare and his contemporaries had a strong impulse to intensify the Aristotelian tragic flaw by associating it with the Christian doctrine of personal responsibility for actions, a concept that stems from the belief in the significance of free will,[4] and hence one that sometimes was far removed from the Greek spirit. For instance, if the climax of *Hamlet*—the mistaken slaying of Polonius—were only a piece of bad luck, the sort of joke the gods like to play on mankind, the play means one thing. On the other hand, if it were a morally determinate decision for Hamlet to kill what he thought was the King behind the arras, the whole action of the play, and especially the catharsis at its conclusion, means something quite different. I have already hinted at what I take to be the point of personal responsibility in the climax and its resolution— the setting-up of human will in opposition to divine will, the resulting tragic error, and the reconciliation at the end when divine will is accepted. But this is a complex matter, and too lengthy to treat here.[5]

Instead, let us take another typical Shakespearean climax, that in *Antony and Cleopatra*. If one searches for that incident to which the fatal conclusion by cause and effect inevitably reverts, there is only one answer. The loss of Actium was the loss of Egypt, certainly, but the outcome of Actium could be prophesied, in a meaningful universe, after the scene in which, against the advice of all his followers, Antony was ruled by Cleopatra and decided to fight at sea. The seventh scene of the third act therefore represents the climax, or crisis, since in this scene the fatal decision was reached to fight from weakness rather than from strength.

The question arises immediately: why was not Antony's desertion

---

[4] By "personal responsibility" I mean the concept that all decisions governing action in this life have a significance for one's fate in the next world; and therefore that mankind's free will places upon him the sole responsibility to choose correctly between good and evil, for more is at stake than the immediate result of the action concerned.

[5] Fuller treatment may be found in Bowers, "Hamlet as Minister and Scourge," *PMLA*, LXX (1955), 740–749, and in "The Death of Hamlet," *Studies in the English Renaissance Drama: In Memory of Karl Holzknecht*, ed. J. W. Bennett, O. Cargill, and V. Hall, Jr. (New York: New York University Press, 1959), pp. 28–42.

in pursuit of Cleopatra during Actium the truly decisive action, for we are told that up to that time Antony seemed to have perhaps a slight advantage in the battle? The answer involves the true nature of climax, which in Shakespearean tragedy is usually the episode that shows us the decision. The fatal action may follow immediately, as it does in *Hamlet,* or be somewhat delayed, as in *Antony and Cleopatra.* But the moral responsibility of the decision itself is overriding. It is overriding because, in the Christian terms that Shakespeare perforce utilized, arbitrary action is meaningless without moral determinism. Motivation alone provides the magic significance for actions; otherwise, Christian free will and the personal responsibility for deeds could not exist. Motivation is the reason, or cause, why men behave as they do in specific incidents. When the actions in this world have a crucial bearing on one's actions in the next, a degree of responsibility for choice is felt in Christian literature that is alien to the Greek. If responsibility for action is so weighty, then the causes for action come under scrutiny as being in the highest degree significant. To the Christian, certainly, motivation was the key to action and to its reward or punishment by the rules of the land as well as those of the spirit. Christian tragedy, therefore, put its weight largely on the effects of premeditation, for conscious choice alone had a major religious meaningfulness. Premeditation means decision, and therefore significant motivation leading to morally determinate action.[6]

These considerations dictate the choice of the seventh scene in Act III, where the fatal decision is made. The play itself indicates the relative importance. Antony's flight in battle was quickly narrated by an onlooker. But the decision to fight this battle at sea is carefully prepared. Antony's subjection to Cleopatra has led to his desertion of his wife and to an attempt to split the Roman Empire by setting Cleopatra up as Empress of the East with himself as Emperor. That Cleopatra has been urging Antony to fight at sea is clear from her opening words to Enobarbus in this seventh scene, upbraiding him for his remark (apparently in some council) that it was not fit for Cleopatra to be in the wars. She warns him she will not stay behind. Antony, entering, announces they will fight by sea, a statement immediately applauded by Cleopatra. Against the protests of Canidius, Enobarbus, and finally the Soldier, Antony stubbornly adheres to his plan with-

[6] I draw this most useful phrase from Elder Olson, *Tragedy and the Theory of Drama* (Detroit: Wayne State University Press, 1961), pp. 37–41. Actually, Olson's statement is, "Plot is a system of actions of a morally determinate quality," and he regards the phrase as a generalization of Aristotle's *spoudaios.* I am, perhaps, applying the sense more narrowly than he would approve.

out giving any reasons.[7] Canidius, after Antony's departure, correctly assigns the cause:

> his whole action grows
> Not in the power on't: so our leader's led,
> And we are women's men.

These lines concentrate the various references in the play to Antony's effeminacy in allowing Cleopatra to dictate his course of life while he sinks in pleasure and his political powers melt away. Insofar as this effeminacy in accepting female rule results from the force of his passionate attachment to Cleopatra, the results to the Elizabethans exemplify the conquest of reason by emotion, or passion, what they called the will. To this rich theme is appended the parallelism of the conflict of East and of West, Egypt and Rome, the pleasure versus the rational or governing principle, the male versus the female position in the chain of being, and much else, so that the effect of this personal decision is given a peculiar significance by the vastness of its setting and the complexity of its moral and psychological texture. The emphasis, it is clear, is not really on a mistaken military decision. Shakespeare has made it evident that Antony knows beforehand the decision is a wrong one, and yet he embraces it and persists against all opposition because he has set his will over his reason and is a woman's man who has allowed Cleopatra to have the decisive voice in a matter in which he, not she, was competent. In doing so, he has abnegated the responsibility of his generalship and therefore deserves defeat. The decision itself, viewed externally, is of comparatively small importance. It might have been made for the best of motives, whereupon a defeat would have had no more significance than that inherent in the medieval moralizing of a fall from high to low estate. But when made for faulty motives, as the result of a tragic flaw in character that affects the power of choice, the motivation is everything, the action is morally determinate, and on it hinges the tragedy.

Nevertheless, Actium is not wholly inevitable although its ill success has been abundantly prophesied. We must not forget that *Antony and Cleopatra* is in some sense a double tragedy, and that the fatal decision did not originate with Antony. What leads Cleopatra to demand her part in the wars? It is not enough to aver, as she does, that she is paying for the military preparations and so should have a voice. It is not enough that Octavius has declared war against her personally, and not directly against Antony. The key is that she "will

[7] The closest he comes to an explanation is that he can conquer by land if defeated at sea. The wholesale desertion of his forces after Actium exposes the speciousness of this argument.

appear there [in the wars] for a man." If Antony is portrayed as increasingly effeminate as his reason is buried under his passions, so Cleopatra is shown as increasingly masculine. It is not entirely a good joke that she swaggers about wearing Antony's sword "Philippan" when he has been drunk to bed and decked in her clothing. She has always used domination as her weapon to keep him in her toils, and she knows no other method.[8] After her experience when Antony was absent in Rome, she will allow him no course of action apart from her. To the Elizabethans brought up to believe in the hierarchical tradition of womanly obedience to male authority, Cleopatra has stepped out of her proper sphere, and her hubris in insisting on acting the male part was so athwart Nature as to demand punishment. Deficiency is the fault of Antony, excess that of Cleopatra. Equal guilt on the part of both protagonists, then, lies in their reversal of the roles intended by Nature to man and woman. Without true experience, Cleopatra is playing at being an Amazon Queen. She is so little prepared for the realities that accompany her play-acting that she turns Egyptian woman in the battle, doffs the masculine responsibilities that she had usurped, and flees in fear, "the breeze upon her, like a cow in June."

In reverse, therefore, Cleopatra repeats Antony's error in allowing her passion, or desires, to overcome her reason, thereby to assume command in a project for which she was not fitted, and finally to turn female coward when her hubris falters. This double error sums up to perfection the whole enveloping relationship of these two people both to each other throughout the play and to the outside world. Each is caught in the tragic point of weakness in his character, and a decision is made that will have its inevitable outcome in defeat. In a tragic universe ruled by law, any decision made for reasons of such levity in the face of an issue of so great momentousness can only be fatal.

In *Antony and Cleopatra* the climax loads the decision with the fullest significant import, and this is suitable, and indeed necessary, for high tragedy. When the outcome is less serious, Shakespeare can direct his audience to the central theme of his play by a curious inversion of the significance of the climax. For example, in the comedy *Much Ado About Nothing* the comic spirit plays with the ancient inversion of all normally expected values. The two wittiest and most intelligent people in the play—Beatrice and Benedict—have the least self-knowledge of anyone except perhaps Dogberry, and a relatively stupid villain has the most. Thus these two smart people utterly mistake their true emotions both in themselves and in the other.

Nothing in this play works out as it should. What any audience

[8] See Charmion's advice to humor Antony, and Cleopatra's contemptuous rejection (I. iii. 6–12).

would expect to be the main line of the counteraction, Don John's feeding of Claudio's jealousy of the Duke, dissolves into nothingness and leaves the villain for the moment with no plan in mind until a fresh plot is almost thrust upon him by an underling. The grave Leonato is convinced by the more volatile Antonio that Pedro is going to propose to Hero. This Leonato, as governor of the town and chief magistrate, is too preoccupied with his daughter's approaching marriage to sift Dogberry's information that would have prevented the disaster that falls upon this marriage. Benedict never does manage to fight a duel with Claudio. Nobody gets quite straight what Pedro had said to Claudio about Hero in the garden. The joke on Beatrice and Benedict is planned to culminate in a mirthful exposure of the deceit, this promised in a scene in which each will think the other in love. But no such scene ever takes place, and each falls genuinely in love with the other and reveals it almost instantly, and in private, instead of providing merriment to the onlookers.

These statements are all true, and they add up to an almost Shandyan muddle in which no expectation is ever gratified in the anticipated manner. Nevertheless, if one were to seek for the key to this comedy's inversion of life's normal values, in which wit is used chiefly for self-deception instead of enlightenment, and the more truth is sought the farther removed it is from recognition, one need only seek out the climax, which should concern the major theme. Indeed it does. The requirement for a happy ending is the discovery of some concrete evidence that will clear Hero from the deceptive accusations that have been accepted as true. Hence when we search back through the plot for that scene where the vital evidence is found, we see it in Act III, scene iii, in which the watch under Dogberry overhear the drunken boasts of Borachio. That the simplest and stupidest characters in the play stumble upon the truth[9] and that they fail to secure the hearing of the intelligent characters, who cannot be bothered to attend the narrative of these simpletons, provides us with a key action to the wryly comic theme that is more basic than any other episode in the play.

To my mind, the high point of subtlety in Shakespeare's treatment of the climax as the key to point of view appears in *1 Henry IV*. Truly, if critics had observed the implications of this scene, much misapprehension about the play would have been prevented. In terms of the plot the climax can only be Act III, scene ii, in which, seemingly, King Henry weans Hal from his dissolute life and sets him on the

---

[9] As Borachio bitterly recognizes when he taunts Don Pedro and the assembled company: "What your wisdoms could not discover, these shallow fools have brought to light. . . ."

road to Shrewsbury, the conquest of Hotspur, and the acceptance of his duties as Prince of Wales. By himself, it is implied, King Henry cannot subdue the rebels. By himself, Hal can have no national forces to lead. A scene of high drama can be anticipated in which the father pleads with his son to join him against a common danger: and, on the surface, Shakespeare gives us just that. The King reproves his son for his wild courses and refuses to accept Hal's submission, perhaps because he thinks it too coldly offered. Hal's formal request for pardon receives a quick "God pardon thee!" and sixty-odd lines of further reproof mixed with a lesson on kingship. Hal quietly promises to be himself, that is, to reform. But the King pushes on as if the Prince had not spoken, and delivers the ultimate insult that he really expects Hal, through fear, to join Hotspur's party against him. Stung at last, Hal forsakes his formal protestations and in an emotional speech vows to defeat Percy and reconcile himself to his father by his deeds. Immediately Henry clinches his victory with,

> A hundred thousand rebels die in this!
> Thou shalt have charge and sovereign trust herein.

Every indication points to Henry's having prepared this interview with particular care, as was his way, leaving nothing to chance. The rising tide of his emotion, and finally the obviously calculated insult at the right moment, are characteristic of his methods. Are we to believe, then, that the King has truly won over his son by this contrivance, has broken down Hal's indifference, detached him from Falstaff and the idle tavern life that was corrupting him and returned the Prince to the great world of affairs that was to be the training for the hero-king Henry V? If we are to believe so, then we must take it that a real conflict of wills was present and that it was resolved in classic fashion in a turnabout of motive and action, a true peripeteia. The King would have been right, and Hal wrong. Hal would have been convinced of the error of his ways by the force of his father's speech and would have been, in a manner of speaking, converted.

Such a scene might well have been an exciting and significant one; but Shakespeare did not write it so. The true point of this climax is that no peripeteia takes place. Hal makes no decision that he had not previously planned. With or without this scene the play would have had the same ending, for a few hours before, Hal had formally decided to reconcile himself to his father and to join in subduing the rebels.[10] There is no tug of war in which Hal is placed between Fal-

[10] Hal to Poins at the end of II. iv: "I'll to the court in the morning. We must all to the wars. . . ."

staff and what he represents, and King Henry and what he represents. The famous "I know you all" soliloquy, at the very beginning of the play, effectively disposes of any dramatic suspense that might have developed from a genuine inability in the Prince to make up his mind about his future. From the start of the play, therefore, Shakespeare has deliberately cast off the legitimate suspense that might have been generated by a lack of Hal's firm commitment. The soliloquy shows Hal to be plain enough. He is amusing himself for the nonce. When an emergency arises he will break through the clouds like the sun and show himself in his true majesty. He is not in the least deceived by Falstaff, nor does he have more than a partial interest in their tavern life.

I pass over the possible moral question that modern sensibility has quite wrongly raised in connection with this soliloquy. Neither Shakespeare nor his audience were egalitarians, nor was it demeaning to accept the fact that kings were not common men fully responsible to the ordinary law. Kings had their own code of conduct, and the responsibility for their actions was primarily to God. We can be confident that Shakespeare would have been surprised to hear the modern denigration of Hal on the basis of this speech. It is not a character speech at all, as Kittredge has observed, but a time-saving plot device, rather on the clumsy side, deliberately to remove from the audience any suspense that Hal was actually committed to his low-life surroundings. A comparison, indeed, may be made with the fifth soliloquy in *Hamlet*,

> 'Tis now the very witching time of night,
> When churchyards yawn, and hell itself breathes out
> Contagion to this world. . . .

This soliloquy has no other purpose than to prevent the audience from feeling an illegitimate suspense in the closet scene that is to follow. When Hamlet promises that the soul of the matricide Nero will not enter his firm bosom, and that he will speak daggers to Gertrude but use none, he is warning the audience that he plans to take a very high line with his mother and, in effect, to frighten her into repentance—a feat that he actually performs. But the audience must not fear for the Queen's life no matter how violently he behaves.[11]

When a playwright deliberately throws away dramatic suspense, one of his main stocks in trade, it is well to look into his motives. In

---

[11] Bowers, "Hamlet's Fifth Soliloquy, III. ii. 406–417," *Essays in Shakespeare and Elizabethan Drama in Honor of Hardin Craig*, ed. R. Hosley (Columbia: University of Missouri Press, 1962), pp. 213–222.

Hamlet it is clear that Shakespeare for very good reasons is determined that the audience should not take the wrong point of view about Hamlet's violent actions in the closet scene. So concerned is he with manipulating the audience to guide the reactions he wants in an episode yet to come that he is willing to sacrifice part of the superficial drama of the scene in order to emphasize to the audience the true nature of the conflict between mother and son.

Similarly, the outright manipulation of the audience was a necessity in *1 Henry IV*. The standard pattern of the plot would have produced a Prince Hal more acted upon than acting himself. Suspense would have developed from his indecision before the three ways of life open to him, each with its separate and conflicting ideals. Then in the climax he would have brought the play to a successful conclusion with his victory at Shrewsbury. This is a possible plot, but it is not Shakespeare's. Recent critics are so occupied with abusing Hal as a cold-blooded prig that they fail to see what Shakespeare was desperately trying to convey in his shaping of the action into a plot. What kind of a play is it in which the Prince from the start reveals to the audience his whole future course of action and therefore destroys the pleasurable uncertainty the audience would feel in the development of the suspense and its resolution? What kind of a play is it in which, faced with three laws of life, Hal chooses all, and none? What kind of a play is it in which the climax goes through all the motions of a decision, but no decision is actually made, for none is needed?

The answer is an obvious one. This is a play about a future hero-king who rose far above ordinary humanity. As in the old fairy tale of the Bear's Son, this future hero had a wild and careless youth, which Shakespeare is concerned to rationalize.[12] We could scarcely expect him to take personally the primitive beef-and-blood picture of Hal in *The Famous Victories*. Hal is to rise superior to the Machiavellian kingship of his father, even though Henry's policy was aimed at a strong central monarchy that any Tudor subject knew was absolutely required for peace and stability. He is to rise superior to Hotspur's narrow chivalric code of honor based on the outmoded feudal ideals that could become a force for evil when used without intelligence. Moreover, the practical value of these ideals was being made obsolete by the nascent central royal authority. He is to rise superior to the chaotic forces of the self-seeking pleasure that denies responsibility in favor of hedonism, as embodied in Falstaff. Three principles of self-

[12] If anything, Shakespeare shows Hal revolting against the principles of his father and dissociating himself from them by his refusal to join in the court life. This is, in brief, the rationalization of Hal's low-life career.

seeking are portrayed in this play, each trying to control the future king.[13]

Shakespeare's difficulty in some part resembled that of Milton in *Samson Agonistes* in that his hero can demonstrate superiority for most of the play only by endurance in the rejection of false values offered to tempt him—that is, by a refusal to be acted upon from without—until the time comes for his own positive individual action that cuts the knot and resolves the whole dramatic problem. Once we learn to read the plot, we see what Shakespeare intends to convey to us through the action. Indeed, he was so concerned to insure the audience's point of view that he ventured in the "I know you all" soliloquy to erect the plainest signpost he could contrive. He thereby tried to avoid the confusion that would have lain in any suspense about Hal's future course. In the action he deliberately shows Hal as a committed man biding his time. The time comes, and Hal makes his anticipated move toward the life of superior glory that lay ahead for him. King Henry may think he has converted his erring son, but Shakespeare tells us the contrary in his plot. That the climax is no climax, in respect to any decision not made before, should alert us to Shakespeare's clear intentions. Hal is his own man, and as his own man he chooses his own course of action in his own way. He is not influenced in any manner by the attempts of others to engage him, because from the start he knows the synthesis that lies ahead for him in the ideals of kingship, chivalry, and the proper use of materialism. This is what Shakespeare tells us through the plot, and we should pay attention to its evidence.

These are examples from three plays of Shakespeare's methods of guiding the audience to a specific point of view when, in his opinion, an exactness of response is necessary, and he cannot trust to the normal trial-and-error dramatic method in which an audience evaluates the dozens of small pieces of conflicting evidence and comes to a generally anticipated collective judgment. It is obvious that something important is at stake when Shakespeare uses extraordinary methods to manipulate the audience's point of view, and that critics need to inquire into these circumstances. By evidence of such nature we can demonstrate Shakespeare's conscious intentions and in some part pull back the veil from the concealed figure of the dramatist, who is the despair of the critic seeking after a certainty that the dramatic form must usually hide.

[13] In this sense Falstaff and his crew represent in concentrated form the commons, which are antigovernment, since their duty is to be governed, generally contrary to their true desires. Thus they avoid responsibility as much as possible and concentrate on their private concerns. Hotspur allows his feudal ideals to overcome his patriotism; the commons are, in their own self-seeking way, equally unpatriotic.

BERTRAND H. BRONSON

"All This for a Song?"

When good queen bess, in her large wisdom, ordered Lord Burleigh to give the poet Spenser £100 for his excellent verses, Burleigh is said to have exclaimed in protest, "What! all this for a song?" It can be inferred from the late files of the *Congressional Record* that a similar view is alive today in certain quarters. During the 1961 debates on the National Defense Education Act, an amendment was introduced in the House, "that no part of the appropriations . . . shall be available for fellowships in the humanities and social sciences field." Earlier, word had reached the press that part of the fellowship funds would be allocated to the study of folklore and "other things like that"; and the bad publicity that followed had so alarmed the committee that already they had cut the funds by a million dollars before bringing up the bill for debate. Congress was mollified by this evidence of discretion; but anxiety was not entirely dispelled.

> I know of no reason [declared the mover of the amendment] why under the National Defense Education Act there should be studies of . . . English folklore, and American folklore. What is the difference between English and American folklore? I will be pleased to have any member of the committee tell me the difference and why we should be providing fellowships under the National Defense Act to study folklore, jazz, the theater, and so forth. [*Congressional Record*, 87th Cong., 1st Sess., p. 8268. House Debate, 17 May 1961.]

The cash value of *The Faerie Queene* or of *Henry V* would, it may readily be granted, puzzle anyone to establish. As a prudent treasurer, Burleigh saw no need to lay out any of the national wealth in the encouragement of poetry and drama, whatever his private liking for a song or a play. The congressman, in turn, whether or not he got satisfaction from speaking the tongue that Shakespeare spoke, saw the matter in the same light, although as a realist he might set a high value

BERTRAND H. BRONSON is Professor of English at the University of California at Berkeley.

on a Broadway success. But, contemporary with Burleigh, there was one who saw things in truer perspective, who wrote with proud eloquence:

> And who in time knowes whither we may vent
> The treasure of our tongue, to what strange shores
> This gaine of our best glorie shall be sent
> T'inrich unknowing nations with our stores? . . .
> What powres it shall bring in, what spirits command,
> What thoughts let out, what humors keep restrain'd:
> What mischiefe it may powrefully withstand,
> And what faire ends may thereby be attain'd?

The odd thing is that neither Burleigh nor the congressman could see these products as national assets, nor was able to imagine any connection they might have with their country's interests at home or abroad. For the practical and utilitarian value to a nation of the theater, jazz, or songs is so much easier to demonstrate than is their absolute value. Indeed, their worth as propaganda is so obvious that folklore in one or more of its manifestations—song, dance, dress, or other handicrafts—is exploited to the utmost by countries behind the Iron Curtain. Certainly, Russian ballet has been one of their most positively ingratiating and valid exports to foreign parts; and it can be argued that Louis Armstrong and Benny Goodman have been two of our most successful ambassadors. Is there any nearer way of allaying suspicion, banishing rancor between peoples, reaffirming the common ties of humanity, and building mutual trust than by sharing popular entertainment together? "No man," Dr. Johnson sagely observed, "is a hypocrite in his pleasures." And when beauty joins pleasure to excite admiration, how much the better! Can we neglect to foster such useful intermediaries of understanding?

Fortunately, the humanities do not have to be vindicated here, in an assembly committed to their recognition, on an occasion so memorably auspicious. If I have raised the issue in a defensive way, it is only because I am concerned with them primarily in one of their humblest walks, and intend to plead that even there they are worthy of serious and prolonged investigation.

Our civilization has become so deeply committed to print for the normal conveyance of its ideas that we tend to ignore the subtler influences of hearsay in our lives. But the latter can be of great importance, and it is the more necessary to be awake to this fact because of their relative obscurity. The persistence of oral tradition in a literate, cosmopolitan, urban society or any segment of it such as the present company is worth investigation. What sorts of lore—limericks, songs, stories, proverbs, superstitions, games, social conventions—are conveyed habitually in speech from person to person, generation to generation, and at what ages, in what contexts. these form a study richly contributory to a knowledge of our communal living. Even limiting ourselves to songs, we can find matter to occupy us for a long time.

Folk song, to be sure, is a warmly human, natural, and lovable phenomenon, and there can be no complaint against those who wish only to keep it alive and to put it to its natural uses: to dance or to work to it, to express their feelings of joy or love or sadness through it. But because it *is* so spontaneous and universal, it deserves serious attention. There are a hundred ways of approaching it: through social studies of family tradition, or the way of life of its bearers—in the woods, on the plains, on ships, on trains, in the mines; of its regional or geographical dissemination; of its persistence through time as fragmentary history by, and of, the generations; of its disclosure of national character; of its psychological significance in choice of subject matter, character prototypes, themes continually reformulated; of its accepted conventions in the telling of stories; of its deeply rooted preferences in the patterns of melody.

There must be few among you who are not familiar with half a dozen of those British-American ballads of which there are records as far back as the seventeenth century and which may very likely be a good deal older than the earliest records. They are so rooted in our tradition that the same acquaintance could be assumed almost anywhere in the country. Any similar gathering would know "Barbara Allen" from childhood and probably, under varying names, a handful of such songs—perhaps "Lord Thomas and Fair Eleanor," "Lady Isabel and the Elf-Knight," "Lord Lovel," "The Two Sisters," "The Gypsy Davy," or "Lord Randal"—not learned from books but from other singers. If only we could immediately pool all the versions of these known to the present company, we should have in our hands the materials of a very interesting research project. The factors, thus visibly exemplified, of stability and variation, perpetually at odds, would yield fascinating data.

Variation-form in Western composed music has been intensively studied. Yet, although everyone would admit its importance in the ceaseless fluctuation of traditional text and tune, one finds little or no discussion of variation as a phenomenon in folk song. Narrative change has received attention, and verbal change has been noticed incidentally. But musicology in this country is too young a science to have condescended to scrutinize folk song, and melodic change here has gone unanalyzed. Obviously, text and tune are interdependent, exercising mutual influences. But when we analyze, variational effects, musical and verbal, have to be separately described. The *story* of a ballad identifies itself almost automatically, given a number of exemplars. But we cannot go far in studying a *melodic* theme without beginning to wonder about its identity. What *is* a tune, in fact? Does a series of notes in common time constitute the same tune as a similar series in another meter? Are the tunes of "Dixie" or "Yankee Doodle" the same tunes if sung in the minor as in the major? Yes, we might say, if you allow that one is incorrect. In this case there is an established norm. But what if none exists? Is a tune with phrases repeating, as ABAB, the same with similar phrases in the order ABBA? Can a tune ranging from its lower to upper dominant (or fifth) keep its identity when, with requisite adjustments, it is stated in a form ranging from tonic to upper octave?

A composer, working in variation forms, will put a theme through all sorts of gymnastics. He states his point of departure, and his object is to excite and sustain our interest by ingenious and imaginative transformations of the melodic idea. Since the norm is fixed, he can invent with the utmost freedom, altering one element after another at pleasure. In folk song the situation is very different. True, most of the kinds of variation appear in miniature—as figuration, ornament, changes of cadence, dynamics, mode, pitch, rhythm; suppression of phrase, contraction or expansion; and so on. But these variations have occurred, in the chances of oral tradition, without reference to one another, and mostly without conscious intent—indeed, usually in spite of it. For the traditional folk singer, no archetype exists except the one he learned, the one in his head. There is and can be no true original of a genuine folk song. The beginning is out of sight and, if the original survived, it would be only as another version, unauthoritative and without control over the derivatives that are perpetuating it. What, then, constitutes a folk song's essential identity? Of what is each statement of its tune a variation? Can we say that its identity lies in the sum of persistent resemblances to apparently kindred tunes? That may not carry us far, but, as with the study of other living species of which the prototypes have disappeared, it must force us to comparisons.

Comparisons are not necessarily odious—indeed, they can be fascinating—but they are burdensome, time-consuming, and full of vexation when they are not superficial. Because we have no archetype to start from, we must begin with a miscellaneous gathering of tunes, collected, with whatever diligence, at the mercy of chance; each one differing from every other at least in minute particulars and therefore unique, but having enough in common to strike us as varying forms of the same melodic idea. What we are pursuing is the precise objective nature of that sensed community.

How shall we start comparing if we do not know that any one characteristic is more symptomatic than any other? If we start with tunes that look alike in their opening notes, we find them wandering apart as they proceed. Or we find more similarity in the *second* phrase of others—or the third—or the fourth—than in the first. Some tunes whose melodic lines are nearly alike may be in quite different meters: 4/4, 6/8, 3/2. Shall we discount on the side of meter or of line? Some tunes have four phrases, some five, some six, some eight. Should this fact be counted essential? The tunes appear in different modes, different scales: how much weight does this deserve in analysis? The difficulty is to set things in order of importance.

In each phrase, the notes that carry metrical emphasis seem more indicative of the melodic line than the notes between stresses. This fact is encouraging, for it suggests the possibility of skeletal abridgment, a shorthand of the tune that may avoid a note-by-note comparison, without too serious a loss. Perhaps, then, at certain points, as the end of a phrase, the shape of the tune is more dependent than elsewhere on the particular note that occupies that position. In this case, phrasal cadences in relation to one another will be significant factors. Close comparison begins to bring out other diagnostic elements: how high the tune rises above its tonic, how far it falls below, within what portion of its range it is comfortably at home, and where, throughout the tune, characteristic phenomena occur. Particular features may not always seem of equal weight. Meter, though never to be ignored, seems less individualizing than might have been anticipated, but sometimes a typical rhythmic habit can be highly indicative.

Very significant is the question as to which notes of the diatonic series are employed by a tune, for these establish its modal character. In our British-American songs the occurrence of chromaticism is a suspicious circumstance. I do not mean microtonal shading, or a singer's intonation. In our older tradition, there is no modulation of the familiar harmonic kind; and it follows that every note has a meaningful, implicit reference to the tonic—most often the final note—of the tune. We testify instinctively to the tonic's latent power by our surprise when a tune ends on another note. Equally significant, in our tradition, is the *absence* of a note or notes from the diatonic octave. Many of our Appalachian tunes, in the veins of which flows a deal of Scottish blood, lack one, and more often two, notes of the scale; and of course the position of these gaps, in relation to the tonic, is as important melodically as, in other tunes, is the *presence* of the particular notes that fill them.

The melodic benefits of folk song stemming from these simple but numerous differences are greater than its harmonic deprivations. For, besides the four favorite (seven possible) heptatonic modes, our tunes may make use of six hexatonic and five pentatonic modal patterns, each of which to a sensitive ear has its own distinctive capabilities. Our folk song, this amounts to saying, is closer to the medieval *variety* than to the modern *simplicity* of major and minor with chromatic blurring, repeated at differing pitches. And something of that ancient feeling, and emotional response, for modality must have filtered down in a tradition that still prefers these patterns to the familiar sun and shade of today's major and minor. It is not a question of merely pedantic interest, for those persistent, instinctive reactions must antedate and underlie all the quaint theorizing that runs from Plato down almost to the eighteenth century in music of the Western world.

How specific the semantic meaning of the modes was felt to be in an ordered universe where every note of the terrestrial diatonic scale had its counterpart above in the planetary spheres, and where these influences, still echoing adjectivally as martial, mercurial, saturnine, or venereal, were palpable on earth in humors, bodily organs, in days of the week, hours of the day, so that the whole universal system may be said to have been full of sympathetic vibrations and celestial overtones—how specific may be readily illustrated in a quotation, contemporary with Shakespeare, and useful to today's professors of musical therapy:

The Dorian *Moode* [writes Dowland, the great lutenist] is the bestower of wisedome, and causer of chastity. The *Phrygian* causeth wars, and enflameth fury. The *Eolian* doth appease the tempests of the minde, and when it hath appeased them lulls them asleepe. The *Lydian* doth sharpen the wit of the dull, & doth make them that are burdened with earthly desires, to desire heavenly things. . . . Every habit of the mind is governed by songs.

The wealth of modal possibilities can be pictured in a seven-pointed star that also exhibits interrelationships between modes (Fig. 1). Each point stands for a distinct heptatonic scale, the initial letter indicating its postclassical name, as Ionian, Mixolydian, etc. At the angles between the points hexatonic scales are indicated, each of which shares all its notes with the heptatonics on either side—when all three are pitched on a common tonic or "keynote"—and therefore assigned a double initial. At the innermost angles are the pentatonic scales, numbered π^1 to π^5. Each of these, lacking the semitones that differentiate the fuller scales, shares all its notes with the hexatonics and heptatonics to which the diagram connects it. Typically, a tune made out of the notes of any one of these schemes has its individual feeling and quality because of the position of gaps, or of semitonal notes, with relation to the basic note (tonic) of the tune. But, because of the scalar correspondences indicated, the pentatonics are, so to speak, the common denominators by means of which a tune may pass most easily from one mode to another in the chances of oral transmission. The passage may occur naturally and even unconsciously; but it may also take place by means of a plagal-authentic shift effective throughout the system, that connects the modes in a more organic way. It will be

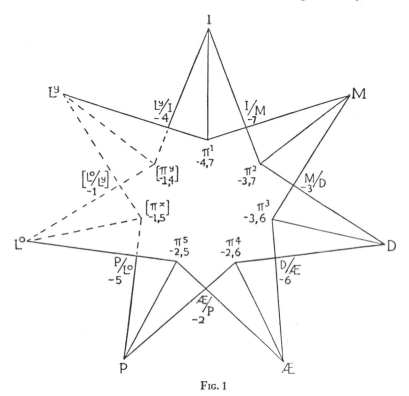

Fɪɢ. 1

seen over all that there are eighteen legitimate modal patterns—of which, however, our tradition habitually repudiates three.

If we are to keep track of all these data in a large, comparative study, we shall find ourselves staggering under a load of statistics so multifarious as to be quite unmanageable and indeed discouraging. For we may want to take out and study in various correlations any of the elements or factors noted in our search for norms. It seems time, therefore, to cast about for some means of controlling the oppressive mass of detail. In this extremity, it naturally occurs to us to inquire of those electronic robots, clothed in power and magic, which speak with sibylline utterance in our day and which can answer the hardest questions in the twinkling of an eye. Might they not be entreated on our behalf to idle away a vacant moment in aesthetic relaxation? After all, we shall not need the thunder and lightning of the greater gods. All we ask at present are a little counting and a few correlated statistics. A mere "drudging goblin" would almost do our business.

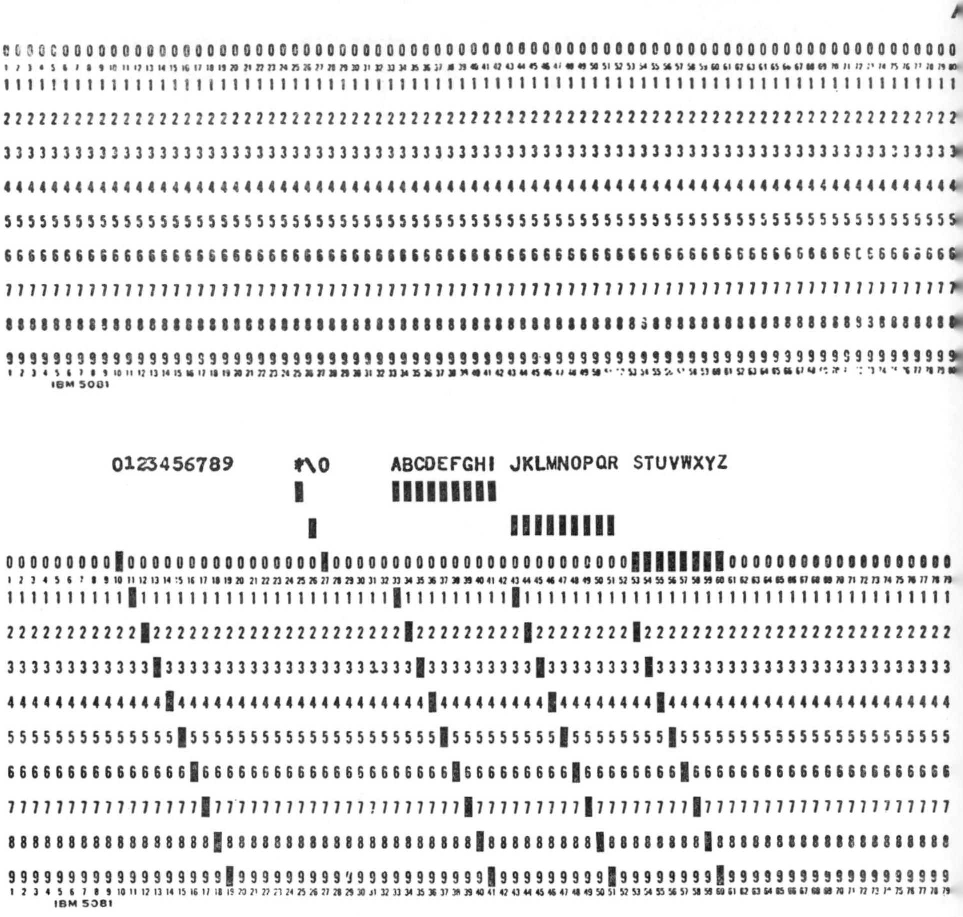

Fig. 2

Looking intently at the familiar IBM card (Fig. 2, *A*) with a hopeful eye, it dawns upon us that those serried ranks of figures on dress parade can just as well stand for the degrees of a musical octave as for less Pythagorean entities. Since with a double punch to the column they translate into letters, we could use the first eight letters of the alphabet, if we wished, for a higher octave, and the middle series for a lower (Fig. 2, *B*). Three octaves would more than cover the vocal range we need. Taking only the stressed notes, of which in a typical tune in our folk tradition there are normally four to a phrase, we could register the skeletal outline of eight such phrases on less than half the length of a card. Elsewhere a punch could indicate which modal scale was being employed, and space could be saved for noting accidental sharps or flats. The rest of the card could be given over to whatever data we thought important to tabulate. With some initial experiment, we might come to the Oracle with an interpretative card looking like Figure 3, *A*. Registering the desired data for a single tune, with the punches interpreted in alphabetical and numerical symbols, we should have a result that could be easily read, as in Figure 3, *B*. But of course the Sibyl understands the punches as readily as our familiar letter and numerical languages, and the punched card, like Figure 3, *C*, is all she needs to answer the sort of questions we have in mind.

Armed, then, with a pack of cards on each of which is punched the information about a single tune to be collated in statistical comparisons, we approach the Sacred Grove. Once admitted, and doffing our sandals, we ask the Priest such questions as the following: Say, an it please thee, how many tunes lie in the authentic range, how many in the plagal, how many extend through both? How many share the same melodic mode, and which are they? Is there a correspondence between the mode in which they are found and the region whence they came? or the region and the metrical pattern? Pray collect all tunes with a mid-cadence on the same degree and say what the probability is of the corresponding first phrase cadencing on a particular degree. We entreat thee, arrange in order the linear identities of tunes, by accented notes from the beginning, as far as identity goes; and tell us also where the most frequent correspondences lie over all. So may we learn the points of greatest stability in that ideal image of the tune which exists in the collective mind of the singers, and begin thence to deduce that abstract copy, or paradigm, "toward which the whole creation moves."

It could not be that the god would send us away empty-handed. We emerge, in fact, with a pile of folded sheets in exchange for our cards. What is stamped on the sheets might look like the specimen shown in Figure 4, the order from left to right being arbitrarily determined. The order downward answers also to a series of factors of predetermined, graduated importance.

Supposing, to give specific illustrative point to our generalizations, we had elected to focus on that most familiar of all ballads in English, "Barbara Allen." Supernatural assistance has not, alas! enabled us to anticipate and analyze the versions of the present company. Instead,

A

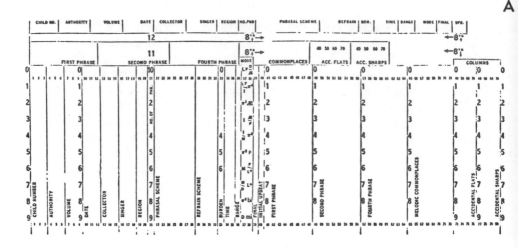

B

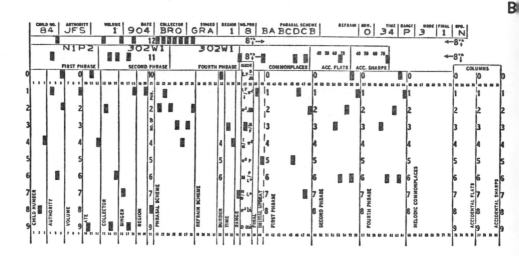

C

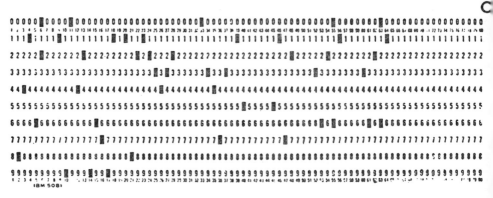

Fig. 3

we have been obliged to scour through libraries, comb collections, both printed and manuscript, of various dates, and transcribe phonographic recordings of sundry kinds, in order to amass a comparable body of evidence—two hundred–odd copies of the song. By this search, we have at least added a spatial and a temporal dimension to the evidence.

```
84CJSS    904GHA  PAL    1  48CD      068A3  1 1      1551    6A7W5
84CJSS    906GHA  LOC    1  48CD      054A3  1 5      A6A6    AB7W5
84CJSS    907SHA  LOC    1  48CD      054A3  1 5      A6A6    AB7W5
84CJSS    906SHA  STO    1  48CD      054A3  1 1      3311    6A7W5
84CJSS    906SHA  GRA    1  48CD      054A3  1 1      3411    3A7W5
84CJSS    905SHA  LAC    1  48CD      054A3  1 1      3441    6A7W5
84  NC    2859CHA         1  48CD      034A3  1 1      3531    3A7W5
84EFR     850RIM         1  48CD      034A3  1 1      3531    3A7W5
84  CF    85              48CD      034A3  1 1      3531    3A7W5
34CJSS    921SHA  RIC    1  48CD      034A3  1 5      3541    6A7W5
84JIF     1904FOX  CAR    3  48CD      068A3  1 1      3531    6B7W5
34W'M     928MAC  LAN    20 48CD      044A3  1 1      3631    4A7W5
84CJSS    918SHA  MAC    25 48AC      032A4  1 5      6543    322W1
34JFS     7924CLA  CRE    1  48CD      032A4  1 1   3152W1    4465
34CJSS    908SHA  SAY    1  48CD      054P1  1 N      11PN    333W2
84  PBS   91 BAR  COB    21 48AC      044P1  1 5      311N    122W3
84  RS    928SMI  COM    25 8BABCDC8  034A5  1 0      1425    652W1      652W1
34JFS     1904BRO  GRA    1  8BABCDC8  034P3  1 N      N1P2   302W1      302W1
34JFS     1904BRO  VAI    1  5BCDC   5 034P3  1 N      102N   P33W2
34CJSS    906SHA  CHA    1  48CD      054P3  1 N      3310   153W2
84  PBV   91 BAR  WIL    21 48CD      044P3  1 1      33NN   343W2
84  FK    891KID  WAR    1  6BCDCD  56 034P3  1 N      1321   1PW2
84  FK    891KID  HOL    1  48CD      034P3  1 N      13P4   13PW2
84  PBV   93 BAR  HAR    21 48CD      034P3  1 N      13P4   13PW2
84  CS    927SAN  DAV    29 48CD      068P3  1 N      13P4   13PW2
84CJSS    906SHA  STO    1  48AC      068P3  1 N      121N   53PW2
34CJSS    905SHA  DUR    1  5BCDC   5 054P3  1 N      1300   22PW2
84EHL     939LIN  HAR    21 48CD      044P3  1 3      332N   N54W3
84CJSS    907SHA  CHA    1  48CD      054P3  1 N      3310   165W3
34  PQS   906GRA  HOR    1  48AC      0X8P4  1 5      6311   633W2
84MOE     939EDD  HOU    23 48CD      034P4  1 N      131N   514W2
84CJS8    1932SHA  SLO    26 48CD      032P  0 1 1      1541   141W3
84CJS     1932SHA  HEN    26 48CD      032P  1 1 1      1551   141W3
34  GQ    925GRE  QUI    2  8BABCDAB  044A8  A C      5353   535WA      535WA
34PWJ     913JOY         3  48CD      044A8  1 5      3131   535WA
34  GQ    925DUN  GIL    2  48CD      034P8  1 1      3541   P21N
34  GQ    925GRE  JOH    2  48CD      044A  0 A 7      ACD8   AA5WA
34  JJ    3790JOH         2  48CD      044A  0 A 5      ACTD   AC5WA
84  CQ    925DUN  GIL    2  48AB      044P  0 1 N      1N32   1NPW1
34  WC    1876CHR         2  48CD      034P  0 1 1      3131   3534
84  WC    1876CHR         2  48AC      034A  2 1 3      3A57   5AAW5
84  WC    1876CHR         2  6BCDCD  56 044A  2 A 5      ACB8   AC5WA
84BNE    10935BAR  FRE    21 48AC      034P  8 1 2      2NON   N3NW1
84  DS    937SCA  CAL    25 48CD      034A3  1 5      5AA4   5AAW5
84  PBS   907BAR  CLA    22 4ABC      044A6  1 5      5AA5   5AA5
84A<D     9295TO  DAV    25 6ABCBC  56 044A1  1 5      6663   6663
84  VR    1946RAN  MCC    24 4ABA      032P  1 1 P      1441   1441
84  VR    1946RAN  MCD    24 4ABC      024P  0 N N      1431   143W1
84MOE     939EDD  DAR    23 48CD      044A7  1 4      5A75   5A7W6
34HMB     940BEL  CHA    24 4ABC      034A7  1 4      5AA5   5AAW5
34HMB     940BEL  CAS    24 5ABCC   5 044A7  1 4      5AA5   5AAW5
84JHC     925COX  BAR    25 4ABC      044A7  1 4      5AA5   5AA5
84A<D     929DAV         25 4ABC      044A7  1 5      5AA5   5AA5
84CJSS    917SHA  SLO    26 48CD      044M7  1        5751   5755
84JAF    22909BAR  HAL    22 48CD      034A7  1 4    45A74   45A7W5
84CJSS    917SHA  TOW    26 48CD      044A7  1 4      5AA4   5AA5
```

FIG. 4

In brief, what the sibylline leaves seem to say—for oracular responses are seldom crystal clear—is that the tunes of "Barbara Allen," with negligible anomalies excepted, fall into four rather unequal groups, members of which are found on both sides of the Atlantic with varying frequency. One class is mainly English, consistently major and heptatonic, and divided about equally between the authentic and plagal ranges (Fig. 5, A). Many variants, especially in southwestern England, lean to 5/4 time (Fig. 5, B). The over all shape of examples

FIG. 5

in the authentic range is from tonic to dominant and back to tonic in the first phrase; rising in the second phrase to the octave, but falling back from the seventh degree to the fifth for a middle cadence. The melodic curve of the third phrase is often rather like the second; and the fourth resembles the first, but seldom closely, so that the phrasal scheme is generally ABCD.

Another class is mainly Scottish, with a darker modal cast, from Dorian to Aeolian (Fig. 5, C). It favors common time, often commencing with a dotted meter; and it typically rises at the middle and final cadences from the lower fifth or flat seventh to the tonic.

A third class, which includes many American variants, is habitually in that pentatonic scale which lacks the fourth and seventh degrees (Fig. 5, D). Its members are mostly plagal tunes, frequently in 3/4 or 3/2 time. Its most consistent features are a rather chaconne-like rhythm, and a middle cadence with a feminine ending that rises like a query from the major third to the fifth degree. The query is answered in the musical rhyme of the final cadence, typically from lower sixth to tonic.

The fourth class is composed almost entirely of American variants of a tune that goes back at least to the seventeenth century. Whether its origins are Scottish, Irish, or English is uncertain. Its usual form nowadays is only the second half of the ancient double-strain tune; and the final makes a rather dubious tonic without the missing half to rationalize it (Fig. 5, E). The middle cadence of the remaining half commonly falls from the octave or seventh to the fifth. This class is composed mostly of pentatonic tunes lacking their third and sixth, but there are also a good many hexatonic variants lacking only their third. Over all, the first and third classes have perhaps a good deal in common, while the Scottish, or second group, is the most distinct—though it has affiliations with other songs than the "Barbara Allen" tribe. The fourth class, too, is of frequent occurrence in other connections.

But we must not forget that "Barbara Allen" is a song; and all this while the words have been left languishing. Returning, then, to the text, we may ask first whether the welter of change, "each way in move," shows any traces of a *current* of tradition; and whether, against "the everlasting wash of air" and the ever present erosive action of forgetfulness, which alters while it gradually obliterates, there stand out harder substances that resist destruction, or if perhaps there may even be re-creative forces at work.

At the start, the name of the place where the action occurs has clung in memory with surprising tenacity. "Scarlet Town," which is not to be found on any map, and which may even be an inspired corruption of a known locality, has stood firm in the popular imagination. Reading (town), for which it might once have been a punning substitute, has not been taken up, nor has London, though they both occur sporadically. But place has often thinned to vaguenesses like "in the town," "in the west country," or "way down South"; and where the localizing impulse has grown so weak, it has tended to drop out, usually taking with it the line which emphasizes Barbara's local potency: "made *every* youth cry wellaway."

Two contrasting seasons for the central event have made strong claims to permanent acceptance: autumn and spring. Autumn, the time when green or yellow leaves were falling, was the choice of the first surviving Scottish version, of the early eighteenth century. Whether the Scots have a special weakness for the pathetic fallacy has not been determined. Burns, we recall, protested its absence:

> Ye banks and braes o' bonnie Doon,
> How can ye bloom sae fresh and fair?
> How can ye chant, ye little birds,
> And I sae weary fu' o' care!

At any rate, the opposite choice has been greatly preferred, perhaps because it sharpens the pathos, the poignancy, of the death of young lovers:

> All in the merry month of May,
> When green buds they were swelling.

Analysts suggest that the reason most suicides occur in fine weather is because of the clash between that and the private unhappiness.

The lover's name has never been felt to matter: it could be Green, Gray, Grame, Groves; and Jimmy, Willie, Sweet William, or just nothing at all. But Allen in some form has clung through thick and thin, being built into rhymes and echoed in the melodic cadences. Better rhyming has sometimes prompted "Ellen"; and thereupon the first name may become an epithet, "barbarous." But that word is rather too literary, and Barbara has generally held her ground.

The reproachful death bells have seldom been forgotten, even in regions where one may suppose bells to be rare; and sometimes, to clinch their message, they have stirred up a chorus of birds to the same import. But when even the birds say "Hard-hearted Barbara Ellen," bells are no longer needed, and sometimes are forgotten.

To make a good ending, Barbara's remorse and death used, as the earlier texts indicate, to be judged sufficient. But not latterly: familiar formulas from other songs have suggested themselves, and the conclusion is drawn out at length. Barbara orders her mother to make her bed, her father to dig her grave; if Jimmie dies as it might be today, she dies as it might be tomorrow, of love in the one case, in the other of sorrow. They are buried in churchyard and choir, respectively, and the old favorite rose-and-briar ending, symbolic or, as some say, metempsychotic, is appended. Frequently the metaphor fades, and the briar springs from Willie, the rose from Barbara. What matters is that they twine in a true-love knot.

A fact that seems to have escaped attention is the very interesting metamorphosis which has befallen Barbara herself in her lifetime. Tradition has gradually transformed her, subtly but surely, without much conscious assistance from anyone. This characteristic process is worth a closer look.

The first known reference to the song's existence is in Pepys's diary, January 2, 1666, when, at end of a very long day, that indefatigable man hurries off in the evening to my Lord Bruncker's, where he finds a numerous company—"but, above all, my dear Mrs. Knipp, with whom I sang, and in perfect pleasure I was to hear her sing, and especially her little Scotch song of 'Barbary Allen.'" How much older the song may be we cannot surely say, but the frequent mention of old songs, like "Greensleeves," in earlier literature makes the lack of a single casual Elizabethan allusion to Barbara an argument for a mid-seventeenth-century origin. Pepys calls it a Scottish song, and Mrs. Knipp, like Maxine Sullivan some years later, may have picked it up and given it an urban currency by singing it on the stage. It has even been wildly conjectured that the song was a covert attack on Barbara Villiers, Countess of Castlemaine. We have no Scottish text so early; no recorded tune in Scotland for another century, in England for two centuries. But an English broadside text was printed in London in Pepys's own day, and its most salient features—with powerful assistance from Percy's *Reliques*, a work continually reprinted after 1765 —have been perpetuated in the traditional memory. "Barbara Allen's Cruelty," it was called, and unexplained cruelty was her chief characteristic trait. It has been a main business of tradition to rationalize this quality and explain it away. In the broadside, when the young man's servant comes to summon her, she ruthlessly replies:

> If death be printed in his face,
>   And sorrow's in him dwelling,
> Then little better shall he be
>   For bonny Barbara Allen.

This *anticipative* obduracy, inessential to the narrative, has disappeared from the popular mind, though her reluctant and tardy arrival is remembered:

> So slowly, slowly she got up,
>   And so slowly she came to him,
> And all she said when she came there,
>   "Young man, I think you are a dying."

In the broadside, his appeal for her pity is met by the retort:

> "If on your death-bed you be lying,
>   What is that to Barbara Allen?
> I cannot keep you from your death;
>   So farewell," said Barbara Allen.

So stony a heart was too much for the popular sensibility, which went to work on motivation. In the earliest Scottish copy, printed about fifty years later, in Ramsay's *Tea Table Miscellany*, and also reprinted by Percy, she is not cold but bitterly resentful:

> "O the better for me ye's never be
>   Tho your heart's blood were a spilling.

> "O dinna ye mind, young man," said she,
>   "When ye was in the tavern a drinking,
> That ye made the healths gae round and round,
>   And slighted Barbara Allen?"

In the Scottish copy, he has no reply, but turns his face to the wall with a kind adieu. She leaves the deathbed with visible reluctance and a parting sigh, and goes home to announce her imminent death.

Not so the early broadside. Walking "on a day," Barbara hears the death bell, turns round to see the funeral procession, orders the corpse to be set down, and takes a long look, all the while loudly laughing. Again the popular mind has recoiled, and in copy after American copy, we find verses like these:

> The more she looked, the more she grieved,
>   She busted out to crying.
> "I might have saved this young man's life
>   And kept him from hard dying."

Sometimes self-reproach changes even to self-exculpation:

> "Oh mother dear, you caused all this;
>   You would not let me have him."

Thus, little by little, and partly through mere abridgment and condensation, a kindlier, more sympathetic image has been wrought in tradition. If Barbara was once a "real person," as Phillips Barry believed that she must have been, she has certainly mellowed with age!

"Barbara Allen" is unquestionably and by all odds the best known, most favorite traditional ballad among English-speaking peoples in the twentieth, and like enough the nineteenth, century. This is a curious fact, and one not very easy to explain. By ordinary standards, one must acknowledge that the story has few of the elements that make a smash hit. The action is far from violent; there is little suspense in it, and a minimum of surprise. The "hero"—if he may so be called—is pallid in every sense: he is acted upon, and hardly acts at all—unless to throw up the sponge in round one constitutes an act. For although he pleads he is misunderstood in some variants, far more of them have no trace of his defense; yet the song flourishes. There is no love triangle, no defiance of conventional morality, no struggle, no complication, no delay. Where is the heroic spirit of the common man, the indomitable will to live, come what may? Here is neither hope nor courage: only abject surrender. As the first choice of the English-speaking peoples, it is a strange phenomenon.

The psychological problem—and I think it is a real one—must be consigned to the experts. But before we leave it, we may remind ourselves that the idea of love as a destructive power has been a potent concept for almost as long as the records of Western civilization can be traced. By the ancients it was looked upon as a seizure, a calamity, a madness; and the lover's madness was a disease also well known to the Middle Ages. In all early literature, as in the best-loved ballads, love is an illness from which few or none recover. Because of it, Barbara's lover is doomed. Her own observation is as clinical as cruel: "Young man, I think you're dying." But what she does not as yet realize is that the disease is infectious. After her rash exposure, *her* death is almost equally predictable, and imminent. She can do nothing to avert it: Love strikes unerringly where he will, and "caught is proud and caught is debonair." "But these are all lies," protests Rosalind cynically: "Men have died from time to time, and worms have eaten them, but not for love." It may be true—but we wish they had! Truly, we wish they had. The ideal of a love so complete and entire as to be essential to the continuance of life is a conceptual archetype persisting through the ages, through all literature, the greatest—and the least. While we scorn the spinelessness of Barbara's lover, some ray of this compelling magic touches him and transfigures him at last; and Barbara herself is redeemed by the *Liebestod*.

To descend to more humdrum matters. I think we may lay it down as axiomatic that whatever is under no external necessity to be remembered will be forgotten if it is possible to forget it. Survival depends partly on ease of recollection. In this sense, "Barbara Allen" is an extremely memorable song. It is next to impossible to get the narrative twisted. There are but two characters, and they are at once delineated by word and act in crisis. The heroine's name is not only unforgettable by virtue of syntactical management but itself serves as a mnemonic for the stanzaic rimes, calling back the successive phases of the narrative: dwelling, swelling, telling, knelling; while the double rime is its own reminding device, requiring special heed and a matching musical cadence to parallel and reinforce it.

So we return once more to the tunes, which are the vital element in which the story exists—the air it breathes, and the breath of its life.

Frequency Counts of ABCD Tunes of Seven Most Popular Ballads
(Child Nos. 4, 12, 53, 73, 84, 200, 243)

Authentic Tunes (277)

ACCENT—POINTS →

SCALE—DEGREES ↓

	1	2	3	4	5	6	7	8
4		2	1					
3	4				1	3		
2	1	3	2			11	7	
1	9	(60)	30	3	28	(140)	43	23
VII	1	5	11	1	15	18	52	5
VI	8	11	13	3	37	19	37	7
V	(92)	(80)	(60)	32	(105)	29	(101)	(112)
IV	41	38	42	38	32	37	11	2
.III	(76)	27	(59)	15	21	11	17	4
II	4	13	34	7	3	4	7	18
I	48	39	23	(172)	28	5	2	6
VII	1			3				
VI								
V								
IV								
III								
II								
0					7			

Mixed Tunes (73)

	1	2	3	4	5	6	7	8
1		1	1	1	2	6	4	
VII		(37)			1	(38)	3	1
VI		1	2		15	16	3	1
V	(42)	6	(46)	1	(40)	7	(45)	(65)
IV	2	1	4	1	5	1	3	1
III	12	14	2	3	3	3	13	1
II		3	10	6				2
I	15	7	7	(59)	4		1	1
VII	1	1						
VI		2	1	1	1	1		
V	1			3			1	1
IV								
III								
II								
0					2			

Plagal Tunes (165)

	1	2	3	4	5	6	7	8
VI		3	1		2	8	1	1
V	10	12	5	4	21	(70)	23	(66)
IV	2	3	15	3	11	19	22	10
III	24	(60)	14	1	(46)	26	(63)	17
II	1	9	(37)	12	5	14	28	(59)
I	(111)	(61)	(54)	(57)	(69)	20	16	4
VII		4	17	3	1	3	8	1
VI	3	6	14	5	3	2	3	
V	14	6	7	(78)	4	4		3
IV		1	1	2				
III					1			
II							1	1
0					3			

FIG. 6

We find, when we extend our correlation of the tunes to a comparative analysis of the whole body of most common and typical British-American folk tunes, that those of "Barbara Allen," in spite of superficial differences and casual exceptions or anomalies, fall into the central norm of our tradition (Fig. 6). They act as we should expect them to do, and require no extra will-to-remember. They end on the tonic, their mid-cadences are usually at the fifth. Their rhythms are simple and familiar. Their length is the common four-phrase length; their phrasal patterns are habitually progressive, ABCD; and in their individual shapes the phrases are typical. Their ranges stay within normal bounds; their melodic modes are among the commonest: major or near-major pentatonics, or (for Scotland) Dorian/Aeolian.

These normal likings gain their importance from being so widespread and universal in our traditional culture. Things need not have gone this way; they might have turned out otherwise. To make these the prevailing patterns, there had to be an infinite number of rejections, conscious or instinctive, or alternative choices or different appeals. Thus, in the long course of time, racial music traditions tend to establish their idiosyncratic distinctions and habitual characters. The psychological and aesthetic implications of these musical facts are far-reaching and profound. When someone asks, why all this fuss and bother, this endless trouble and expenditure of time on an old song, the answer is: because this old song, in its mere, sheer *commonness*, strikes to our very roots. There is no obligation on these old things to survive. They have lived on in the minds and hearts of countless men and women, untainted by compulsion, for the purest and most disinterested reason possible to be conceived: because they have continued to give joy and solace, on the basic levels of artistic experience, to generation after generation of our humankind. "The proper study of mankind is man"; and so long as this precept remains valid, folk song will continue to be an important subject for human inquiry.

NOTE: What is said above of "Barbara Allen" echoes and expands the summary statement on this ballad in the author's *Traditional Tunes of the Child Ballads*, II (1962), 321. Figure 1 has already appeared in the same work (p. xii) and earlier in the *Musical Quarterly*, XXXII (1946), 44. Figure 6 was printed in the *Journal of the International Folk Music Council*, IX (1957), 27.

FREDERICK A. POTTLE

Boswell Revalued

We have just lived through a period of rapidly shifting sensibility, one of those times of crisis in literary history when it becomes necessary to readjust the reputations of the classics, to see them in the perspective of a significantly novel literature which our own age has created. Boswell would in any case have had to undergo revaluation. But the case of Boswell is considerably different from, let us say, the case of Shelley, a classic whose claims we are seeing sharply challenged. We have recovered in this century no important new poems of Shelley, whereas the last thirty years have witnessed tremendous significant additions, not merely to our knowledge of Boswell's life, but also to the canon of his works. In a very real sense, Boswell has been a part of the literature of our time. The *London Journal*, though written just two hundred years ago, was first published in November 1950 as a trade book in full competition with contemporary nonfiction. Up to the present time, it has had a world circulation in English of well over 750,000 copies and has been translated into Danish, Swedish, Finnish, French, German, and Italian. This huge popular demand for a new work of an author long since dead is unique in publishing history. For proof that the process of revaluation now going on is not merely academic, one can point to small newspapers all over the country, for example, to the following paragraph from the *Allendale County Citizen*, Allendale (pop. 13,000), South Carolina, 20 April 1951:

The Allendale Library board met Friday, April 13, at 10 o'clock at the home of Mrs. Jim Glen with Mrs. Lawton Maner as co-hostess.

Prior to the business meeting Mr. Tom O'Connor [editor and publisher of the *Citizen*] reviewed the "London Journal" of James Boswell, biographer of Dr. Samuel Johnson. Up to this point Boswell was an uninteresting character to be written in college themes and passed on as quickly as possible. (Our instructor also left out what Mr. O'Connor

FREDERICK A. POTTLE is Sterling Professor of English at Yale University.

termed the "purple passages" in Boswell's diary.) The speaker advised to skip those passages. (Does anyone have an unexpurgated edition around?) At any rate Tom O'Connor has brought alive a dead and vapid personality and made it interesting.

What are the most important points that appear to be emerging in present-day critical thinking with regard to Boswell? Let me lay the ground for my attempted answer by listing briefly those tremendous recent additions to Boswell's writings and to the materials for writing his life which I have just mentioned. What, in short, are the Boswell Papers which Yale University acquired fourteen years ago?

They consist essentially of Boswell's private archives, reunited by Lt.-Col. Ralph H. Isham from Malahide Castle, Ireland, and Fettercairn House, Scotland, after having dropped completely out of sight for one hundred and thirty years. At the center stands Boswell's journal in all its varieties, from fully written narrative to abbreviated and cryptic notes. Then comes his large and interesting correspondence, including many copies of his own letters and a surprising number of originals which he got back from the recipients. Then various kinds of personalia supporting the journal: memoranda, registers of letters, expense accounts, the "Book of Company and Liquors at Auchinleck"—a visitors' book with a detailed record of what the guests drank.[1] Then miscellaneous compositions of a less personal sort: verse (quantities of it, nearly all bad), anecdotes, language exercises, legal notes and papers. Finally, book manuscripts: a holograph manuscript (not printer's copy) of *An Account of Corsica;* the original manuscript of *The Journal of a Tour to the Hebrides with Samuel Johnson*, prepared to serve as printer's copy; nearly all of the manuscript of the *Life of Johnson*, a manuscript that is at once first draft, revised draft, and printer's copy.

What changes does this new material make in Boswellian biography? Does Boswell emerge a different man from what we had supposed?

The new papers extend enormously the chronicle of Boswell's life and will make it perhaps the richest in authentic detail of any English biography. They do not change in any important respect the conception of Boswell's character which serious scholars and really informed critics have had since the publication of his letters to his most intimate friend, the Reverend William Johnson Temple, over one hundred years ago. These letters, which had never been part of Boswell's archives, drifted over to France after Temple's death and were

---

[1] This was separated from the archives before they came to Yale and is now in the Hyde Collection.

rescued, about 1840, from a shopkeeper in Boulogne, one Mme Noël, who was using them to wrap small parcels. There had originally been perhaps two hundred of them, the first written when Boswell was a boy of eighteen, the last as he lay on his deathbed, and though Mme Noël had already dispersed half of them, enough survived to form a surprisingly adequate *biographia epistolaris*. But they were read only by specialists. The general or popular estimate of Boswell's character up to 1950 was based almost entirely on two essays of very wide circulation written by Thomas Babington Macaulay: the review of Croker's Boswell, 1831, and the "Essay on Johnson," 1856. For generations, one or the other of these essays was required reading for every high-school student in America. The trade-book publication of Boswell's journal and selected letters will alter very considerably the general or popular estimate of Boswell's character, for the simple reason that Boswell's own writing will for the first time be getting as wide a circulation as Macaulay's.

Macaulay's method was the method of paradox. His thesis in essence was, "This man wrote the greatest of all biographies *because* he was a fool." Even the general public, now that it has read some of Boswell's autobiography, will see that, though brilliant, this is much too simple.

The great difference that the new Boswell material does make is to render untenable any simple formula for handling him. Most of the Macaulayan adjectives are properly applicable, but one must be very careful to tie them up to the right portions of the evidence. He was one of the most paradoxical literary characters on record, combining in uneasy equilibrium a host of contradictory traits. The easy way out is to say that he thought he was, or pretended to be, *this* and was really *that*. Nothing is farther from the truth. He *was* a well instructed and sincerely devout Christian with an unusual capacity for worship, and he was also a notable fornicator. He savored as few others have the delights of intellectual conversation, and he was a sensualist. He was weak of will, and he sat up all night through four nights in one week to record Johnson's conversation. He loved Scotland deeply, and he preferred to live in England. He was inordinately proud of his ancestry and his status as a gentleman, and he associated with the lowest of low people. He was an affectionate husband, painfully dependent on his wife, and he was unfaithful to her and kept her sitting up for him when he knew she was mortally ill. He was a thoughtful and indulgent father who found it difficult to endure his children's company. He was dissipated and restless, and he carried on an extensive legal practice. He was often gloomy to the point of suicide, and Mrs. Thrale gave him a perfect score in good humor. (Johnson got zero.) He was stately and Spaniard-like in his bearing, and he played the clown with or without provocation. He was proud and he deferred to

Johnson. He was independent and he licked Lonsdale's boots. He did and said many foolish things, but he was not a fool.[2]

Having said this, one has immediately to bow to established linguistic usage and admit that in one important sense he *was* of course a fool. He was the kind of fool we mean when we say, "I don't see how Jones could have been such a fool." We mean that we can't understand how Jones, whom we know to be an intelligent man, could have performed so foolish an action. Boswell could be counted on at all periods of his life to analyze a situation shrewdly and accurately; he could not be counted on to follow the course of action he knew to be right. One may safely impugn Boswell's judgment, but one should be very careful not to underestimate his intelligence. He was not a dimwit; he was possessed of a bright, eager intelligence. I am prepared to say that he had a better mind than most of the critics who have treated him with contempt.

The proof of Boswell's intelligence has always been before us in the *Life of Johnson*, but it has been strangely ignored. The Johnsonian conversations in that book cover a wide range of topics and often deal with matter of considerable subtlety. The vividness of Boswell's reporting shows that his mind is keeping up with Johnson's in everything he sets down, and is doing it with ease and delight. The great superiority of Boswell's *Life of Johnson* to Eckermann's *Conversations with Goethe* is not due to the fact that Johnson was the better subject. It is due primarily to the fact that Boswell was a greater artist, but secondarily to the fact that he had a keener intelligence than Eckermann. The public will come to see that Boswell had a good mind, that he was well educated, and that he was endowed with a great literary gift, though a gift of a peculiar and limited kind.

The public will learn, what scholars have always known, that he was not English but Scots; that he was not a social climber but the representative of an ancient and well-connected family. Readers of the *Life of Johnson* have always noticed Boswell's humble deference to Johnson's wisdom and goodness, but they will now perhaps notice Johnson's deference to Boswell's social status. The relationship was one of generous and recognized condescension on both sides.

The public (as well as some scholars) will learn that Boswell was not a man of leisure nor by profession a man of letters, but a lawyer; that in that profession he was for twenty years regular, ambitious, and hard-working. I do not know how often it has been noticed that the dates of the conversations with Johnson from the time that Boswell became an advocate to 1781 all fall either between 12 March

[2] F. A. Pottle, "The Life of Boswell," *Yale Review*, XXXV (Spring 1946), 455, with slight revision. Much else in the present essay is adapted from the same source.

and 12 June or between 12 August and 12 November, that is, fall in the vacations of the Court of Session in Edinburgh. Boswell never gained a commanding position at the Scots bar, but he always had plenty of business. He was considerably more successful in point of fees than Walter Scott was. There can be little doubt that if he had held on in Edinburgh, he would have been made a judge.

People generally will come to see that though Boswell was vain, intemperate, and incontinent, he was personally very attractive, especially to women. I do not speak without warrant. Since Boswell is no longer on hand to receive his fan mail, I have read a good deal of it for him since 1950.

So far as literary critics and literary historians are concerned, the effect of the new papers will be to demonstrate that Boswell was primarily a journalist. All his significant books—*The Journal of a Tour to Corsica, The Journal of a Tour to Hebrides*, the *Life of Johnson*—were quarried out of his journal. Though the *Life* will probably always be considered his greatest artistic achievement, critics and historians will come to see that his central, his unique performance lies in the private record of which he published only samples. It is a rare kind of journal in that it is consistently dramatic. I do not mean merely that he records a good deal of dialogue, cast as in a play, with stage directions and characterizations of the speakers, though that is part of what I mean. I refer primarily to his consistent practice of giving each recorded moment its own proper emotional tone, not that of the time of writing. Those who have read the journal of his tour of Switzerland in 1764 will perhaps remember his vivid account of the excitement and uneasiness he felt as he strolled along the bank of the wintry Areuse while he waited to see whether Rousseau was going to give him an interview. He had a letter from Rousseau's protector, Lord Marischal, that was sure to gain him admission, but he had chosen instead to present a letter of his own in which he described himself as a man of singular merit. The journal records his internal dialogue: "Is not this romantic madness? . . . Could I not see him as any other gentleman would do? . . . If my bold attempt succeeds, the recollection of it will be grand as long as I live. But perhaps I may appear to him so vain, or so extraordinary, that he may be shocked by such a character and may not admit me. I shall then be in a pretty situation, for I shall be ashamed to present my recommendations."[3] The whole thing is so natural and convincing that one never stops to consider that he must have written it hours

---

[3] Journal, 3 December 1764, *Boswell on the Grand Tour: Germany and Switzerland, 1764* (New York: McGraw-Hill, 1953) (hereafter cited as "*Germany and Switzerland*"), pp. 216–221.

or days afterward—after the doubt and the suspense had been completely resolved.

A really thoughtful analysis of Boswell's art and a definition of his genius have been long overdue. We have been strangely content with the great Boswellian paradox, which is this: Ask any group of respected literary critics to name the ten greatest prose works in English, and the chances are high that the *Life of Johnson* will turn up on most of the lists. Ask the same critics to name the ten greatest authors of English prose, and not one of them will ever think of Boswell. Now this, as I have said, would seem to be sheer paradox. Abstractly considered, nothing would seem to be more completely a truism than the proposition that the author of a great book is a great author. But when we are invited to apply it to Boswell, we boggle. What are the causes of this inconsistency?

If I may trust my own feelings, we find it hard to think of Boswell as a great author because we are in doubt as to what, or how much, he has created. Though we may admire the *Life* intensely, we feel somehow that it wrote itself, or that Johnson wrote it. The wit and wisdom of the book are certainly Johnson's, and the wit and wisdom appear to be presented in Johnson's own words. Boswell's function, we are likely to feel, was that of a mere recorder. He somehow made on the spot a verbatim record of what was said, like a court stenographer, and his artistic activity consisted of nothing more exacting than tidying up his records and perhaps cutting them a little.

Before I state an even more fundamental cause of doubt, I should like to present three passages from the *London Journal*.

DIALOGUE AT CHILD'S

I CITIZEN. Pray, Doctor, what became of that patient of yours? Was not her skull fractured?

PHYSICIAN. Yes. To pieces. However, I got her cured.

I CITIZEN. Good Lord.[4]

When I went home in the evening, I felt myself quite dissipated by running about so much. I was indolent and careless and could not fix to anything. Even this my journal was in danger of being neglected. Near a whole week had elapsed without my writing a single page of it. By way therefore of penance for my idleness, and by way of making up for the time lost and bringing up my business, I determined to sit up all this night; which I accordingly did, and wrote a great deal. About two o'clock in the morning I inadvertently snuffed out my candle, and as my fire was long before that black and cold, I was in a great dilemma how to proceed.

---

[4] 18 December 1762, *Boswell's London Journal, 1762–1763* (New York: McGraw-Hill, 1950), p. 94, or p. 101 of the Signet Book edition of the same (1956).

Downstairs did I softly and silently step to the kitchen. But, alas, there was as little fire there as upon the icy mountains of Greenland. With a tinder-box is a light struck every morning to kindle the fire, which is put out at night. But this tinder-box I could not see, nor knew where to find. I was now filled with gloomy ideas of the terrors of the night. I was also apprehensive that my landlord, who always keeps a pair of loaded pistols by him, might fire at me as a thief. I went up to my room, sat quietly till I heard the watchman calling, "Past three o'clock." I then called to him to knock at the door of the house where I lodged. He did so, and I opened it to him and got my candle relumed without danger. Thus was I relieved and continued busy till eight next day.[5]

I walked up to the Tower in order to see Mr. Wilkes come out. But he was gone. I then thought I should see prisoners of one kind or other, so went to Newgate. I stepped into a sort of court before the cells. They are surely most dismal places. There are three rows of 'em, four in a row, all above each other. They have double iron windows, and within these, strong iron rails; and in these dark mansions are the unhappy criminals confined. I did not go in, but stood in the court, where were a number of strange blackguard beings with sad countenances, most of them being friends and acquaintances of those under sentence of death. Mr. Rice the broker was confined in another part of the house. In the cells were Paul Lewis for robbery and Hannah Diego for theft. I saw them pass by to chapel. The woman was a big unconcerned being. Paul, who had been in the sea-service and was called Captain, was a genteel, spirited young fellow. He was just a Macheath. He was dressed in a white coat and a blue silk vest and silver, with his hair neatly queued and a silver-laced hat, smartly cocked. An acquaintance asked him how he was. He said, "Very well"; quite resigned. Poor fellow! I really took a great concern for him, and wished to relieve him. He walked firmly and with a good air, with his chains rattling upon him, to the chapel.[6]

It will, I think, be granted that these scenes are as firmly grasped and as vividly realized as scenes from fiction, say, from Smollett. Yet we doubt whether they can be art, or at least whether they can be important art, *because these things really happened*, because the circumstances are historical, because Boswell aimed at circumstantial accuracy. Johnson himself has expressed this doubt in a remark recorded by Boswell in this very volume:

He said that great parts were not requisite for a historian, as in that kind of composition all the greatest powers of the human mind are quiescent. "He has facts ready to his hand, so he has no exercise of invention. Imagination is not required in any high degree; only about as much as is

[5] 21 March 1763, *ibid.*, pp. 224 and 204, respectively.
[6] 3 May 1763, *ibid.*, pp. 250–252 and 224–225, respectively.

used in the lower parts of poetry. Some penetration, accuracy, and colouring will fit a man for such a task, who can give the application which is necessary."[7]

The concern for circumstantial accuracy must be stressed. It is not the same thing as the use of matter-of-fact detail or reliance on the commonplace. Boswell is not Wordsworth. Wordsworth often uses matter of history, generally of his own history, as the basis of a poem, and he prefers commonplace events and scenes to the magic ring and the dragon's wing. But Wordsworth aims always to transfigure the commonplace, and he never hesitates to change circumstances when by so doing he can make his poetical point better. He was not solitary when he saw the daffodils at Ullswater; he did not meet the old leech-gatherer stirring the waters of a pool on the lonely moor, but begging in the highway. There is no question of Wordsworth's artistry, for he deliberately invests the objects of his vision with the light that never was on sea or land. It does not enter Boswell's head to transfigure or to consecrate; he is content to realize. He does not report *all* the circumstances, but he never changes any that he does report. He grasps and renders in the mode of average human perception. His style is a plate-glass style, so transparent as to be practically invisible.

No one could ever feel that the *Life of Johnson* wrote itself if he had studied any portion of the bale of manuscript at Yale showing the book in all the stages of its composition: outlines, draft, finished text. The marks of thoughtful planning and of anxious revision are everywhere. Nor could one who had read Boswell's journal doubt that he was acutely aware of the central problem of biography long before he began his great book.

I observe continually how imperfectly, upon most occasions, words preserve our ideas. . . . In description we omit insensibly many little touches which give life to objects. With how small a speck does a painter give life to an eye! The vivid glances of Garrick's features, which cannot be copied in words, will illuminate an extent of sensation, if that term may be used, as a spark from a flint will throw a lustre in a dark night for a considerable space around it.[8]

Breakfasted early with the Commissioner, and came to town with him in his chaise. The great lines of characters may be put down. But I doubt much of it be possible to preserve in words the peculiar features of mind which distinguish individuals as certainly as the features of different countenances. The art of portrait painting fixes the last, and musical sounds with all their nice gradations can also be fixed. Perhaps language

[7] 6 July 1763, *ibid.*, pp. 293 and 260, respectively.

[8] Journal, 16 September 1769, *Boswell in Search of a Wife, 1766–1769* (New York: McGraw-Hill, 1963), pp. 292–293.

may be improved to such a degree as to picture the varieties of mind as minutely. In the mean time we must be content to enjoy the recollection of characters in our own breasts, or by conversation and gestures with people acquainted with the particular persons as much as we are. I cannot portray Commissioner Cochrane as he exists in my mind.[9]

I told Erskine I was to write Dr. Johnson's life in Scenes. He approved.[10]

The last extract is the first record of Boswell's decision to organize the *Life* around the dramatically cast conversations with Johnson which he had been entering in his journal for seventeen years. It was written four years before Johnson's death.

No one who had read transcripts of genuine shorthand or magnetic tape recordings of actual conversations would ever suppose that Boswell's were of that sort. We now know that he almost never recorded conversations on the spot. His usual practice was to make an abbreviated and cryptic minute in the privacy of his own room soon after the events in question. Unless he made these minutes, his memory of the past seems not to have been remarkable. But given them, and given time and patience, he could at almost any distance of time recall in detail everything that had ever happened to him. He never pretended that his records were word-for-word echoes of what was said. They are obviously in the first place epitomes or miniatures: much more was said than he has preserved. At the end of the first extended conversation in his journal—one which he and his friend Andrew Erskine had with David Hume on 4 November 1762—he says he has "preserved the heads and many of the words"[11] of a two-hour conversation. That covers it nicely. These topics were really discussed, and the crucial words, the joints or pivots, are *ipsissima verba*. But the whole is an imaginative reconstruction.

Besides, though we are apt to forget it, there is a great deal in the best passages of conversation in the *Life of Johnson* that was not spoken by anybody. Consider, for example, the following delicious passage from the *Life*, 1 April 1775:

Next morning I won a small bet from Lady Diana Beauclerk, by asking him as to one of his particularities, which her Ladyship laid I durst not do. It seems he had been frequently observed at the Club to put into his pocket the Seville oranges, after he had squeezed the juice of them into the

[9] Journal, 19 October 1775, *Boswell: The Ominous Years, 1774–1776* (New York: McGraw-Hill, 1963), p. 168.

[10] Journal, 12 October 1780, *Private Papers of James Boswell from Malahide Castle in the Collection of Lt. Colonel Ralph Heyward Isham*, ed. Geoffrey Scott and F. A. Pottle (privately printed, 1932), XIV, 132.

[11] *Ibid.*, I, 126–129 or pp. 100–104 of the de luxe edition of *Boswell's London Journal, 1762–1763* (London: Heinemann, 1951).

drink which he made for himself. Beauclerk and Garrick talked of it to me, and seemed to think that he had a strange unwillingness to be discovered. We could not divine what he did with them; and this was the bold question to be put. I saw on his table the spoils of the preceding night, some fresh peels nicely scraped and cut into pieces. "O, Sir, (said I,) I now partly see what you do with the squeezed oranges which you put into your pocket at the Club." JOHNSON. "I have a great love for them." BosWELL. "And pray, Sir, what do you do with them? You scrape them, it seems, very neatly, and what next?" JOHNSON. "I let them dry, Sir." BosWELL. "And what next?" JOHNSON. "Nay, Sir, you shall know their fate no further." BOSWELL. "Then the world must be left in the dark. It must be said (assuming a mock solemnity,) he scraped them, and let them dry, but what he did with them next, he never could be prevailed upon to tell." JOHNSON. "Nay, Sir you should say it more emphatically:—he could not be prevailed upon, even by his dearest friends, to tell."

Now, granting that in this case Boswell remembered verbatim just what he and Johnson said and all that they said (which is unlikely), he had in writing it up to provide the setting and the gestures. Only about 50 per cent of the passage is direct quotation. Much of the peculiar vividness of Boswell's representations comes from his sparing but effective use of stage directions—"assuming a mock solemnity." The superiority of his records of Johnson's conversations to those of his rival, Mrs. Piozzi, resides largely in these dramatic touches.

Dr. Johnson to the contrary, it takes just as much imagination to express vividly the non-verbal matter of one's own personal experience as it does to express vividly the matter of a fiction. Between perception and verbal communication of the quality of perception a great gulf is fixed, as Boswell knew only too well. To fall back on Johnson's terms, Boswell has as much *Imagination* as Scott or Dickens, though he has nothing like as much *Invention*. Theoretical criticism has always attached more importance to invention than practical or unreflective criticism does. In actual practice—when we do not theorize—we allow a high degree of imagination to make up for a lack or weakness of invention.

I suppose when we reflect there always comes into our minds Aristotle's dictum that poetry is a more philosophical and a higher thing than history: that history relates what has happened, poetry what may happen.[12] But this is not as exclusive as it sounds: it surely does not say that no history can be poetry. It merely states a tautology, namely, that the poet (artist) who keeps within the limits of the historical is limited. He hasn't the range of the inventive artist. His success is dependent on his luck or his skill in finding in real life

[12] *Poetics* ix. 1–3.

matter *as good as* that which poets invent. And Aristotle admits it: "Even if he happens to take a subject from history, he is none the less a poet for that; for there is nothing to hinder certain actual events from possessing the ideal quality of a probable or necessary sequence; and it is by virtue of representing this quality in such events that he is their poet."[13] The imaginative journalist is like the imaginative photographer. Dr. Johnson really existed, but he is as fine a character as the creations of Scott or Dickens. No extended day-by-day journal runs much chance of being continuously great art, but stretches of it may be. The London journal of 1762–63 may be. The Hebridean journal of 1773 may be. The John Reid journal of 1774 may be. The decision must be made empirically—by reading.

Yet I think when we talk in this traditional way we leave out a very real element of the situation. Surely—and this applies to more than naïve readers—we derive pleasure from graphic and trustworthy reconstructions of the past, not in spite of their being historical but because of it. I have come to the point where I am not sure what my answers should be. Boswell's Dr. Johnson is as vivid as a fiction, but our pleasure in him would be spoiled if we found he *was* a fiction. We want to believe that the historical Johnson was just like that. On the other hand, we should feel uneasy if some one proposed to demonstrate that Sterne's Uncle Toby was not really invented but had historical existence. Why is this? Is it merely because of our jealousy of the artistic integrity of two works which we admire? Because we feel that the *Life of Johnson* was designed to show a Johnson larger than his context, because it invites us to extend and complete him, whereas any more of Uncle Toby would strain or burst the pattern? ("BOSWELL. You tell us nothing of your Émile's father. ROUSSEAU. Oh, he hadn't any. He didn't exist.")[14]

Carlyle, in an essay devoted specifically to Boswell, maintained that imaginative biography is *better* than fiction. Critics, he says, insist that the poet should inform the finite with the infinite, ennoble the actual into the ideal. But as a matter of fact, he goes on, Time itself, "which is the outer veil of Eternity," invests Boswell's *Johnsoniad* with a felt infinitude. A truly *poetic* meaning is implied in the word "Past," a meaning that becomes ever clearer as we have more of the past to look through. "On which ground indeed must Sauerteig have built, and not without plausibility, in that strange thesis of his: 'That History, after all, is the true Poetry; that Reality, if rightly interpreted, is grander than Fiction.'"

[13] *Ibid.* ix. 9 (Lane Cooper's translation).
[14] Journal, 15 December 1764, *Germany and Switzerland*, p. 258.

Thus for Boswell's *Life of Johnson* has Time done, is Time still doing, what no ornament of Art or Artifice could have done for it. Rough Samuel and sleek wheedling James *were*, and *are not*. Their Life and whole personal Environment has melted into air. The Mitre Tavern still stands in Fleet Street: but where now is its scot-and-lot paying, beef-and-ale loving, cocked-hatted, pot-bellied Landlord; its rosy-faced assiduous Landlady with all her shining brass-pans, waxed tables, well-filled larder-shelves; her cooks, and bootjacks, and errand-boys, and watery-mouthed hangers-on? Gone! Gone! The becking Waiter who, with wreathed smiles, was wont to spread for Samuel and Bozzy their supper of the gods, has long since pocketed his last sixpence; and vanished, sixpences and all, like a ghost at cock-crowing. The Bottles they drank out of are all broken, the Chairs they sat on all rotted and burnt; the very Knifes and Forks they ate with have rusted to the heart, and become brown oxide of iron, and mingled with the indiscriminate clay. All, all has vanished; in very deed and truth, like that baseless fabric of Prospero's air-vision. Of the Mitre Tavern nothing but the bare walls remain there: of London, of England, of the World, nothing but the bare walls remain; and these also decaying (were they of adamant), only slower. The mysterious River of Existence rushes on: a new Billow thereof has arrived, and lashes wildly as ever around the old embankments; but the former Billow with *its* loud, mad eddyings, where is it?—Where!—Now this Book of Boswell's, this is precisely a revocation of the edict of Destiny; so that Time shall not utterly, not so soon by several centuries, have dominion over us. A little row of Naphtha-lamps, with its line of Naphtha-light, burns clear and holy through the dead Night of the Past: they who are gone are still here; though hidden they are revealed, though dead they yet speak. There it shines, that little miraculously lamplit Pathway; shedding its feebler and feebler twilight into the boundless dark Oblivion,—for all that our Johnson *touched* has become illuminated for us: on which miraculous little Pathway we can still travel, and see wonders.[15]

It is better in these puzzling shades not to allow ourselves to be intimidated by valiant but premature systems: better to pay more attention to the intuition that tells us that the *Life of Johnson* is great art than to the theory that finds no place of honor for its author.

I have impinged on one mystery, and shall now broach another. What formal principle makes Boswell's salvaging of the past so graphic? Why is that little conversation at Child's so memorable? Some principle of selection is operating, no doubt, but what is the principle? Carlyle said it was an open and loving heart. Boswell him-

[15] Thomas Carlyle, "Boswell's Life of Johnson," in *Critical and Miscellaneous Essays* (this essay originally 1831), paragraphs 20, 21, and 22. In paragraph 19 Carlyle himself had assumed by implication the onus of Sauerteig's "strange thesis": "In worth as a Book we have rated [the *Life of Johnson*] beyond any other product of the eighteenth century."

self said that he had a pliant ease of manners and could tune himself so to the tone of any bearable man that that man felt as free with him as with another self.[16] I accept both these explanations and should like to point also to what I may call Boswell's invincible mediocrity (I use the word in the sense of Latin *mediocritas*), his habit of apprehending the world imaginatively but in terms of average human perception. The combination of mediocrity of perception with great expressive power is obviously a rare one; most artists distort or color. But this still leaves us very far from where we wish to be. What are the formal equivalents of an open and loving heart, of tunability, of mediocrity?

In any case, one thing is clear. Boswell's style is extraordinarily modern. I do not mean by this to imply an absolute superiority so far as we are concerned. The great circulation of the *London Journal* has been generally attributed to the grossness of some of its subject matter; the book has been called high-class pornography, which of course some of it is if one uses the word pornography in its strict etymological sense. But anyone who thinks that mere dirt will sell an autobiography has a very naïve notion of the publishing business. *Boswell's London Journal* undoubtedly had wider circulation because it contained a strong and exciting element of sex, but it had wide circulation because it was well written. And it had wider circulation because it handled its element of sex in a modern manner. Smollett's novels are, shall we say, as robust as *Boswell's London Journal*, but if one were by good luck to discover a completely new Smollett novel of the quality of *Roderick Random* or *Peregrine Pickle*, one could not make a successful trade book out of it. Scholars, men of letters, readers with a special interest in the eighteenth century might acclaim it, but the general reading public would have none of it. Its style would be too much of a barrier, would rouse in the general reader too many unpleasant recollections of the classics he had to read when he was in school. Boswell writes like one of us. His style raises few feelings of strangeness in the minds of readers whose taste has been fixed by Maugham, Hemingway, Joyce, Faulkner, Salinger. I should hesitate to maintain with Carlyle that Boswell is the greatest of eighteenth-century authors. But I am certain that he is the only eighteenth-century author who could have competed with *Kon-Tiki*.

[16] Journal, 29 December 1764, *Germany and Switzerland*, pp. 304–305.

LIONEL TRILLING

The Fate of Pleasure:
Wordsworth to Dostoevsky

Oᶠ ᴀʟʟ ᴄʀɪᴛɪᴄᴀʟ ᴇꜱꜱᴀʏꜱ in the English language, there is none that has established itself so firmly in our minds as Wordsworth's Preface to *Lyrical Ballads*. Indeed, certain of the statements that the Preface makes about the nature of poetry have come to exist for us as something like proverbs of criticism. This is deplorable, for the famous utterances, in the form in which we hold them in memory, can only darken counsel. A large part of the literate world believes that Wordsworth defines poetry as the spontaneous overflow of powerful feelings. With such a definition we shall not get very far in our efforts to think about poetry, and in point of fact Wordsworth makes no such definition. Much less does he say, as many find it convenient to recall, that poetry is emotion recollected in tranquillity. Yet the tenacity with which we hold in mind our distortions of what Wordsworth actually does say suggests the peculiar power of the essay as a whole, its unique existence as a work of criticism. Its cogency in argument is notable, even if intermittent, but the Preface is not regarded by its readers only as an argument. By reason of its eloquence, and because of the impetuous spirit with which it engages the great questions of the nature and function of poetry, it presents itself to us not chiefly as a discourse but rather as a dramatic action, and we are prepared to respond to its utterances less for their truth than for their happy boldness.

This being so, it should be a matter for surprise that one especially bold utterance of the Preface has not engaged us at all and is scarcely ever cited. I refer to the sentence in which Wordsworth speaks of what he calls "the grand elementary principle of pleasure," and says of it that it constitutes "the naked and native dignity of man," that

LIONEL TRILLING is Professor of English at Columbia University.

it is the principle by which man "knows, and feels, and lives, and moves."

This is a statement which has great intrinsic interest, because, if we recognize that it is bold at all, we must also perceive that it is bold to the point of being shocking, for it echoes and it controverts St. Paul's sentence which tells us that "we live, and move, and have our being" in God (Acts 17:28). And in addition to its intrinsic interest, it has great historical interest, not only because it sums up a characteristic tendency of eighteenth-century thought, but also because it bears significantly upon a characteristic tendency of our contemporary culture. Its relation to our contemporary culture is chiefly a negative one—our present sense of life does not accommodate the idea of pleasure as something which constitutes the "naked and native dignity of man."

The word "pleasure" occurs frequently in the Preface. Like earlier writers on the subject, when Wordsworth undertakes to explain why we do, or should, value poetry, he bases his explanation upon the pleasure which poetry gives. Generally he uses the word in much the same sense that was intended by his predecessors. The pleasure which used commonly to be associated with poetry was morally unexceptionable and not very intense—it was generally understood that poetry might indeed sometimes excite the mind but only as a step toward composing it. But the word has, we know, two separate moral ambiences and two very different degrees of intensity. The pleasures of domestic life are virtuous; the pleasures of Imagination or Melancholy propose the idea of a cultivated delicacy of mind in those who experience them; the name of an English pipe-tobacco, "Parson's Pleasure," suggests how readily the word consorts with ideas of mildness. None of these propose what Byron had in mind when he wrote, "O pleasure! you're indeed a pleasant thing, / Although one must be damn'd for you no doubt." The *Oxford English Dictionary* takes due note of what it calls an "unfavorable" sense of the word: "Sensuous enjoyment as a chief object of life, or end, in itself" and informs us that in this pejorative sense it is "sometimes personified as a female deity." The Oxford lexicographers do not stop there but go on to recognize what they call a "strictly physical" sense, which is even lower in the moral scale: "the indulgence of the appetites, sensual gratification." The "unfavorable" significations of the word are dramatized by the English career of the most usual Latin word for pleasure, *voluptas*. Although some Latin-English dictionaries, especially those of the nineteenth century, say that *voluptas* means "pleasure, enjoyment, or delight of body or mind in a good or a bad sense," the word as it was used in antiquity seems to have been on the whole morally neutral and not necessarily intense. But the English words derived from *voluptas* are charged with moral judgment and are rather excited. We understand that it is not really to the minds of men that a voluptuous woman holds out the promise of pleasure, enjoyment, or delight. We do not expect a voluptuary to seek his pleasures in domesticity, or in the Imagination or Melancholy, or in smoking a pipe.

It is obvious that any badness or unfavorableness of meaning that the word "pleasure" may have relates to the primitiveness of the enjoyment that is being referred to. Scarcely any moralist will object to pleasure as what we may call a secondary state of feeling, as a charm or grace added to the solid business of life. What does arouse strong adverse judgment is pleasure in its radical aspect, as it is the object of an essential and definitive energy of man's nature. It was because Bentham's moral theory asserted that pleasure was indeed the object of an essential and definitive part of man's nature that Carlyle called it "the Pig-philosophy." He meant, of course, that it impugned man's nature to associate it so immediately with pleasure. Yet this is just how Wordsworth asks us to conceive man's nature in the sentence I have spoken of—it is precisely pleasure in its primitive or radical aspect that he has in mind. He speaks of "the grand *elementary* principle of pleasure," which is to say, pleasure not as a mere charm or amenity but as the object of an instinct, of what Freud, whose complex exposition of the part that pleasure plays in life is of course much in point here, was later to call a "drive." How little concerned was Wordsworth, at least in this one sentence, with pleasure in its mere secondary aspect is suggested by his speaking of it as constituting the *dignity* of man, not having in mind such dignity as is conferred by society but that which is *native* and *naked*.

When Carlyle denounced Bentham's assertion that pleasure is, and must be, a first consideration of the human being, it was exactly man's dignity that he was undertaking to defend. The traditional morality to which Carlyle subscribed was certainly under no illusion about the crude force of man's impulse to self-gratification, but it did not associate man's dignity with this force—on the contrary, dignity, so far as it was personal and moral, was thought to derive from the resistance which man offers to the impulse to pleasure.

For Wordsworth, however, pleasure was the defining attribute of life itself and of nature itself—pleasure is the "impulse from the vernal wood" which teaches us more of man and his moral being "than all the sages can." And the fallen condition of humanity—"what man has made of man"—is comprised by the circumstance that man alone of natural beings does not experience the pleasure which, Wordsworth believes, moves the living world. It is of course a commonplace of Wordsworth criticism that, although the poet set the highest store by the idea of pleasure, the actual pleasures he represents are of a quite limited kind. Certainly he ruled out pleasures that are "strictly physical," those which derive from "the indulgence of the appetites" and "sensual gratification," most particularly erotic gratification. His living world of springtime is far removed from that of Lucretius: nothing in it is driven by the irresistible power of *alma Venus*. This is not to say that there is no erotic aspect to Wordsworth's mind; but the eroticism is very highly sublimated—Wordsworth's pleasure always tended toward *joy*, a purer and more nearly transcendent state. And yet our awareness of this significant limitation does not permit us to underrate the boldness of his statement in the Preface about the primacy of pleasure and the dignity which derives from the principle of pleasure, nor to ignore its intimate connection with certain radical aspects of the moral theory of the French Revolution.

For an understanding of the era of the Revolution, there is, I think, much to be gained from one of the works of the German economic historian Werner Sombart, whose chief preoccupation was the origins of capitalism. In his extensive monograph, *Luxury and Capitalism*, Sombart develops the thesis that the first great accumulations of capital were achieved by the luxury trades in consequence of that ever increasing demand for the pleasures of the world, for comfort, sumptuousness, and elegance, which is to be observed in western Europe between the end of the Middle Ages and the end of the eighteenth century. As a comprehensive explanation of the rise of capitalism, this theory, I gather, has been largely discredited. Yet the social and cultural data which Sombart accumulates are in themselves very interesting, and they are much to our point.

Sombart advances the view that the European preoccupation with luxury took its rise in the princely courts and in the influence of women which court life made possible; he represents luxury as being essentially an expression of eroticism, as the effort to refine and complicate the sexual life, to enhance, as it were, the quality of erotic pleasure. The courtly luxury that Sombart studies is scarcely a unique instance of the association of pleasure with power, of pleasure being thought of as one of the signs of power and therefore to be made not merely manifest but conspicuous in the objects that constitute the *décor* of the lives of powerful men—surely Egypt, Knossos, and Byzantium surpassed Renaissance Europe in elaborateness of luxury. But what would seem to be remarkable about the particular phenomenon that Sombart describes is the extent of its proliferation at a certain period—the sheer amount of luxury that got produced, its increasing availability to classes less than royal or noble, the overtness of desire for it, and the fierceness of this desire. Sombart's data on these points are too numerous to be adduced here, but any tourist, having in mind what he has even casually seen of the secondary arts of Europe from the centuries in question, the ornaments, furniture, and garniture of certain stations of life, will know that, as to the amount of luxury produced, Sombart does not exaggerate. And any reader of Balzac will recognize the intensity of the passions which, at a somewhat later time, attended the acquisition of elaborate and costly objects which were desired as the means or signs of pleasure.

What chiefly engages our interest is the influence that luxury may be discovered to have upon social and moral ideas. Such an influence is to be observed in the growing tendency of power to express itself mediately, by signs or indexes, rather than directly, by the exercise of force. The richness and elaboration of the objects in a princely establishment were the indexes of a power which was actual enough, but they indicated an actual power which had no need to avow itself in action. What a prince conceived of as his dignity might, more than ever before, be expressed by affluence, by the means of pleasure made overt and conspicuous.

And as the objects of luxury became more widely available, so did the dignity which luxury was meant to imply. The connection between dignity and a luxurious style of life was at first not self-evident —in France in 1670 the very phrase *bourgeois gentilhomme* was thought to be comical. In the English translation of the title of Molière's comedy, *The Cit Turned Gentleman*, it was funny too, but the English laugh was neither so loud nor so long as the French. Tocqueville believed that it was the relatively easy growth of the English class of gentlemen, that is to say, the acceptance of the idea that the outward sign of status eventually conferred real status, which made an event like the Revolution of France unnecessary in England. Yet in France as in England, the downward spread of the idea of dignity, until it eventually became an idea that might be applied to man in general, was advanced by the increasing possibility of possessing the means or signs of pleasure. That idea, it need scarcely be said, established itself at the very heart of the radical thought of the eighteenth century. And Diderot himself, the most uncompromising of materialists, as he was the most subtle and delicate, could not have wanted a more categorical statement of his own moral and intellectual theory than Wordsworth's assertion that the grand elementary principle of pleasure constitutes the native and naked dignity of man, and that it is by this principle that man knows, and lives, and breathes, and moves.

Nothing so much connects Keats with Wordsworth as the extent of his conscious commitment to the principle of pleasure. But of course nothing so much separates Keats from his great master as his characteristic way of exemplifying the principle. In the degree that for Wordsworth pleasure is abstract and austere, for Keats it is explicit and voluptuous. No poet ever gave so much credence to the idea of pleasure in the sense of "indulgence of the appetites, sensual gratification," as Keats did, and the phenomenon that Sombart describes, the complex of pleasure-sensuality-luxury, makes the very fabric of his thought.

Keats's preoccupation with the creature-pleasures, as it manifests itself in his early work, is commonly regarded, even by some of his warmest admirers, with an amused disdain. At best it seems to derive from the kind of elegant miniscule imagination that used to design the charming erotic scenes for the lids of enameled sweetmeat- and snuffboxes. At worst it seems to be downright vulgar in the explicitness of its concern with luxury. The word itself had a charm for Keats, and in his use of it he seems on the point of reviving its Middle English meaning which is specifically erotic and nothing but erotic; for Chaucer, *luxures* were lusts and *luxurie* was licentiousness. Women present themselves to Keats's imagination as luxuries: "All that soft luxury / That nestled in his arms." A poem is described as "a posy / Of luxuries, bright, milky, soft and rosy." Poetry itself is defined by reference to objects of luxury, and even in its highest nobility, its function is said to be that of comforting and soothing.

Nor is the vulgarity—if we consent to call it that—confined to the early works; we find it in an extreme form in a poem of Keats's maturity. The lover in *Lamia* is generally taken to be an innocent youth, yet the most corrupt young man of Balzac's scenes of Parisian life would scarcely have spoken to his mistress or his fiancée as Lycius speaks to Lamia when he insists that she display her beauty in public for the enhancement of his prestige. Tocqueville said that envy was the characteristic emotion of plutocratic democracy, and it is envy of a particularly ugly kind that Lycius wishes to excite. "Let my foes choke," he says, "and my friends shout afar, / While through the thronged streets your bridal car / Wheels round its dazzling spokes." I am not sure that we should be at pains to insist that this is wholly a dramatic utterance and not a personal one, that we ought entirely to dissociate Keats from Lycius. I am inclined to think that we should suppose Keats to have been involved in all aspects of the principle of pleasure, even the ones that are vulgar and ugly. Otherwise we miss the full complication of that dialectic of pleasure which is the characteristic intellectual activity of Keats's poetry.

The movement of this dialectic is indicated in two lines from an early poem in which Keats speaks of "the pillowy silkiness that rests / Full in the speculation of the stars"—it is the movement from the sensual to the transcendent, from pleasure to knowledge, and knowledge of an ultimate kind. Keats's intellect was brought into fullest play when the intensity of his affirmation of pleasure was met by the intensity of his skepticism about pleasure. The principle of pleasure is for Keats, as it is for Wordsworth, the principle of reality—by it, as Wordsworth said, we *know*. But for Keats it is also the principle of illusion. In "The Eve of St. Agnes," to take the most obvious example, the moment of pleasure at the center of the poem, erotic pleasure expressed in the fullest possible imagination of the luxurious, is the very essence of reality: it is all we know on earth and all we need to know. And it is the more real as reality, and it is the more comprehensive as knowledge, exactly because in the poem it exists surrounded by what on earth denies it, by darkness, cold, and death, which make it transitory, which make the felt and proclaimed reality mere illusion.

But we must be aware that in Keats's dialectic of pleasure it is not only external circumstances that condition pleasure and bring it into question as the principle of reality, but also the very nature of pleasure itself. If for Keats erotic enjoyment is the peak and crown of all pleasures, it is also his prime instance of the way in which the desire for pleasure denies itself and produces the very opposite of itself.

> Love in a hut, with water and a crust,
> Is—Love, forgive us—cinders, ashes, dust;
> Love in a palace is perhaps at last
> More grievous torment than a hermit's fast.

This opening statement of the second part of *Lamia* is not, as it is often said to be, merely a rather disagreeable jaunty cynicism but one of Keats's boldest expressions of his sense that there is something perverse and self-negating in the erotic life, that it is quite in the course of nature that we should feel "Pleasure . . . turning to Poison as the bee-mouth sips." He insists on the seriousness of the statement in a way that should not be hard to interpret—referring to the lines I have just quoted, he says,

> That is a doubtful tale from faery land,
> Hard for the non-elect to understand.

That faery land we know very well—in "To a Nightingale" Keats's epithet for the region is "forlorn"; it is the country of La Belle Dame Sans Merci, the scene of erotic pleasure which leads to devastation, of an erotic fulfilment which implies castration.

Keats, then, may be thought of as the poet who made the boldest affirmation of the principle of pleasure and also as the poet who brought the principle of pleasure into the greatest and *sincerest* doubt. He therefore has for us a peculiar cultural interest, for it would seem to be true that at some point in modern history the principle of pleasure came to be regarded with just such ambivalence.

This divided state of feeling may be expressed in terms of a breach between politics and art. Modern societies seek to fulfil themselves in affluence, which of course implies the possibility of pleasure. Our political morality is more than acquiescent to this intention. Its simple and on the whole efficient criterion is the extent to which affluence is distributed among individuals and nations. But another morality, that which we may describe as being associated with art, regards with a stern and even minatory gaze all that is implied by affluence, and it takes a dim or at best a very complicated view of the principle of pleasure. If we speak not only of the two different modes of morality, the political and the artistic, but also of the people who are responsive to them, we can say that it is quite within the bounds of possibility, if not of consistency, for the same person to respond, and intensely, to both of the two moral modes: it is by no means uncommon for an educated person to base his judgment of politics on a simple affirmation of the principle of pleasure, and his judgment of art, and also his judgment of personal existence, on a complex antagonism to that principle. This dichotomy makes one of the most significant circumstances of our cultural situation.

A way of testing what I have said about the modern artistic attitude to pleasure is afforded by the conception of poetry which Keats formulates in *Sleep and Poetry*. This poem does not express everything that Keats thought about the nature and function of poetry, but what it does express is undeniably central to his thought, and, for the modern sensibility it is inadmissible and even repulsive. It tells us that poetry is gentle, soothing, cheerful, healthful, serene, smooth, regal; that the poet, in the natural course of his development, will first devote his art to the representation of the pleasures of appetite, of things that can be bitten and tasted, such as apples, strawberries, and the white shoulders of nymphs, and that he will give his attention to the details of erotic enticement amid grateful sights and odors, and to sexual fulfilment and sleep. The poem then goes on to say that, as the poet grows older, he will write a different kind of poetry, which is called nobler; this later kind of poetry is less derived from and directed to the sensuality of youth and is more fitted to the gravity of mature years, but it still ministers to pleasure and must therefore be strict in its avoidance of ugly themes, it must not deal with those distressing matters which are referred to as "the burrs and thorns of life": the great end of poetry, we are told, is "to soothe the cares, and lift the thoughts of man."

Such doctrine from a great poet puzzles and embarrasses us. It is, we say, the essence of Philistinism.

The conception of the nature and function of poetry which Keats propounds is, of course, by no means unique with him—it can be understood as a statement of the common assumptions about art which prevailed through the Renaissance up to some point in the nineteenth century, when they began to lose their force.[1] Especially in the eighteenth century, art is closely associated with luxury—with the pleasure or at least the comfort of the consumer, or with the quite direct flattery of his ego. The very idea of Beauty seems to imply considerations of this sort, which is perhaps why the eighteenth century was so much drawn to the idea of the Sublime, for that word would seem to indicate a kind of success in art which could not be called Beauty because it lacked the smoothness and serenity (to take two attributes from Keats's catalogue) and the immediacy of gratification which the idea of Beauty seems to propose. But the Sublime itself of course served the purposes of egoism—thus, that instance of Sublime which was called the Grand Style, as it is described by its great English exponent in painting, Sir Joshua Reynolds, is said to be concerned with "some instance of heroic action or heroic suffering" and its proper effect, Reynolds explains, is to produce the emotion which Bouchardon reported he felt when he read Homer: "His whole frame appeared to himself to be enlarged, and all nature which surrounded him diminished to atoms."[2]

[1] One of the last significant exponents of the old assumptions was the young Yeats. He was "in all things pre-Raphaelite"—a partisan, that is, not of the early and austere pre-Raphaelite mode, but of the later sumptuous style, tinged with a sort of mystical eroticism—and he stubbornly resisted the realism of Carolus Duran and Bastien-Lepage which was being brought back to England by the painters who had gone to study in Paris. His commitment to the "beautiful," as against truthful ugliness, was an issue of great moment between him and his father.

[2] All writers on the Sublime say in effect what Bouchardon says—that, although the sublime subject induces an overpowering emotion, even fear or terror, it does so in a way that permits us to rise superior to it and thus gives us occasion to have a good opinion of our power of intellect and of ourselves generally. The Sublime has this direct relation to comfort and luxury, that it induces us "to regard as small those things of which we are wont to be solicitous" (Kant, *Critique of Aesthetic Judgment*). A more ambitious treatment of my subject would require a much fuller exposition of the theory of the Sublime. Of this theory, which so much occupied the writers on art of the eighteenth century, it can be said that it has much more bearing upon our own literature than modern critics have recognized, although the scholars have set forth in very attractive form all that the critics need to know. The classic study in English is Samuel H. Monk's *The Sublime*, first published in 1935, now available as an Ann Arbor Paperback.

In connection with the art of the eighteenth century I used the disagreeable modern word "consumer," meaning thus to suggest the affinity that art was thought to have with luxury, its status as a commodity which is implied by the solicitude it felt for the pleasure and the comfort of the person who was to own and experience it. Certainly Wordsworth was pre-eminent in the movement to change this state of affairs,[3] yet Wordsworth locates the value of metrical language as lying in its ability to protect the reader from the discomfort of certain situations that poetry may wish to represent, and he compares the effect of such situations in novels with their effect in Shakespeare, his point being that in novels they are "distressful" but in Shakespeare they are not.[4] It was, we know, an explanation which did not satisfy Keats, who was left to puzzle out why it is that in *King Lear* "all disagreeables evaporate." He discovers that this effect is achieved by "intensity," and we of our day are just at the point of being comfortable with him when he disappoints our best hopes by hedging: he is constrained to say that the "disagreeables" evaporate not only by the operation of intensity but also by "their being in close connection with Beauty & Truth." But we do at last find ourselves at one with him when, in his sonnet "On Sitting Down To Read King Lear Once Again," he dismisses all thought of pleasure and prepares himself for the pain he is in duty bound to undergo:

> . . . Once again, the fierce dispute
> Betwixt damnation and impassioned clay
> Must I burn through; once more humbly essay
> The bitter-sweet of this Shakespearean fruit.

He is by no means certain that the disagreeables really will evaporate and that he will emerge whole and sound from the experience, and he prays to Shakespeare and "the clouds of Albion" that they will guard

[3] "Men . . . who talk of Poetry as of a matter of amusement and idle pleasure; who will converse with us as gravely about a *taste* for Poetry, as they express it, as if it were a thing as indifferent as a taste for rope-dancing, or Frontiniac or Sherry" (Preface to *Lyrical Ballads*).

[4] The strength of Wordsworth's impulse to suppress the "distressful" is suggested by the famous passage in *The Prelude* in which the poet explains how his childhood reading served to inure him to the terrors of actuality. He recounts the incident, which occurred when he was nine years old, of his seeing a drowned man brought up from the bottom of Esthwaite Lake. He was, he says, not overcome by fear of the "ghastly face," because his "inner eye" had seen such sights before in fairy tales and romances. And then he feels it necessary to go further, to go beyond the bounds of our ready credence, for he tells us that from his reading came "a spirit" which hallowed the awful sight

> With decoration and ideal grace
> A dignity, a smoothness, like the works
> Of Grecian Art, and purest poesy.

him against wandering "in a barren dream," and that, when he is "consumed in the fire," they will contrive his Phoenix-resurrection.

This we of our time can quite understand. We are repelled by the idea of an art that is consumer-directed and comfortable, let alone luxurious. Our typical experience of a work which will eventually have authority with us is to begin our relation to it at a conscious disadvantage, and to wrestle with it until it consents to bless us. We express our high esteem for such a work by supposing that it judges us. And when it no longer does seem to judge us, or when it no longer baffles and resists us, when we begin to feel that we *possess* it, we discover that its power is diminished. In our praise of it we are not likely to use the word "Beauty": we consented long ago—more than four decades ago—to the demonstration made by I. A. Richards in collaboration with Ogden and Wood that the concept of Beauty either could not be assigned any real meaning or was frivolously derived from some assumed connection between works of art and our sexual preferences, quite conventional sexual preferences at that. "Beauty: it curves: curves are beauty," says Leopold Bloom, and we smile at so outmoded an aesthetic—how like him! With a similar ironic tolerance we read the language in which the young Yeats praised beauty in "The Secret Rose" (1896)—he speaks of those who are so fortunate as to be "heavy with the sleep / Men have named beauty."[5]

In short, our contemporary aesthetic culture does not set great store by the principle of pleasure in its simple and primitive meaning, and it may even be said to maintain an antagonism to the principle of pleasure. Such a statement of course has its aspect of absurdity, but in logic only. There is no psychic fact more available to our modern comprehension than that there are human impulses which, in one degree or another, and sometimes in the very highest degree, repudiate pleasure and seek gratification in—to use Freud's word—unpleasure.

The repudiation of pleasure in favor of the gratification which may

---

[5] Mr. Bloom's observation (which goes on to "shapely goddesses Venus, Juno: curves the world admires" and "lovely forms of women sculped Junonian") follows upon his lyrical recollection of his first sexual encounter with Molly; Yeats's phrase occurs in the course of a poem to Maud Gonne. I think it is true to say of Joyce (at least up through *Ulysses*) and of Yeats that they were among the last devotees of the European cult of Woman, of a Female Principle which, in one way or another, *zieht uns hinan*, and that Molly and Maud are perhaps the last women in literature to be represented as having a transcendent and on the whole beneficent significance (although Lara in *Dr. Zhivago* should be mentioned—it is she who gives that novel much of its archaic quality). The radical change in our sexual mythos must surely be considered in any speculation about the status of pleasure in our culture. It is to the point, for example, that in Kafka's account of the spiritual life, which is touched on below, women play a part that is at best ambiguous.

be found in unpleasure is a leading theme of Dostoevsky's great *nouvelle, Notes from Underground*. Of this extraordinary work Thomas Mann has said that "its painful and scornful conclusions," its "radical frankness . . . ruthlessly transcending all novelistic and literary bounds" have "long become parts of our moral culture." Mann's statement is accurate but minimal—the painful and scornful conclusions of Dostoevsky's story have established themselves not only as parts of our moral culture but as its essence, at least so far as it makes itself explicit in literature.

Notes from Underground is an account, given in the first person, of the temperament and speculations of a miserable clerk, disadvantaged in every possible way, who responds to his unfortunate plight by every device of bitterness and resentment, by hostility toward those of mankind who are more unfortunate than he is, and also by the fiercest contempt for his more fortunate fellow beings, and for the elements of good fortune. He hates all men of purposeful life, and reasonable men, and action, and happiness, and what he refers to as "the sublime and the beautiful," and pleasure. His mind is subtle, complex, and contradictory almost beyond credibility—we never know where to have him, and in our exhaustion we are likely to explain his perversity in some simple way, such as that he hates because he is envious, that he despises what he cannot have: all quite natural. But we are not permitted to lay this flattering unction to our souls— for one thing, he himself beats us to that explanation. And although it is quite true, it is only a small part of the truth. It is also true that he does not have because he does not wish to have; he has arranged his own misery—arranged it in the interests of his dignity, which is to say, of his freedom. For to want what is commonly thought to be appropriate to men, to want whatever it is, high or low, that is believed to yield pleasure, to be active about securing it, to use common sense and prudence to the end of gaining it, this is to admit and consent to the *conditioned* nature of man. What a distance we have come in the six decades since Wordsworth wrote his Preface! To know and feel and live and move at the behest of the principle of pleasure—this, for the Underground Man, so far from constituting his native and naked dignity, constitutes his humiliation in bondage. It makes him, he believes, a mechanic thing, the puppet of whoever or whatever can offer him the means of pleasure. If pleasure is indeed the principle of his being, he is as *known* as the sum of 2 and 2; he is a mere object of reason, of that rationality of the Revolution which is established upon the primacy of the principle of pleasure.

At one point in his narrative, the protagonist of *Notes from Underground* speaks of himself as an "anti-hero." He is the eponymous ancestor of a now numerous tribe. He stands as the antagonistic opposite to all the qualities which are represented by that statue of Sophocles which Professor Margarete Bieber tells us we are to have in mind when we try to understand the Greek conception of the hero, the grave beauty of the countenance and physique expressing the strength and order of the soul; the Underground Man traces his line of descent back to Thersites. It is in his character of anti-hero that he addresses the "gentlemen," as he calls them, the men of action and reason, the lovers of the "sublime and the beautiful," and brags to them, "I have more life in me than you have."

More life: perhaps it was this boast of the Underground Man that Nietzsche recalled when he said, "Dostoevsky's Underman and My Overman are the same person clawing his way out of the pit [of modern thought and feeling] into the sunlight." One understands what Nietzsche meant, but he is mistaken in the identification, for his own imagination is bounded on one side by that word "sunlight," by the Mediterranean world which he loved: by the tradition of humanism with its recognition of the value of pleasure. He is ineluctably constrained by considerations of society and culture, however much he may despise his own society and culture, but the Underground Man is not. To be sure, the terms of the latter's experience are, in the first instance, social; he is preoccupied by questions of status and dignity, and he could not, we may suppose, have come into existence if the fates of the heroes of Balzac and Stendhal had not previously demonstrated that no object of desire or of the social will is anything but an illusion and a source of corruption, society being what it is. But it is the essence of the Underground Man's position that his antagonism to society arises not in response to the deficiencies of social life, but, rather, in response to the insult which society offers to his freedom by aspiring to be beneficent, to embody "the sublime and the beautiful" as elements of its being. The anger that Dostoevsky expresses in *Notes from Underground* was mobilized not by the bad social condition of Russia in 1864 but by the avowed hope of some people that a good social condition could be brought into being. He had in mind a particular expression of this hope, a Utopian novel of the day, Chernyshevsky's *What Is To Be Done?*[6] His disgust was

[6] "A Utopian novel of the day" does not, of course, give anything like an adequate notion of the book's importance in the political culture of Russia. Dostoevsky chose his antagonist with the precision that was characteristic of him, for Chernyshevsky, who thought of himself as the heir of the French Enlightenment, by his one novel exercised a decisive influence upon the Russian revolutionaries of the next two generations, most notably upon Lenin, who borrowed its title for one of his best-known pamphlets and whose moral style was much influenced by the character Rakhmétov. This paragon of revolutionists, although very fond of the luxury in which he was reared,

aroused by this novel's assumption that man would be better for a
rationally organized society, by which was meant, of course, a society
organized in the service of pleasure. Dostoevsky's reprobation of this
idea, begun in *Notes from Underground,* reached its climax in Ivan
Karamazov's poem of The Grand Inquisitor, in which again, but this
time without the brilliant perversities of the earlier work, the disgust
with the specious good of pleasure is the ground for the affirmation of
spiritual freedom.

I have taken the phrase "specious good" from a passage in Wallace
Fowlie's little book on Rimbaud, in which Mr. Fowlie discusses what
he calls "the modern seizure and comprehension of spirituality."
Without evasion, Mr. Fowlie identifies a chief characteristic of our
culture which critics must inevitably be conscious of and yet don't
like to name. If we are to be aware of the spiritual intention of
modern literature, we have to get rid of certain nineteenth-century
connotations of the word "spiritual," all that they may imply to us of
an overrefined and even effeminate quality, and have chiefly in mind
what Mr. Fowlie refers to when he speaks of a certain type of saint
and a certain type of poet and says of them that "both the saint and
the poet exist through some propagation of destructive violence." And
Mr. Fowlie continues: "In order to discover what is the center of
themselves, the saint has to destroy the world of evil, and the poet has
to destroy the world of specious good."

The destruction of what is considered to be specious good is surely one of the chief literary enterprises of our age. Whenever in
modern literature we find violence, whether of represented act or of
expression, and the insistence upon the sordid and the disgusting, and
the insult offered to the prevailing morality or habit of life, we may
assume that we are in the presence of the intention to destroy specious
good, that we are being confronted by that spirituality, or the aspira-
tion toward it, which subsists upon violence against the specious good.

The most immediate specious good that a modern writer will seek
to destroy is, of course, the habits, manners, and "values" of the
bourgeois world, and not merely because these associate themselves
with much that is bad, such as vulgarity or the exploitation of the disadvantaged, but for other reasons as well, because they clog and
hamper the movement of the individual spirit toward freedom, be-

embraces an extreme asceticism because, as he says, "We demand that men may have
a complete enjoyment of their lives, and we must show by our example that we demand it, not to satisfy our personal passions, but for mankind in general; that what
we say we say from principle and not from passion, from conviction and not from
personal desire." Only one pleasure is proof against Rakhmétov's iron will—he cannot
overcome his love of expensive cigars.

cause they prevent the attainment of "more life." The particular systems and modes of thought of the bourgeois world are a natural first target for the modern spirituality. But it is not hard to believe that the impulse to destroy specious good would be as readily directed against the most benign society, which, by modern definition, serves the principle of pleasure.

In the characteristically modern conception of the spiritual life, the influence of Dostoevsky is definitive. By the same token, the influence of Nietzsche is merely marginal. For however radical Nietzsche was in his criticism of the existing culture, the terms of his adversity were, as I have remarked, essentially social and humanistic. The moral and personal qualities suggested by a particular class, the aristocracy, had great simple force with him and proposed to his imagination a particular style of life. Despite the scorn he expressed for liberal democracy and socialist theory as we knew them, he was able to speak with sympathy of future democracies and possible socialisms, led to do so by that element of his thought which served to aerate his mind and keep it frank and generous—his awareness of the part played in human existence by the will to power, which, however it figures in the thought of his epigones and vulgarizers, was conceived by Nietzsche himself as comprising the whole range of the possibilities of human energy, creativity, libido; the claims of any social group to this human characteristic had weight with him. And he gave ready credence to the pleasure that attends one or another kind of power; if he was quick to judge people by the pleasures they chose—alas for those who preferred beer to wine and *Parsifal* to *Carmen!*—the principle of pleasure presented itself to him as constituting an element of the dignity of man. It is because of this humanism of his, this naturalistic acceptance of power and pleasure, that Nietsche is held at a distance by the modern spiritual sensibility. And the converse of what explains Nietzsche's marginality explains Dostoevsky's position at the very heart of the modern spiritual life.

If we speak of spirituality, we must note that it is not only humanism that is negated by the Underground Man but Christianity as well, or at least Christianity as western Europe understands it. For not only humanism but the Christianity of the West bases reason upon pleasure, upon pleasure postponed and purified but analogous in kind to worldly pleasure. Dostoevsky's clerk has had his way with us: it would seem to be true that, in the degree that the promises of the spiritual life are made in terms of pleasure—of comfort, rest, and beauty—they have no power over the modern imagination. If Kafka, perhaps more than any other writer of our time, lends the color of reality to the events of the spiritual life, his power to do so lies in his characterizing these events by unpleasure, by sordidness and disorder, even when, as in *The Castle*, the spiritual struggle seems to yield a measure of success. He understood that a divinity who, like St. Augustine's, could be spoken of as gratifying all the senses, must nowadays be deficient in reality, that a heaven which is presented to us as well-ordered, commodious, beautiful—as *luxurious!*—cannot be an object of hope. He was set on the road to this understanding by Dostoevsky, who, more dramatically and cogently than anyone before him, expresses the modern aversion from pleasure. Yeats tells us that "Berkeley in his youth described the summum bonum and the reality of Heaven as physical pleasure, and thought this conception made both more intelligible to simple men." To simple men perhaps, but who now is a simple man? How far from our imagination is the idea of "peace" as the crown of spiritual struggle! The idea of "bliss" is even further removed. The two words propose to us a state of virtually infantile passivity which is the negation of the "more life" that we crave, the "more life" of spiritual militancy. We dread Eden, and of all Christian concepts there is none which we understand so well as the *felix culpa* and the "fortunate fall"; not, of course, for the reason on which these Christian paradoxes were based, but because by means of the sin and the fall we managed to get ourselves expelled from that dreadful place.

I have tried to make explicit, although surely in a way that is all too summary, a change in the assumptions of literature which everybody is more or less aware of. In undertaking to do this, my first intention has been historical and objective. But it must be obvious that my account of the change has not been wholly objective in the sense of being wholly neutral. It asks a question which is inevitably adversary in some degree, if only by reason of the irony which is implicit in the historical approach to a fact of moral culture. It suggests that the modern spirituality, with its devaluation of the principle of pleasure, because it came into being at a particular time may be regarded as a contingent and not a necessary mode of thought. This opens the way to regarding it as a mode of thought which is "received" or "established" and which is therefore, like any other received or established mode of thought, available to critical scrutiny.

And that possibility is by no means comfortable. We set great store by the unillusioned militancy of spirit which deals violently with the specious good. Upon it we base whatever self-esteem we can lay claim to—it gives us, as one of D. H. Lawrence's characters says of it (or something very much like it), our "last distinction"; he feels that to question it is a "sort of vulgarity."[7] To what end, with what intention, is it to be questioned? Can an adversary scrutiny of it point away from it to anything else than an idiot literature, to "positive heroes" who know how to get the good out of life and who have "affirmative" emotions about their success in doing so? The energy, the consciousness, and the wit of modern literature derive from its enterprise of violence against the specious good of whatever poor "pleasure" may be offered to us by the universe or by our general culture in its quotidian aspects. We feel an instinctive resentment of questions which tend to suggest that there is fault to be found with the one saving element of our moral situation—that extruded "high" segment of our general culture, with its exigent, violently subversive spirituality, with its power of arming us against, and setting us apart from, all in the general culture that we hate and fear.

Then what justification can there be for describing with any irony at all the diminished status of the principle of pleasure which characterizes this segment of our culture?

Possibly one small justification can be brought to light by reference to a famous passage in the *Confessions* of St. Augustine, the one in which Augustine speaks of an episode of his adolescence and asks why he entered that orchard and stole those pears. Of all the acts of his unregenerate days which he calls sinful and examines in his grim, brilliant way, there is none that he nags so persistently, none that seems to lie so far beyond the reach of his ready comprehension of sin. He did not steal the pears because he was hungry. He did not steal them because they were delicious—they were pears of rather poor quality, he had better at home. He did not steal them to win the admiration of the friends who were with him, although this comes close, for, as he says, he would not have stolen them if he had been alone. In all sin, he says, there is a patent motivating desire, some good to be gained, some pleasure for the sake of which the act was committed. But this sin of the stolen pears is, as it were, pure—he can discover no human reason for it. He speaks again of the presence of the companions, but although their being with him was a necessary condition of the act, it cannot be said to have motivated it. To the mature Augustine, the petty theft of his youth is horrifying not only because it seems to have been a sin committed solely for the sake of sinning, but because, in having no conceivable pleasure in view, it was a sort of negative transcendence—in effect, a negation—of his humanity. This

[7] Gerald Crich, in chapter xxix of *Women in Love*.

is not strange to us—what I have called the high extruded segment of our general culture has for some time been engaged in an experiment in the negative transcendence of the human, a condition which is to be achieved by freeing the self from its thralldom to pleasure. Augustine's puzzling sin is the paradigm of the modern spiritual enterprise, and in his reprobation of it is to be found the reason why Dostoevsky contemned and hated the Christianity of the West, which he denounced as, in effect, a vulgar humanism.

To be aware of this undertaking of negative transcendence is, surely, to admire the energy of its desperateness. And we can comprehend how, for the consumer of literature, for that highly developed person who must perforce live the bourgeois life in an affluent society, an aesthetic ethos based on the devaluation of pleasure can serve, and seem to save, one of the two souls which inhabit his breast. Nearly overcome as we are by the specious good, insulted as we are by being forced to acquire it, we claim the right of the Underground Man to address the "gentlemen" with our assertion, "I have more life in me than you have," which consorts better with the refinement of our sensibility than other brags that men have made, such as, "I am stronger than you," or "I am holier than thou." Our high culture invites us to transfer our energies from the bourgeois competition to the spiritual competition. We find our "distinction"—last or penultimate—in our triumph over the miserable "gentlemen," whether they are others or ourselves, whether our cry be, "I have more life in me than you have" or "I have more life in me than I have." Now and then it must occur to us that the life of competition for spiritual status is not without its sordidness and absurdity. But how else are we to live?

But this is a matter for the novelist—for that novelist we do not yet have but must surely have one day, who will take into serious and comic account the actualities of the spiritual career of our time.

More immediately available to our awareness and more substantive and simple in itself is the effect which the devaluation of pleasure has upon the relation between our high literature and our life in politics, taking that word in its largest possible sense. There was a time when literature assumed that the best ideals of politics were naturally in accord with its own essence, when poetry celebrated the qualities of social life which had their paradigmatic existence in poetry itself. Keats's *Poems* of 1817 takes for its epigraph two lines from Spenser which are intended to point up the political overtone of the volume: "What more felicity can fall to creature / Than to enjoy delight with liberty." Even when Wordsworth is deep in Toryism and Stoic Christianity, it is natural for him to assert the utopian possibility.

Paradise and groves
Elysian, Fortunate Fields—like those of old
Sought in the Atlantic Main—why should they be
A history only of departed things,
Or a mere fiction of what never was?

He goes on to say categorically that these imaginations may become, at the behest of rationality and good will, "a simple produce of the common day." But the old connection between literature and politics has been dissolved. For the typical modern literary personality, political life is likely to exist only as it makes an occasion for the disgust and rage which are essential to the state of modern spirituality, as one particular instance of the irrational, violent, and obscene fantasy which life in general is, as licensing the counter-fantasy of the poet.

In a recent essay,[8] William Phillips described in an accurate and telling way the dichotomy that has developed between modern literature and a rational and positive politics and went on to explain why, for literature's sake, the separation must be maintained. "It now looks," Mr. Phillips said, "as though a radical literature and a radical politics must be kept apart. For radical politics of the modern variety has really served as an antidote to literature. The moral hygiene, the puritanism, the benevolence—all the virtues that sprout on the left—work like a cure for the perverse and morbid idealism of the modern writer. If writing is to be thought of as radical, it must be in a deeper sense, in the sense not simply of cutting across the grain of contemporary life but also of reaching for the connections between the real and the forbidden and the fantastic. The classic example is Dostoevsky. . . ."

The situation that Mr. Phillips describes will scarcely be a matter of indifference to any one of us who, while responding to the force of the perverse and morbid idealism of modern literature, has no wish to think about society only in the apocalyptic way which this literature proposes. We can but feel a discomfort of mind when we regard the hostile separation of politics and literature, two modes of thought which, we might well believe, naturally seek union with each other. And we are led to ask—even at the risk of being hygienic—whether the perverse and morbid idealism of modern literature is not to be thought of as in some sense political, whether it does not express a demand which in its own way is rational and positive and which may have to be taken into eventual account by a rational and positive politics.

If we do ask this question, we will be ready to remind ourselves that the devaluation of the pleasure principle, or, as perhaps we ought

[8] "What Happened in the 30's," *Commentary*, September 1962.

to put it, the imagination of going *beyond the pleasure principle* is, after all, not merely an event of a particular moment in culture. It is, as Freud made plain in his famous essay, a fact of the psychic life itself. The impulse to go beyond the pleasure principle is certainly to be observed not only in modern literature but in all literature, and of course not only in literature but in the emotional economy of at least some persons in all epochs. But what we can indeed call an event in culture is that at a particular moment in history, in our moment, this fact of the psychic life became a salient and dominant theme in literature, and also that it has been made explicit as a fact in the psychic life and forced upon our consciousness by Freud's momentous foray into metapsychology. And this cultural event may indeed be understood in political terms, as likely to have eventual political consequences, just as we understood in political terms and as having had political consequences the eighteenth-century assertion that the dignity of man was to be found in the principle of pleasure.

We deal with a change in quantity. It has always been true of some men that to pleasure they have preferred what the world called unpleasure. They imposed upon themselves difficult and painful tasks, they committed themselves to strange, "unnatural" modes of life, they sought out distressing emotions, in order to know psychic energies which are not to be summoned up in felicity. These psychic energies, even when they are experienced in self-destruction, are a means of self-definition and self-affirmation. As such, they have a social reference—the election of unpleasure, however isolated and private the act may be, must refer to society if only because the choice denies the valuation which society in general puts upon pleasure; and of course it often receives social approbation in the highest degree, even if at a remove of time: it is the choice of the hero, the saint and martyr, and, in some cultures, the artist. The quantitative change which we have to take account of is: what was once a mode of experience of a few has now become an ideal of experience of many. For reasons which, at least in this essay, must defy speculation, the ideal of pleasure has exhausted itself, almost as if it had been actually realized and had issued in satiety and ennui. In its place, or at the least, beside it, there is developing—conceivably at the behest of literature!—an ideal of the experience of those psychic energies which are linked with unpleasure and which are directed toward self-definition and self-affirmation. Such an ideal makes a demand upon society for its satisfaction: it is a political fact.

What I have called the spirituality of modern literature can scarcely be immune from irony, and the less so as we see it advancing in the easy comprehension of increasing numbers of people, to the point of its becoming, through the medium of the stage and the cinema, the stuff of popular entertainment—how can irony be withheld from an accredited subversiveness, an established moral radicalism, a respectable violence, an entertaining spirituality? But although the anomalies of the culture of the educated middle class do indeed justify an adversary response, and perhaps a weightier one than that of irony, yet a response that is nothing but adversary will not be adequate.

We often hear it said nowadays, usually by psychoanalysts and by writers oriented toward psychoanalysis, that the very existence of civilization is threatened unless society can give credence to the principle of pleasure and learn how to implement it. We understand what is meant, that repressiveness and oppression will be lessened if the principle of pleasure is established in our social arrangements, and we readily assent. Yet secretly we know that the formula does not satisfy the condition it addresses itself to—it leaves out of account those psychic energies which press beyond the pleasure principle and even deny it.

It is possible to say that—whether for good or for bad—we confront a mutation in culture by which an old established proportion between the pleasure-seeking instincts and the ego instincts is being altered in favor of the latter.[9] If we follow Freud through the awesome paradoxes of *Beyond the Pleasure Principle,* we may understand why the indications of this change should present themselves as perverse and morbid, for the other name that Freud uses for the ego instincts is the death instincts. Freud's having made the ego instincts synonymous with the death instincts accounts, more than anything

---

[9] I said something to this effect when, in "On the Modern Element of Modern Literature" (*Partisan Review*, January–February 1961), I commented on the status of tragedy in our culture. I ventured the opinion that the tragic mode is not available to us—this was not, I said, a mark of our spiritual inferiority—because we do not think of the degradation or downfall of the protagonist as a deplorable event: what he loses in the worldly way we judge to be well lost for the sake of the reality and truth, the ultimate self-realization, which we understand tragedy to bring. I based my generalization on our response to the fate of Kurtz in *Heart of Darkness* and Aschenbach in *Death in Venice.* Lionel Abel in the brilliant chapter on tragedy in his *Metatheatre,* says that a tragedy—a *real* tragedy, of which Mr. Abel believes there are only a very few—must have for its protagonist a "daemon," that is to say, a person who, "having lived through tragic destruction . . . becomes divine, a daemon." The tragic destruction is the extirpation of "merely" human feeling: the daemonic existence comes with the protagonist's survival of the death of the pleasure-seeking instincts. Kurtz and Aschenbach become daemons, or nearly, but our emotions don't take into account the "destruction" or fall as the traditional emotions in response to tragedy were supposed to do.

For a full and detailed account of the modern devaluation of that good fortune the destruction of which once pained us in tragedy, see Thomas Munro, "The Failure Story: A Study of Contemporary Pessimism," *Journal of Aesthetics and Art Criticism,* Vol. XVII, No. 2 (December 1958).

else in his dark and difficult essay, for the cloud of misunderstanding in which it exists. But before we conclude that *Beyond the Pleasure Principle* issues, as many believe, in an ultimate pessimism or "negation," and before we conclude that the tendencies in our literature which we have remarked on are nothing but perverse and morbid, let us recall that although Freud did indeed say that "the aim of all life is death," the course of his argument leads him to the statement that "the organism wishes to die only in its own fashion," only through the complex fulness of its appropriate life.

PERRY MILLER

New England's Transcendentalism:
Native or Imported?

TRANSCENDENTALISM, a fairly parochial disturbance in and around
Boston in the 1830's and 1840's, may be of interest to all serious students of American culture, wherever they reside, because it is at least
an instructive episode in the history of the American intellect. Its intrinsic importance must not be exaggerated, but the issues it presents
invest it with a fascination.

Perhaps a good way of attempting to place New England's Transcendentalism in a proper perspective is to review briefly the fortunes
of Emerson's reputation in literary discourse of the last century. Indeed, the critical estimation of all the group around him has followed
the same fluctuations—with, as we shall see, one exception. As Emerson repeatedly insisted, this was no organized band. They were simply
a number of young people who around 1830 found themselves sharing a set of new ideas of which their elders disapproved. They were
steadily ridiculed and finally attacked, especially after 1838 when
Emerson delivered "The Divinity School Address" at Harvard. The
graduate students had invited him; thereafter the faculty took away
from the students the right to invite anybody.

Emerson was denounced by the greatest pundit of the Divinity
School, Andrews Norton—who had been Emerson's mentor and was
popularly known as "the Unitarian Pope"—for purveying "the Latest
Form of Infidelity." What did Norton mean by infidelity? He made
clear that the essence of Emerson's heresy was a trust in intuition, in
direct perception of truth. Confident as was the Unitarian reliance on
the powers of the human reason, Norton was certain that men have
never by unassisted reason been able to attain assurance concerning
fundamentals. But Emerson blandly asserted,

PERRY MILLER was, before his recent death, Powell M. Cabot Professor of American Literature at Harvard University.

The intuition of the moral sentiment is an insight of the perfection of the laws of the soul. These laws execute themselves. They are out of time, out of space, and not subject to circumstance.

It is not difficult to see wherein this notion would outrage the clergy, or indeed the faculty of Harvard College, or anybody who holds forth to an audience in time and space in an effort to instruct them on something which they are presumed not to know of themselves.

Emerson added insult to injury in a once famous passage which his Unitarian colleagues felt was a rude caricature of their pulpit manner:

I once heard a preacher who sorely tempted me to say I would go to church no more. Men go, thought I, where they are wont to go, else had no soul entered the temple in the afternoon. A snow-storm was falling around us. The snow-storm was real, the preacher merely spectral, and the eye felt the sad contrast in looking at him, and then out of the window behind him into the beautiful meteor of the snow. He had lived in vain. He had no one word intimating that he had laughed or wept, was married or in love, had been commended, or cheated, or chagrined.

After all, we should not be too hard put to it to understand why dignified gentlemen of the stature of Andrews Norton would snort with rage when not only did they have to hear nonsense of this nature delivered from the pulpit of Divinity Hall but also to behold their students greeting it as wisdom. What minister then or now (or for that matter what professor in his classroom) who, instead of expounding doctrine or sticking to his subject matter, should talk to his audience of how often he had been in love, how many times married, and how frequently he had been chagrined and cheated, could expect to hold their attention for more than one relation?

Emerson himself never, of course, made such a ludicrous parade of his inward life on the lecture platform as this passage, had he taken it literally, would have obliged him to exhibit. But many of those who gathered around him—who in public opinion were known as his followers—invited the derision of proper Boston by conduct which, according to the standards of the day, was manifestly absurd. Jones Very, we can now perceive, was veritably insane. Margaret Fuller, possessed by her "mountainous me," indulged in extravagances of costume, rhetoric, and eventually of sexual daring which could bring only the most severe reprobation upon the ideas which she was supposed to have taken from the saintly Mr. Emerson. And indeed, in the considered opinion of respectable Boston and likewise of all solid New England, the supreme example of the pernicious consequences of Emerson's bland tuition was Henry Thoreau. Here was a youth who resolved not to be spectral as against the snowstorm. So he fled from all civic responsibilities, did not marry, begot no children, never held a steady job, paid no taxes, and lived alone as a hermit. No wonder that many then feared Transcendentalism to be, as Emerson ironically remarked, a "conspiracy against State Street."

The revolution in popular esteem was somehow wrought along with the Civil War. For thirty years after the "Divinity School Address" Emerson was officially ostracized from Harvard Yard, never officially asked to speak. But at long last, coincident with the election of Harvard's revolutionary President William Eliot, Emerson was chosen an overseer—on which board his first vote was for the retention of compulsory chapel! Harvard has long since done public penance for this neglect of one of its most distinguished children by naming its hall of philosophy for Emerson. In the lobby is a statue made by Daniel French; if you look at it carefully, especially when there are no other people about, you will see that it frequently lights up with an amused grin. By the end of the century, Oliver Wendell Holmes can write a biography of Emerson; Barrett Wendell considers him a pillar of the orthodox New England mentality, along with Longfellow and Lowell. Indeed, as early as 1876 O. B. Frothingham, in what was generally taken to be the definitive treatise, *Transcendentalism in New England*, presented the whole business as an American counterpart of the great German philosophical assertion of idealism. The once outcasts of Unitarian New England were now saluted as worthy equivalents of Kant, Fichte, and Schelling. So Frothingham could enthrone Emerson and surround him with his courtiers—Parker, Ripley, Hedge. Interestingly enough, however, in this work of canonization, Henry Thoreau is left out. Emerson and even the firebrand Parker might be made respectable, but not Thoreau.

Yet in the most complacent days of Emerson's elevation there were a few dissenting murmurs. Both Henry Adams and Charles Eliot Norton could be irritated by the dogmatic blindness of Emerson's resolute optimism. Their affectionate objections were, as the event proved, only mild prefigurations of the revolt which in the 1920's became a savage condemnation of what Santayana indelibly smeared as the "genteel tradition." Oddly enough the incendiary of 1838 now appeared the symbol of all that was most repulsive, evasive, emasculated in this blanket of gentility. He was now denounced not because he had preached a trust in intuition but because he was pale, sexless, and an imitator. He was demoted from the eminence he had so painfully acquired, on the grounds that he was entirely derivative. And by this time, the attitude of rejection of his optimism was an orthodoxy beyond any that Unitarianism ever dreamed of. Yet the fascination and complexity of the story increase as we note that in the 1920's the surge of Thoreau's reputation really gathered momentum.

I think it fair to say that the period when the favorite sport of commentators on American letters was making fun of Mr. Emerson came to an end with the passing of the vogue of H. L. Mencken. There has lately been considerable sane discussion of Emerson; while there is no need to reassert some of the extravagances of late nineteenth-century New England patriotism, still we can see him looming large precisely because, however great was his debt to Wordsworth or Coleridge, he was *not* derivative. His sanity, clear perception, and intermittent wit become the more highly prized the less we have to lament his emotional limitations. At the same time, we may welcome a similar steadying of the critical estimate of the group as a whole. Christopher Cranch, for example, has been receiving mature treatment, let alone Theodore Parker and George Ripley, for whom it is long overdue; Margaret Fuller is being rescued from the folds of adoring feminists who did their best to smother all evidences of her intellect. We are attaining a new, and I am sure a salutary, sense that though they were a small band and had little or no effect upon American politics and economy, their real importance is that they were the first (and in many respects most eloquent) protest of the American sensibility against what in their day was rapidly becoming and in ours has implacably remained a "business" civilization.

Inevitably the Transcendentalists' wails about the pressures of making a living or making money seem quaint to us. Their world was as yet so little industrialized or financialized, was still so close to the agrarian pastoralism of the eighteenth century, that we who know Pittsburgh and Wall Street may pardonably wonder what they had to complain about. But precisely here their prescience becomes remarkable. Emerson, with serenity and precision, became their spokesman, as for instance in "Man the Reformer," read before the Mechanics' Apprentices' Library Association in Boston on 25 January 1841:

It cannot be wondered at that this general inquest into abuses should arise in the bosom of society, when one considers the practical impediments that stand in the way of virtuous young men. The young man, on entering life, finds the way to lucrative employments blocked with abuses. The ways of trade are grown selfish to the borders of theft, and supple to the borders (if not beyond the borders) of fraud. The employments of commerce are not intrinsically unfit for a man, or less genial to his faculties; but these are now in their general course so vitiated by derelictions and abuses at which all connive, that it requires more vigor and resources than can be expected of every young man, to right himself in them; he is lost in them; he cannot move hand or foot in them. Has he genius and virtue? the less does he find them fit for him to grow in, and if he would thrive in them, he must sacrifice all the brilliant dreams of boyhood and youth as dreams; he must forget the prayers of his childhood and must take on him the harness of routine and obsequiousness.

One could easily compose an *explication* on this passage longer than this whole paper, simply on the connotations and even the unconscious implications of the superb vocabulary—"inquest," "supple," "intrinsically," "dreams of boyhood." The whole history of the impact of an evolving society upon an intellect utterly unprepared for what it was working upon itself is contained within this passage. But surely the most striking, and the most significant, phrases are in the concluding clauses, where the dreams of boyhood become "prayers," now harnessed to "routine and obsequiousness." Henry Thoreau would put the anguish more memorably: "Everywhere I go, men pursue me and paw me with their dirty institutions." Those of us today who annually on 15 April are pawed by the dirtiest of institutions can barely comprehend what Henry was talking about. Nevertheless, he conceived that the American order, even in that easy period, had already come to be one which pawed men into conformity, into obsequiousness, and above all into routine. And we suspect that the threat of the latter was to him and to Emerson the most repulsive—as it was to prove in the twentieth century to those more humiliatingly subjected to it.

Thus we are obliged to ask the central question: if these Transcendental children of a (to our way of thinking) relatively idyllic America were propelled to express so vehement a revolt against their society, from whence did the vehemence spring? Why a revolt at all? Here is the issue for historical and for critical appreciation.

One factor, a factor that must never be underestimated, was the impact of Europe. But is this to be rated, in the manner of O. B. Frothingham, the sole one, or even the chief one? Margaret Fuller no doubt received early in her tempestuous life the inspiration of Madame de Staël's *Corinne*, and it drove her through the rest of her career. The young men who issued during the early 1830's the various articles that became statements and manifestoes produced writings which are replete with invocations of names which meant nothing to Andrews Norton—strange, weird creatures like Herder, Coleridge, Benjamin Constant, John Paul Richter. The youths who pushed these reviews into the pages of the Unitarian *Christian Examiner*—until at last the editors put a stop to the nonsense—made an elaborate and generally awkward effort to speak the names with nonchalance, as though of course all cultivated persons knew who these authors were. For example, Frederic Hedge in an 1833 article on Coleridge (which years later he modestly claimed was the first in America to ask for a respectful recognition of Transcendentalism) declared with affected casualness, "In a review of Mr. Coleridge's literary life, we must not omit to notice that marked fondness for metaphysics, and particularly for German metaphysics, which has exercised so decisive an influence over all his writings." This innocent observation may seem to us merely Hedge's sharp recognition of historical contiguity, but to his elders in New England it was a flag of revolt, doubly un-furled.

When the faculty of the Harvard Divinity School—and along with them the professors at Harvard College—bestirred themselves to ask who were these foreign people, they discovered that Madame de Staël had had many lovers and that George Sand was still having them. For these reasons, even if not for a variety of more intellectual worries, men like Andrews Norton might justifiably have striven to relegate Emerson, Parker, and Ripley to a side show named the latest form of infidelity—and so of no pertinence to the life of any American mind. These heretics were none of our breeding; they were merely a few (as indeed they were) infatuated appropriators of obscure European notions. If this was all they had to say for themselves—and despite their volubility they seemed to have no more to say—they were a pale imitation of a pretentious and mystagogical German silliness. If this were what they were, then in America they were exotics. They were justifiably excluded from any effect, or even indirect influence, upon the development of American thought.

The exoticism of the Transcendentalists' figure in American life—if I may so use the term—has long figured as a hindrance to our com-prehending their historical role. Nothing, I suppose, can more linger in the fantasy of tourists as a symbol of futility than the "Concord School of Philosophy," so assiduously visited by those who enter with reverence the house sanctified to the memory of Louisa May Alcott. Yet when Louisa May becomes the favorite of posterity above her in-effectual father, what is happening for the moment is a triumph of Andrews Norton over "infidelity." It is an insubstantial victory. If the American hostility to what Norton and his colleagues called the "German disease" was a vindication of their conception of American-ism, then they had yet to reckon with—in fact never did reckon with —the respects in which Transcendentalism was only in part an impor-tation.

I am the last historian in America—I hope—who would endeavor to treat Transcendentalism as wholly, or even primarily, a native phe-nomenon. There is no gainsaying that as an intellectual perturbation it was as much stimulated from abroad as was the assiduous campaign, then fully in progress, for the appropriation to American circumstances of the English Common Law and of portions of the Continental Civil Law. New England Transcendentalism will always signify the effect upon an American provinciality of a European sophistication with which it was not entirely competent to deal—despite the swaggering assurances of such would-be pundits of the *Examiner* as Hedge, Ripley, Brownson, and Parker. But we have always this reflection to disturb us: from this influx—this lesson of discontent against routine, against "sensualism," against externalism in all its forms—came (to an America which by all proprieties should have been the ultimate in content) the message of discontent. And among the most sensitive of Americans, those who could easily have had no cause for discontent, the response was immediate. They instinctively, or intuitively, rebelled against the "sensualism" of a society which had barely begun to exhibit the enormity of its potential.

Once we can perceive the galvanizing effect of European ideas—of those we glibly term "romantic"—upon the domestic situation, we are tempted to suggest that "galvanic" is the wrong adjective:—they were catalytic. They did not so much arouse by imparting new viewpoints as they stirred latent propensities. They inspired these youths to reject all forms of what they called sensualism—and often these were quite indiscriminate in their application of the term. They gave the greatest offense by equating the sensational psychology of John Locke and the Scottish philosophers with profane sensualism. Since the Unitarian liberation from Calvinism had been achieved under the aegis of such thinkers, and since Unitarians were eminently men of probity and self-discipline, they could not help seeing in every invocation of the Germans a nasty aspersion on themselves. The young men never accused their elders of profligacy, but they were becoming so distressed by a society wherein things had leaped into the saddle that in order to object to being ridden they struck at the very foundation of the system they hated. Only when we appreciate fully both the spiritual and social gulf that the "German disease" (as most normal Americans called it) created can we comprehend how divisive was, for example, Hedge's advertising of the German virtues in his 1834 essay on Schiller:

The class of writings, to which this work [a biography of Schiller] belongs, is peculiar, we believe, to modern times. It is characterized by a spirit of fierce disquietude, a dissatisfaction with the whole mechanism of society, and a presumptuous questioning of all that God or man has ordained. It represents a state of being which no word or combination of words can exactly express; a disease peculiar to ardent natures, in early life:

"The flash and outbreak of a fiery mind;
A savageness of unreclaimed blood;"

a keen sensibility to all that is absurd and oppressive in social life, a scorning of authority and custom, a feeling that all the uses of this world are weary and unprofitable, together with the consciousness of high powers, bright visions of ideal excellence, and a restless yearning after things not granted to man.

Assuredly this was not a frame of mind that Harvard College or the Divinity School wanted in the least to cultivate! And even more assuredly, it was no mood in which to get ahead on State Street!

To students aware of the violence of the several European forms of Romantic tumult the words Emerson employed in his aged recollection of the 1830's in New England may seem melodramatic and ludicrously exaggerated. Yet they attest the accuracy of his failing memory, because they recapture what the "ardent natures" of the period deeply felt. "The key to the period," he wrote, "appeared to be that the mind had become aware of itself. Men grew reflective and intellectual." Previously the standard belief had been that "a shining social prosperity was the beatitude of man," but suddenly the conviction arose that the nation existed for the individual. In one of his finest sentences Emerson continues: "The young men were born with knives in their brain, a tendency to introversion, self-dissection, anatomizing of motives." Hence this new race hated "tolls, taxes, turnpikes, banks, hierarchies, governors, yea, almost laws." They rebelled against both theological and political dogmas, against saints "or any nobility in the unseen." If all this was not sedition and subversion, what was it? No wonder the ancient and the honorable of the earth heard here the crack of doom!

Thus our question becomes all the more pressing: why foment such a rebellion in America? We can readily understand how the contagion of the French Revolution excited young Germans to arise against the decrepit and fossilized system of petty principalities. We can comprehend why in France itself the populace were goaded into storming the prisons, burning chateaus, and cutting off the head of King Louis. We can also understand the rage of a Hazlitt or a Byron against the reactionary regime of King George. But in the United States we had no king to execute and no nobility to proscribe. We had got rid of all those encumbrances. America was prosperous, expanding, and there was abundant opportunity for all. From our point of view we may indeed ask where in all the history of the world were careers more open to talent, let alone genius, than in the nation of Andrew Jackson? What could the terms "conservative" or "reactionary" mean in that community? Emerson's motto of "self-reliance," though it may have seemed infidelity to Andrews Norton, now appears to us the banner of the whole age, not just of a few eccentric Transcendentalists. What epoch was ever more self-reliant than that of Fulton and Morse, of steamboats and railroads, of the moving frontier, of the sewing machine and the Hoe press? Where could the individual more unhamperedly express himself? Emerson might sound terribly radical when he declared, "Whosoever would be a man must be a non-conformist," but even in his lifetime the sentence could be inscribed on plaques in the offices of vice-presidents of banks. And why then were there so many efforts to escape the relation to even so loose a society as this, why Brook Farm and the myriad other would-be ideal communities? Henry Thoreau denounced the social order in the time of his Walden sojourn as a "joint stock company." Certainly compared with the regulations imposed upon our living today, our economy of giant corporations and foundations, the America of Thoreau's day was a joyful chaos, a marvelous realm of rugged individualism and free competition which some of our presently styled "conservative" politicians dream can be revived.

The problem of properly evaluating Transcendentalism as a movement of protest in America is further complicated by the fact that in New England, because of local historical circumstances, it was enmeshed in the controversy over the historicity of the miracles related in the New Testament. Norton and the Unitarian critics were not half so much enraged with Emerson for saying that truth is intuitive as they were for his concluding therefrom that in the name of intuitive truth mankind no longer needed the external (and sensual!) support of recorded exceptions to the laws of nature in order to be truly religious. To make the miracles a test of the spiritual mission of Christ was indeed to manacle the conception of a divine teacher to a sensual notion of history; it was to prostitute the possible meaning of the Gospel to exactly the same materiality of the commercial society against which the ardent natures were objecting. A "joint stock company" which pretended to be Christian and then could conceive of Christianity in only this way had already so lost the idea of spirituality as to call for a savageness of unreclaimed blood from those with knives in their brain.

Now a similar attack upon a literal acceptance of the biblical miracles was being levied in Europe. The historian of ideas may rightly see in it one among many manifestations of the new sense of historical process that everywhere was a symptom of the Romantic revolt against the age of static reason. Some of these European expressions exerted an influence in America or at least in New England, particu-

larly Strauss's *Life of Jesus* in 1835. Yet actually these New England-
ers were not so much inspired by the German "higher criticism,"
about which most of them (with the exception of Theodore Parker)
knew very little, as they were by a disgust with the dogmatic way the
Unitarianism in which they were raised had fastened upon the miracles as the sole attestation of spiritual reality. In Europe the debate
over the historicity of the miracles and the quest for a historical Jesus
is indeed an intense intellectual affair, but it is not central to the life
of the mind. Nobody imagined that society would be toppled or
morality destroyed because Strauss or Renan sought to put the Messiah into a historical context. But in Cambridge and Boston the Transcendentalists' reduction of the miracles to the plane of "nature"
seemed infinitely more dangerous even than their denunciations of the
joint stock company of society. Consequently a vast amount of the
literature in the decade or so after Emerson's "Address," and a dispro-
portionate amount of youthful energy, were expended in the sterile
argument. In the larger perspective of American intellectual history
this is not one of the major issues of the century—compared, let us
say, with those of geology and then of evolution in relation to Christian belief. Because New England Transcendentalism could never rid
itself of the incubus thus early fastened upon it, it always presents
itself to a critical world as lamed by a provincial accident. It was
parochial enough to begin with, but its effort to achieve at least an
affectation of cosmopolitanism was sadly hindered by the fanatical
demand of its enemies that it fight on the ground of their choosing.

And then we have a still more annoying puzzle in our endeavor to
place the Transcendentalists both in time and space. They were undoubtedly stirred, even aroused by their importation of the intoxicat-
ing literature of European Romanticism. But the Europeans were in-
toxicating because, primarily, they were conducting a violent reaction
against the eighteenth century. They universally denounced the previous age as one of sterility and frivolity, of the heroic couplet, of the
rules, of the artificial vocabulary, as well as of political oppression.
Especially in Germany was the regime of the petty courts identified
with the corruption of French manners. We may find the image of
those principalities given in *The Marriage of Figaro* charming (the
scene is of course Germany and not the pretended Spain), but such
antics were not so charming to the actual peasants and not at all to the
intellectuals. Therefore the young Americans were avidly reading
writers who burned with anger against the Enlightenment. Yet as
Professor Alfred North Whitehead once remarked, in that casual
profundity of which only he was capable, "the secret of understanding America is that it never had an eighteenth century." Many have

objected against him that the Declaration of Independence is thoroughly of the century, Benjamin Franklin incarnates it, the Constitution is a product of it. Well, in a sense yes, but these manifestations are relatively few. We do not have an eighteenth-century experience in the way in which Voltaire is of the age, or Diderot is, or the German courts were. The American eighteenth century is squeezed in between Jonathan Edwards and the Second Awakening of 1800. It is fortunate for us that our great state papers and our War for Independence could be enacted in this interval, but even then the Enlightenment did not bite deeply into the Protestant, or if you will Puritan, heritage of the seventeenth century. We jump fairly abruptly from the rural, pious, hard-working world of the colonies into the nineteenth-century era of expansion, exploitation, movement, and romantic unrest.

In New England the Enlightenment can be said to have produced Unitarianism, or rather imparted to the provinces an atmosphere in which this could painlessly evolve out of Puritan intellectualism. But New England Unitarianism as compared with Continental Deism—with for example Helvetius—is very, very mild indeed. When therefore these young men with knives in their brain were becoming excited by books and articles denouncing the eighteenth century and they looked about them for something to denounce in their region, about all they could find for a target was this inoffensive Unitarianism. They had no need for resisting traditional Christianity. They were kept from fighting Calvinism because their Unitarian fathers and teachers stood between them and the orthodoxy of the back-country. It was not the Awakening or the Methodists who were oppressing them; it was this liberal Unitarianism that was crushing them in the vise of routine and obsequiousness. They aspired to be rebellious in terms comparable to those of their European heroes and heroines—Novalis, Herder, Madame de Staël, Carlyle—but they could not muster up a really profound revulsion against the past. The best they could manufacture was a revulsion against the very recent past, actually the present. They might suppose that they were being American Byrons but they had no way to get out of the moral patterns that ruled New England from the Puritan foundation and had never been shattered by any eighteenth-century cynicism. Their quarrel with their past was no satanic rebellion but only a shame that America had so little to show in the life of the mind. As Emerson beautifully summed up the American predicament in the opening paragraph of "The American Scholar" in 1837, our festivals so far have been simply a friendly sign of the persistence of a love of letters among a people too busy to produce any. The American task thus was not to reject the eighteenth century and the rule of reason, but to contend with the present: "Perhaps the time is already come when it ought to be, and will be, something else; when the sluggard intellect of this continent will look from under its iron lids and fill the postponed expectation of the world with something better than the exertions of mechanical skill." In this spirit he announced that the day of our dependence on the learning of other lands was drawing to a close—just in the very day that he and his contemporaries were finding a resolution to achieve independence in a voluminous absorption of the new learning of Romantic Europe!

New England Transcendentalism thus is, after all, a peculiarly American phenomenon: while New England did have a past, and sentient young persons like Emerson, Thoreau, and Margaret Fuller were entirely conscious of it, yet in a very real sense they were without a past. Or a more precise way of putting it is simply that they had no experience of the French Revolution and all its woes, no share in the disillusionment which came from committing oneself to the wild hope of the Revolution and then being broken by the Terror. They could read of these matters, and often talk fluently about them, but they did not actually *know*. One need only compare the heartbreaking account in Wordsworth's *The Prelude* with the lighthearted treatment of it in Emerson, particularly in the "Napoleon" chapter of *Representative Men*. Furthermore, in America there were no unrepentant revolutionaries who had to stand with their backs against the wall and maintain the radical stance against the tides of black reaction. We never had a Hazlitt. Perhaps the only American of the era who had at least some awareness of what the agony of keeping his head high amid defeat could be was Herman Melville, but his suffering was as remote from Transcendental comprehension as Hazlitt's.

The Transcendentalists are a part of the international movement historians call Romanticism. Their devotion to the Germans, to Wordsworth, to Victor Cousin, demonstrate their participation in it. Still, we have to say of them that an essential chapter in the biography of Romanticism is entirely missing in the lives of these Americans. It is as though, having barely passed the age of puberty and become adolescents at the age of eighteen, they awoke the next morning to find themselves aged thirty or so, having missed all those turbulent and charming perturbations of age twenty. Wherefore the peculiar pathos of their attempts to appropriate the delirium of a Romanticism they could not experience. There is something gallant and at the same time poignant in their efforts to play the role of men and women of the world. In this contradiction we may find—or at least I fancy we may—the compulsion behind their special veneration of *Nature*, behind Emerson's book so entitled in 1836, which is the heart of all their thinking and feeling. They go to Nature not for solace against the betrayals worked upon them by civilization and by reason, as in the last books of *The Prelude*, but for a source of the resistance which they must begin to put up against the iron lids of American mechanism. It is all they have to save them from routine and obsequiousness. In this respect the supreme statement—even more than Emerson's *Nature*—is, as time has now made clear, Thoreau's *Walden*.

Among the little band there is perhaps only one exception—Margaret Fuller. In 1846, after devouring more of the literature of Romanticism than any of her colleagues, and contributing to the American image of Europe, she at last went there and encountered the reality. She took part in a real revolution, the Roman one of 1848. She nursed wounded and dying men in the hospitals while her husband stood guard on the ramparts. She and he went down in defeat before the soldiers of reaction, and so she learned what Europe meant. One is moved to tears to find that she received from, as she called them, "the clean white hands" of Mr. Emerson, in the midst of the ordeal, a letter saying that Italy needs a great man. She shot back in cold anger, "Mazzini is a great man." But in Concord nobody could understand that. Nobody there could understand that she had bitten deep into the bitter fruit, and all were dismayed at the prospect of having to cope with her upon her return, complete with a husband (at least putative) and a child. Her cruel extinction in 1850 saved them the necessity.

They could therefore rest content with their original formulation of the American problem as an opposition or confrontation between nature and civilization. Out of this arose a happy version of the American genius. He stands amid Nature, and with it to assist him, to guide his steps aright, he will not be sucked into commerce or trade. He can ransom himself, Emerson told the mechanics, from the duties of economy by the rigor and privation of his habits:

For privileges so rare and grand, let him not stint to pay a great tax. Let him be a caenobite, a pauper, and if need be, celibate also. Let him learn to eat his meals standing, and to relish the taste of fair water and black bread. He may leave to others the costly conveniences of housekeeping, and large hospitality, and the possession of works of art. Let him feel that genius is a hospitality, and that he who can create works of art needs not collect them. He must live in a chamber, and postpone his self-indulgence, forewarned and forearmed against that frequent misfortune of men of genius—the taste for luxury.

This taste for luxury—and Emerson clearly implies the luxuries of emotion and the senses as well as those of housekeeping—is the tragedy of genius. But there are many forms of tragedy. In *Walden—* which in part is the record of Henry's endeavor to act out the program Waldo outlined to the mechanics—Thoreau cried in unmistakably oratorical tones, "Simplify, simplify, simplify." The American genius thus stands amid Nature, either literally as did Thoreau or in dreams of it within the city as did Bryant in New York. He does not go to the left bank of Paris and live in a garret. He does not loll in splendor as did Goethe in Weimar. He does not even flee to the Alps of Switzerland, for they are rife with hotels. He stands for the concept of Nature against the iron lids, for Walden against State Street, for Concord against New York.

All this is to say that the Transcendentalists really stand for the moral innocence which they identify with Nature, against the corruptions of civilization. They might read Madame de Staël on Germany or Wordsworth's *Prelude,* but they could not understand why these writers were so up in arms against the eighteenth century. But they could understand that these found in Nature a defense against the wiles of artificiality, and this they could adopt as their defense against what in America was the threat to their innocence. And by this device they did not need to attribute a positive evil to that which they were opposing, as Carlyle would cheerfully behold nothing but depravity in the *ancien régime*. They would not have to say that Unitarians were wicked men, but merely that they had severed their hearts from Nature and so had become corpse-cold.

This maneuver has provided, as I noted to begin with, opportunities for uncomprehending readers to accuse the whole group, but especially Emerson, of having been morally obtuse. But a bit more exercise of a sympathic insight into the historical situation may find in this characterization not an indictment but an evidence of the reaction of a supple intellect to a situation in which any proclamation of an evil American eighteenth century would make no sense. It was not a contradiction in terms for Emerson to announce that our long day of dependence upon the learning of other lands was drawing to a close and in the same oration make an incantation of the great names the young Americans were still reverently studying.

Meek young men grow up in libraries, believing it their duty to accept the views which Cicero, which Locke, which Bacon have given; forgetful that Cicero, Locke, and Bacon were only young men in libraries when they wrote these books.

The peculiar use of the word "scholar" by the Transcendentalists derives its special flavor from this background. They did not mean the professional scholar, delving for forgotten facts amid manuscripts and ancient tomes. The American scholar is a student but all the while a rebel against study. The point was—and still is—that the American independence had to be achieved *through* dependence. This is how America perforce stands in relation to the past. It is not going to achieve independence through violent assertions of the uniquely American quality of our experience or through discounting the influence of Byron on Herman Melville in order to set up some mythological native impetus as the true informing spirit of *Moby-Dick*. Emerson and the Transcendentalists were fully aware of this double pressure, this inner tension. Out of their consciousness comes their curious mingling of sophistication and innocence. This is a quality they variously exhibit, but it is pre-eminently displayed by Emerson and Thoreau. In the final analysis this Americanism is their indestructible virtue. It is their splendid ambiguity. On the one hand they talk of independence and on the other make clear their dependence. This very ambiguity—or possibly antinomy is a better word—is the reason for their growth in stature, despite the fluctuations of critical fashions. In this respect they stand firm, quite apart from the student's personal opinion of the concept of the "Over-Soul" or his liking or disliking the chapter on higher laws in *Walden*. They are spokesmen not merely for a tiny intellectual tempest in the New England teapot, but as representatives of a persistent problem in American culture, compounded of our dread and our joy. Is our culture entirely a satellite of the European or do we have a culture of our own? If our culture is both at once, how do we reconcile the two? Or rather, not reconcile—for that would be the death of us—but how hold them in suspension in order to conduct an active life of the mind by alternating pole to pole? If this conclusion has any validity, it may throw some light on the respects in which these New England writers are not merely local peculiarities but are indeed eminently national and profound expressions of the American spirit.

LOUIS B. WRIGHT

Culture and Anarchy on the Frontier

THE WORD "FRONTIER" carries a great burden of meaning. A semanticist might write a learned essay on the various connotations of this word, which has metaphorical, geographical, and historical implications. In Washington today we have much of the New Frontier—and some hostile critics talk of the anarchy on that frontier. The Census Bureau in 1890 announced that it was now impossible to mark a frontier line in the West, for the West had been settled to the Pacific, and Professor Frederick Jackson Turner three years later wrote his famous essay on the frontier to point out the significance of this event. In Europe the word "frontier" means to most of us the border point where we show our passports and have our luggage examined. It is also that grim line where soldiers eternally watch the opposing country.

For the first time in its history the United States finds itself on this kind of a frontier, for planes and missiles have wiped out the protection of seas and land barriers, and we have to stand guard on a hostile frontier, as European nations have always guarded their borders. This new concept of a hostile frontier has altered nearly every aspect of American life and has had an impact so deep that none of us yet can quite grasp its significance.

It is not my purpose to discuss the changes that the concept of a hostile frontier is making in us, but rather to talk for a few minutes about the conflict that has always raged on the historical and geographical frontier in America between the powers of darkness and the children of light for the soul of the nation. This is a battle that is not yet won; perhaps it will be lost; but it is a conflict that deserves the attention of all literate men and women, particularly in a time when all of our old values and ideals are in jeopardy.

LOUIS B. WRIGHT is Director of the Folger Shakespeare Library. Portions of this essay are adapted from the author's *Culture on the Moving Frontier* (Blooming-ton, Ind.: Indiana University Press, 1955; 2d ed.; New York: Harper Torchbooks, 1961).

Americans have tended to romanticize the historical frontier and to glory in its crudity, fighting, bloodshed, and violence. Almost every western town at intervals celebrates "Frontier Days" and induces its citizens to grow whiskers and dress in Levi's and carry harmless six-shooters as part of the masquerade. Television lives on the slaughter of Indians. More red men had died since the invention of television than could be found in the whole of America in the nineteenth century. We even export this frontier annihilation; in 1962 I observed in Basel the rapt attention which the peace-loving Swiss gave to an Indian raid on "Wagon Train." We have had movies on Billy the Kid and Calamity Jane and a host of other characters who gave color to a West that we like to recall. Highwaymen and saloon gunfighters occupy a favored spot in our fiction and in our imaginations. We think of rough-and-ready settlers in the clearings who could fight off Indians, wrestle a bear, or strangle a mountain lion barehanded. It was one of these characters who declared that he was "agin the guv'ment, school larnin', and the railroads" and aimed to be let alone. Another quick-shooting character in a Kentucky town was at last persuaded to place his talents on the side of law enforcement, but specified that he would take the marshal's job only if he could have his office in easy walking distance of the distillery. The frontier was a region of rugged independence, the stronghold of individuals who did not want to be told by anyone else what to do, or how to do it. The attitude was exemplified in a Nebraska farmer who was urged to attend a meeting where government workers would explain how to grow better wheat. "No, I ain't a-goin'," he replied; "I don't do half as well as I know how now." The notion of a frontier of lawless, independent, non-conforming, and often violent characters is the concept that probably comes to most of us at the mention of the word.

We forget, or we are unaware of, another aspect of the frontier from Jamestown to San Francisco, as the line of civilization slowly moved across the continent. On every frontier, there was a group who sometimes self-consciously and perhaps self-righteously called themselves the "better element." These were the people who struggled to reproduce the best of the older civilization they had left. The struggle was often difficult and the results were frequently discouraging, but the "right-minded folk" never gave up the fight. It was they who brought along preachers and teachers, built churches and schools, and established a settled and orderly society. The instinct for tradition, for the preservation and perpetuation of ancient values, especially noteworthy among people of Anglo-Saxon stock, has exerted a powerful influence in civilizing successive frontiers in this country. Over the centuries we have clung tenaciously to ancient decorum, to old habits of thought, old legal traditions and customs—the elements of cultivated society in the regions whence we came. Whether the frontier was coastal Virginia in the seventeenth century, the forested lands below the Great Lakes in the early nineteenth century, or the slopes of the Sierras during the Gold Rush, the tendency to transplant the past has been the same. In every frontier society an influential element has contrived successfully to reproduce the best of the cultural heritage.

The first settlers in Virginia were not particularly noteworthy for idealism. They came in search of profits, which they hoped to reap in the form of gold nuggets or gold plate that they would take from the Indians as Cortez and Pizarro had done. But it is significant that soon after they landed at Jamestown they built a church; Master Robert Hunt, the first parson, unpacked his library; and George Sandys was soon busily engaged in making an English translation of Ovid's *Metamorphoses*—the first consciously literary work in English America. In this somewhat ribald and riotous colony, a colony as yet without women, the authorities took thought of decorum. Captain John Smith decreed that men assigned to the woodchopping details should not swear over the pain to their blistered hands. The punishment for swearing was one cup of ice-cold water per oath poured down the offender's sleeve.

Twelve years after the first shelter was erected at Jamestown, the colony took steps to establish an institution of classical learning. In 1619, the Virginia Company set aside ten thousand acres of land for a university and announced the collection of £1,500 in cash for that worthy purpose. Other funds were donated for what the company records describe as the "sacred work" of the "foundation of a college in Virginia." Unhappily for the history of American learning, the Indian massacre of 1622 destroyed this hopeful enterprise. Nevertheless, the embryonic university was a symbol of the desire of our first frontiersmen to transplant the culture of Oxford and Cambridge to the banks of the James River.

In all the little settlements on the Atlantic frontier, a similar effort was made throughout the colonial period to establish learning and to reproduce the stable society which the settlers had known in the homeland. Parents were deeply concerned lest their children "grow barbarous in the wilderness"—a phrase and a fear which an investigator of the past frequently encounters. Although dissatisfaction with economic opportunities in the Old World, or grievances against church or state, had been impelling motives that drove most settlers to seek a new life in America, once here, they set about reproducing the kind of society they had left. Despite the claims advanced by certain patriotic historians, colonial Americans showed an astonishing aversion to social experimentation. Most of them yearned for the good old ways of their forefathers, and they succeeded in creating substantial conservative commonwealths. From New England to Carolina, the ruling groups in all the colonies were eager to duplicate as much of old England as possible. Even in colonies like New York and Pennsylvania with large non-English populations, traditional English culture in time became dominant.

The tendency to conserve the traditions of the past, so noteworthy in Virginia, was characteristic of other colonies, though it manifested itself in different ways. New England, for example, duplicated the bourgeois tradition of the commercial classes in old England. Much of what we loosely call Puritanism is essentially bourgeois. Indeed, the code of prudential morality—with its glorification of thrift, diligence, sobriety, and honesty—derives from the ethics of the English middle class evolved in the sixteenth and seventeenth centuries. These ideals were transmitted to America and became the dominant ethical concepts of the trading classes. Benjamin Franklin, whose *Way to Wealth* has been the most widely read of any American work, epitomized the whole bourgeois philosophy, and that philosophy has done more to shape American life than any other creed or dogma.

As Americans pushed westward up the rivers and over the Alleghenies, across the Mississippi Valley and the Great Plains, and eventually over the Sierra to the Pacific Coast, they carried with them a grim determination to remain a civilized people according to a fairly definite notion of what civilization meant to them. The substantial majority of western immigrants feared the disruptive influences of isolation on the frontier more than they feared physical hardships or the scalping knives of Indians. And this fear of what the enveloping crudity of the West might do to them and their children made them all the more zealous to preserve traditions of order and decency. Though fiction has made us believe that gunfighters and saloon keepers were the typical figures of western expansion, the sober truth is that the majority of citizens on the frontier were bent upon establishing a safe and sane community life as nearly as possible like that in the villages and towns which they had left in the East. Western towns were not long without churches and schools, or the benefit of middle-class ethics enforced by public opinion.

The struggle between culture and anarchy in Texas was more dramatic than elsewhere. Everything seems dramatic if not exaggerated in Texas. Even when Texas was a colony of Mexico and Stephen Austin was trying with all his ingenuity to keep peace with the

Mexican government, Protestant missionaries traveled through the land distributing Bibles. A few teachers also tried to maintain some semblance of education. The need for schools was a problem that vexed the leaders of the Republic of Texas, and when Texas finally entered the Union, one of the first acts was to appropriate $2,000,000 for an endowment for schools. This sum was two-fifths of $5,000,000 in bonds turned over to the new state by the federal government. If $2,000,000 sounds like a pittance in Texas today, in 1850 it represented an enormous incentive to public education. Texans were determined not to let their children grow up in a state of nature.

Even the most charitable historians of Texas admit that the state's reputation for lawlessness in the early days was not undeserved. Judge Bean was not the only character west of the Pecos—or east of it for that matter—who took the law into his own hands. But in Texas, as in every other frontier region, the forces at war with the devil prevailed. Early in the state's history missionaries heard the call to come over into Macedonia and do battle, and American missionaries have always relished a challenge. By 1860, one census showed a total of 758 preachers practicing their calling in Texas; at the same time the state had 1,471 physicians and 65 dentists. Whether this represented the proportionate interest of body over soul, no man can say, but these 758 ministers of the gospel were often itinerant and managed to cover a vast territory. They also combined with their godly vocation the duties of teaching and distributing pious literature.

One of the most famous missionaries to Texas was a Methodist, the Reverend Martin Ruter, who arrived in 1838 and remained to wage a long war against iniquity. "Profaneness, gaming, and intemperance are prevailing vices against which we have to contend," he asserted. And of these, the preachers considered intemperance the worst. Hence they made Demon Rum their major target. In 1848 the Sons of Temperance, a national organization, moved into Texas, and such was their influence, that even Sam Houston gave up his bottle and went to work in behalf of temperance. So active were they that they very nearly dried up Texas. For example, in the town of San Marcos, they forced every saloon out of business except one, and they finally bought it out and emptied the liquor in the gutters. Finding himself out of employment, the saloon keeper joined the Sons of Temperance and became an organizer.

The decrease in the number of saloons brought a reduction in the amount of violence and a greater receptivity to what the reformers liked to call "the finer things of life." The *Houston Telegraph* in the 1840's and '50's campaigned vigorously against an excess of homicides which, it pointed out fairly obviously, gave the town a bad name.

The citizens of San Antonio took a firm stand against violence and rounded up a dozen or so of the worst offenders and summarily hanged them. That brought a modicum of peace.

As Texans settled down to less exciting ways of life, they began to think of higher education. Academies and institutes sprang up in various places during the days of the Republic and increased in number after statehood. A college would be created around a single man of learning—or even about one not so learned. Methodist, Baptist, and Presbyterian preachers were all responsible for schools of various sorts. The Presbyterians were the most learned; they concentrated upon the classical languages and added such sciences as they knew. For example, the Reverend Marcus A. Montrose, with a degree from the University of Edinburgh, felt impelled to offer at San Augustine University courses taught by himself in Greek, Latin, history, mathematics, astronomy, navigation, rhetoric, logic, political economy, natural philosophy, chemistry, geology, and botany. For one man that constituted a fair cultural load. In the period before the Civil War, one historian has counted forty academies, thirty colleges, twenty-seven institutes, seven universities, and one medical college, besides various other learned associations and organizations. Few frontier regions could equal Texas in the number of educational institutions. Although the quality was poor and few of these early schools survived, the very fact of their establishment signifies a desire for, and a dream of, higher learning that has been characteristic of the country as a whole.

Texas also had other cultural manifestations in frontier days. Few towns of any size lacked a newspaper of sorts. The Federal Census of 1860 listed sixty-five weekly newspapers, three daily and three tri-weekly papers, and three monthly periodicals. The news that these papers reported was sketchy, chiefly matter reprinted from New Orleans papers, but the papers served as an important medium for the expression of local opinion. Galveston even had a literary periodical, the *Port Folio*. A few bookstores flourished in the larger towns and distributed both practical and literary works ranging from a treatise on horse diseases to *Godey's Lady's Book*. Texans early manifested a profound interest in themselves, and Henderson Yoakum's *History of Texas* (1855) was a best seller, second only in sales to *The Texas Almanac*.

Something more than coincidence is required to account for the mushroom growth of colleges which closely followed the expansion westward. During the nineteenth century denominational academies and colleges were founded literally by the hundreds and many a town was talking of a college before its citizens were housed in permanent structures. If saloons and gambling dives were characteristic of the frontier settlement, they soon met stiff competition from schools and churches. Every western town was proud of citizens who earnestly set about reproducing the orderly and cultivated life of older regions. The schoolteacher, the preacher, occasionally the doctor, but more often an overworked mother with a handful of books and a few sheets of music, struggled to keep alive a desire for learning, an interest in literature, and the mores of a cultivated community.

Faith in education as the way to social and spiritual salvation has been a characteristic of America from the beginning, and it was nowhere better exemplified than on the moving frontier. Someone commented that if a wagon train camped overnight in Ohio, the morning was certain to see a college started at the campsite. Certainly Ohio was bountifully supplied with colleges in the early days, and many of these survived to become significant institutions of our own time. In Michigan, something with the grandiose title of the University of Michigan was established in 1817 in Detroit with a Presbyterian preacher from Princeton as president and a Catholic missionary as vice-president, a remarkable evidence of coexistence on the frontier that, unhappily, did not endure for long in halcyon peace. But it does indicate the determination of frontier citizens to utilize all available resources for the purposes of education.

After the establishment of schools and churches came the organization of literary societies and clubs for intellectual improvement. Little towns of log houses or sod huts boasted lively societies for debate and discussion of literary matters. For example, in the raw little town of Kalamazoo, Michigan, in 1847, the women formed the Ladies Library Association, which not only established a public library "as a means of educating the people and forming a taste for reading"—to quote their bylaws—but met at intervals for public discussion of books. In scores of communities, literary societies, frequently organized and promoted by women, were formed to build libraries and to discuss literature and history. The Ladies History Club of Sioux Falls, South Dakota, organized in 1879, had for its purpose the study of English history. Ten years later the Woman's Club of Watertown, South Dakota, took as its first task the study of English history and followed it with a course of American history—a proper sequence for an intelligent understanding of our development. The Zetetic Club of Weeping Water, Nebraska, founded in 1884, devoted itself to the history of the Reformation and Elizabethan England, and completed its course with a review of the French Revolution. After that it devoted two years to reading Shakespeare. The Woman's Club of Sleepy Eye, Minnesota, chose Shakespeare as the main theme for study but continued with a survey of English history. Shakespeare societies, history societies, even Greek literature societies, flourished in the backwoods and kept alive an interest in the past and in a world beyond the limited horizons of the settlers. One society in a tiny Kansas town devoted a program to "A Higher Life for Hindu Women" and followed this with a number called "Ten Minutes with the Russians," which Kansas, even in the 1870's, apparently thought enough.

Faith in the spoken word was both naïve and touching, and the itinerant lecturer on almost any subject usually received a warm welcome in frontier towns. He might have a few Leyden jars and show the wonders of static electricity; he might lecture on health and the ills of the liver; he might be a phrenologist who offered to appraise the bumps on the heads of members of his audience; or he might lecture on religion, history, Shakespeare, or almost any conceivable topic. Whatever it was, he usually got a representative audience and collected a respectable fee.

If a small town could boast a college or university, it was especially blessed with lecturers who came more often to edify the townsfolk than the students. Professor Theodore Hornberger many years ago made a study of the itinerant lecturers who came to the University of Michigan in the period before the Civil War and afterward. The editor of the Ann Arbor *Argus* in June of 1837 was earnestly campaigning for the formation of a "Society for Improvement in Morals, Literature, and Science," and three years later the editor of the *Washtenaw Whig* was belaboring the students for rowdiness at lectures which the townspeople wanted to hear. The young men quieted down presently and they themselves discussed, presumably to the great pleasure of the audience, the topic, "The History of the Government and the Signs of the Time Are Indicative of a Premature Decay of This Nation." This was followed by another student forum on the announced theme: "The Present System of Collegiate Instruction Is Inconsistent with the True Spirit of Our Republican Institutions." Orations, recitations, and recitals of beautiful passages from literature, whether by students or itinerants, found eager listeners. Many a small town turned out en masse to hear some elocutionist recite Portia's speech on mercy or Lady Macbeth's sleepwalking scene.

Of all the self-appointed missionaries intent upon civilizing the frontier, the most militant and competent were the Scotch Presbyterians, who were particularly active in the eighteenth and early nineteenth centuries. They were a hardy and determined lot who believed that to get into heaven one might have to give the password in Latin or Greek. Their determination is exemplified in a prayer that a Scotch Presbyterian preacher uttered: "O Lord, grant that I may be always right, for thou knowest that I am hard to turn."

Princeton University was the product of Scotch Presbyterian ministers, but before Princeton there were many little academies in the woods where devoted teachers taught Latin, Greek, and Hebrew, as well as other essentials of higher learning. From Princeton many preachers and teachers went out to found schools and colleges all the way across the continent.

Long before the American Revolution, Ulster Scots had established a chain of Presbyterian churches along the frontier from New England to Georgia. These fortresses against the devil paralleled a chain of blockhouses and forts against the French and Indians. The Scotch Presbyterians had an Old Testament faith, and they equated the Indians with the Canaanites. Acting on a text from Joshua, "There is yet much land to be possessed," they were ready to slay the Indians and appropriate the land. Preachers accompanied the settlers into the wilderness, and clergymen who held degrees from the University of Edinburgh, and later from Princeton, lived in the same kind of log cabins as those occupied by their far-flung parishioners. These pioneer parsons rode horseback from clearing to clearing, teaching and preaching as they went. They were a fearless group who exerted an enormous influence over their people. Not only were the preachers spiritual guides but they also frequently served as civil and military leaders as well. Many a fighting parson organized the scattered settlers into an effective militia against the Indians. One of the most famous of the soldier-preachers was the Reverend John Elder, pastor of the church at Derry, Pennsylvania, from 1738 to 1791. Commissioned a captain by the Pennsylvania government, he led a company of rangers and was accustomed to preach with his loaded musket across the pulpit. A graduate of Edinburgh, Elder was a classical scholar equally at home tracing the wanderings of Ulysses or tracking down the most recent Indian marauder.

More famous even than Elder was Dr. John McMillan, who began his ministerial career toward the end of the colonial period and for a generation carried a message of piety and learning through the backwoods of Pennsylvania, Kentucky, and Tennessee. Dr. McMillan was known for his ready wit and his ability to find an apt quotation from the Scriptures or the classics to fit every occasion. Traveling with the Reverend Joseph Patterson to a meeting of the Pittsburgh Presbytery when that town was an outpost of civilization, the two parsons stopped at a tavern for refreshment. The tavern keeper set out two goblets of whisky, the accepted beverage among the Scotch-Irish, lay or clerical. Before drinking, Mr. Patterson proposed a prayer of gratitude for a safe journey and the hospitality about to be received. After the custom of the time, he prayed long and earnestly, reminding God of the accumulated events since the preachers had last passed that way. Dr. McMillan, weary and thirsty, quietly drank his own glass and then downed the other glass too. When Patterson finally said "Amen" and opened his eyes, he was distressed to find only two empty glasses. Remembering a scriptural injunction, Dr. McMillan reminded him: "My brother, you must watch as well as pray."

These hard-riding, long-winded preachers of the Presbyterian faith were the apostles of both religion and learning. They insisted that every child must know at least enough to read the Bible and the Shorter Catechism. They distributed books and tracts. And they often taught the children as well as their parents. They were instrumental in stirring up backward settlements to establish neighborhood schools, and they persuaded itinerant schoolmasters to make their way around the circuits which the preachers rode.

The history of all frontier society was re-enacted in California, but such is the nature of California that whatever is done there is accomplished with greater dramatic emphasis than is characteristic of more somber regions. The conflict between humanism and materialism in California dates from the days of the Gold Rush. In the hysterical scramble to get rich in the gold fields, California drew from the ends of the earth an extraordinary collection of adventurers motivated solely by a crass desire for material gain. But there also came an astonishing number of gold seekers who soon showed that they were unwilling to let even a mining camp remain a barbarous and uncivilized place. Some men brought along their wives, and these women deserve much of the credit for transmitting to the gold towns a little of the cultivation which they believed essential to decent life.

The life of Mrs. Sarah Royce, mother of Josiah Royce, one of the great American teachers of philosophy, provides an illustration of the influence of one unpretentious pioneer woman in conserving traditional values. The story of her heroism is an epic which ought to be required reading for every American. Fortunately she kept a diary, and excerpts from that record were published in 1932 by the Yale University Press under the title of *A Frontier Lady*.

A lady she was, of cultivation and gentle breeding, but with iron in her soul. Through the summer and early autumn of 1849 she and her husband, with their two-year-old daughter, toiled across the Great Plains in an ox-drawn wagon. With snow blocking the passes of the Sierra in October, they abandoned their wagon and made their way mule-back across the mountains. Through all of that weary way,

Mrs. Royce carried a King James version of the Bible and a copy of John Milton's poetry. In mining camps, in boisterous San Francisco, wherever they went, Mrs. Royce was a light of learning. Later, when they had established themselves in Grass Valley, she opened a school for her own and her neighbors' children. Subtly she taught them that life had a higher purpose than getting and spending—that the gold washed from California gravel beds could never be more than a means to an end, an end which ought to be worthy of man's infinite intellectual promise.

With a few good books Mrs. Royce created in Grass Valley a modest center of traditional culture. In some manner she procured an organ which had been brought around the Horn. "There was little time for music during the day except on Sundays," she wrote in her journal, "but at night when the children were all in bed . . . I used to indulge myself in the melodies and harmonies that brought to me the most precious memories of earth, and opened up visions of heaven. And then those bare rafters and cloth walls became for the time a banquet hall, a cathedral."

Mrs. Royce had the courage and faith of the women who made the West a great empire. She also had something beyond mere physical stamina. Like others of her kind, she had a vision of the future in which Californians would transcend materialistic greed and develop those qualities of mind and spirit which made men only a little lower than the angels.

Many years later, when Josiah Royce was a distinguished professor of philosophy at Harvard, he recalled the lessons he had learned in Grass Valley. From his mother he had received a faith that a people should strive to produce a civilization that used its material assets as a means of reaching values which are good, true, and eternal. "What you and I really most need and desire is not the new nor yet the old," he wrote. "It is the eternal." Through a long and useful life, this Californian, brought up in the traditions of an ancient civilization translated to the crudest of frontiers, labored to convince Americans that they should put aside what he called "a dangerous practical materialism" and seek more enduring values. Royce had learned in Grass Valley that men might reach their highest ethical attainments through literature, music, art, and all the stored-up wisdom of the past. His was a vigorous proof of the vitality of what we call the humanities.

Though the geographical frontier that we knew in the nineteenth century no longer exists, we still have cultural frontiers where the battle continues to rage between good and evil for the soul of the nation. Our cities are jungles where the life of the average citizen is daily in greater hazard than ever it was in Dodge City, Kansas, or Tombstone, Arizona. Social tensions are acute and old antagonisms pit neighbor against neighbor. Educationally, intellectually, and spiritually, we live in a period of uncertainty and even chaos. Men and women trained in the humanistic tradition are often in despair as they contemplate the responsibility that rests upon them to provide the leadership necessary to preserve permanent values in the commonwealth.

Society is beset with a materialism, perhaps somewhat less crass than the materialism of the nineteenth century but probably more sinister in its guise of patriotism and public service. The materialism of the present moment is often disguised in a raiment of plausibility. Some of the most vocal theorists in education, for example, urge the glorification of the practical at the expense of everything else. They are confusing the immediate expediency of vocational training with education. In their zeal they insist that the humanities are mere luxuries for those who can afford them, that the generality of men and women should stick to sound vocational courses which will teach the technique of making a living. The fallacy of that doctrine is obvious, for the generality of men and women in a democratic society have something else to do besides exist, however comfortably. They must assert a positive voice in government, for instance, or the whole democratic process fails. The tremendous advance in technology, which places in the hands of the people powers hitherto undreamed of, makes necessary, as never before, broader education for popular leadership. The commonalty of mankind must have minds broad enough and sufficiently informed to enable them to make wise decisions. Our very survival as a planet of breathing organisms depends upon our wisdom.

We must not forget that in the American democratic state leaders are not imposed from above but rise from the ranks. If we neglect to provide a sound humanistic education available to the masses, we shall pave the way to destruction.

The folk wisdom of the earlier frontier recognized this truth. For that reason our ancestors pinned their faith on education and taxed themselves to maintain schools which supplied something more than an apprenticeship in a vocation. Only with the pseudo-sophistication of our own time—with the substitution of graphs and statistics of so-called educational experts for the common sense of the people—has this fundamental truth been called in question. It will be an unhappy day for American civilization when the people turn over education entirely to the experts.

As we have become urbanized and sophisticated, there has come a tendency on the part of the people to abandon many of the social responsibilities which frontier folk accepted as a duty and a privilege. Few of us show much personal concern about any of the educational influences of the present moment.

We have allowed ourselves to become a prey to the minions of Madison Avenue who have become the greatest single influence in the shaping of American character. What they decide is good for advertising, the American nation must accept as doctrine for its children—as well as for its adults. The insidious inanities of soap opera, the daily fare of crime and violence, the sheer cheapness of most of the material that passes over television screens will determine our characters and our behavior. We cannot place all the blame on the presidents and vice-presidents of television chains who determine the programs. We—the people who silently and complacently endure the shoddy and the stupid while the moronic fringe writes fan letters of approval—are to blame.

Today the nation critically needs an enlightened leadership which humanists should be prepared to give. Without the sanity and balance which are the eternal aim of humane learning, the social order would be doomed to disintegration. It may be headed for anarchy anyway, but if we are to be saved, it will depend upon those citizens who have the intellectual and spiritual equipment to battle the demons of the night. As in an earlier period of turmoil when determined and tough-minded citizens preserved traditional values, so now, in another period of transition and upheaval, those who have faith in ancient spiritual values must struggle against the current materialistic cynicism, particularly its manifestation by the hucksters who control the instruments of mass communication. Upon intelligent and cultivated citizens rests the heavy responsibility of saving society from the chaos of the cheap and the tawdry.

NORTHROP FRYE

The Problem of Spiritual Authority
in the Nineteenth Century

W HEN IT WAS SUGGESTED to me that I should contribute a nineteenth-century topic to this Rice University semicentennial series, I
hesitated, because the nineteenth century is far from being what I
hopefully think of, in my furtive non-administrative moments, as my
"field." But there is one aspect of Victorian culture that interests
me a good deal, and that is the extraordinary fertility and suggestive-
ness of its educational theories. I speak of the problem of spiritual
authority, because all educational theory seems to me to be essentially
an application of that problem. I hope also that the subject of educational theory will have some relevance to an anniversary program
of a university, which should be an appropriate time for considering
the function of the university and its relation to the social order.

The source of actual or "temporal" authority in society is seldom
hard to locate. It is always in the near vicinity of whatever one pays
one's taxes to. As long as it can be believed that might is right, and
that the tax-collecting power is not to be questioned, there is no
separate problem of spiritual authority. But the thesis that might is
right, even when as carefully rationalized as it is in Hobbes, has seldom been regarded as much more than an irresponsible paradox.
There has almost certainly never been a period in history when the
taxpayer did not try to cheat the publican, and even the desire to
cheat raises the question of what kinds of authority may be thought
of as overriding the actual one. For self-interest also has a separate
authority.

Spiritual authority is usually connected, of course, with religion,
God being normally thought of as a sovereign spirit. Our cultural
tradition has inherited from the Old Testament a conception of the

NORTHROP FRYE is Professor of English and Principal of Victoria College in
the University of Toronto.

will of God which may often be in the sharpest possible opposition
to the will of man, especially an Egyptian or Babylonian or Philistine
will. But if a religion can find an accredited human representative,
the two kinds of authority again tend to merge. The medieval theory
of the pope's right to temporal power and the post-Renaissance conception of the divine right of kings are examples of an effort to make
the spiritual order a guarantee of the stability of the temporal one.
As far as the normal workings of the human mind can go, the will of
God differs in degree but not in kind from the will of man, and the
metaphors applied to it, such as the metaphor of divine "sovereignty,"
are drawn from the more primitive forms of human society. When
Greek philosophers began to frame ethical conceptions of justice and
righteousness, they ran into similar problems. Their traditional gods, as
they appear in Homer, still had all the arbitrary and whimsical quality
of a human aristocracy, and submitting to a human conqueror would
not be psychologically very different from praying to Poseidon the
irascible earth-shaker. In Christianity the human product of spiritual
authority is supposed to be charity, but Christian charity has usually
been, down to quite recent times, supported by temporal power, and
it may be significant that the word "charity" itself has come to mean
chiefly a form of voluntary taxation.

Ordinary social consciousness usually begins in a sense of antithesis
between what the ego wants and what society will allow it to have.
Hence temporal authority comes to the individual first of all in the
form of an external compulsion. In this stage freedom is identified
with the ego's side of this antithesis. But education, and more particularly education of the reason, introduces us to a form of necessity
or compulsion which is not opposed to freedom but seems to be
rather another aspect of it. To assent to the truth of a geometrical
demonstration is psychologically a contrast to assenting to the will of
a social superior. Hence reason can do what faith, hope, and even love
by themselves cannot do: present us with the model or pattern of an
authority which appeals to the mind but not to the body, which com-
pels but does not enforce. Such authority confers dignity on the
person who accepts it, and such dignity has no context of hierarchy,
nobody at whose expense the dignity is achieved.

The nineteenth-century social and political writers in Great Britain had inherited from Milton a conception of spiritual authority of
this sort, and a singularly lucid and powerful one. For Milton the
source of spiritual authority was revelation from God, more particularly the revelation of the gospel which had spiritualized the law,
and delivered those under the gospel from the sense of external con-
straint. St. Paul tells us that where the spirit of the Lord is, there is

liberty, and those under the gospel should do as they like, because what they like to do is the will of God, not the illusory pseudo-acts suggested by passion or selfishness. For Milton, again, the accredited human agent of spiritual authority is the church in the sense of the society of individuals who are under the gospel, among whom the one who has authority is the apostle or saint, which according to Milton is what the New Testament means by an *episcope* or overseer. Such authority clearly has no relevance to magistrates or penal codes. Revelation from God accommodates itself to man primarily in the form of reason. Reason manifests itself in the decisive acts of a free life ("Reason is but choosing," Milton says in *Areopagitica*, annexing Aristotle's conception of *proairesis* of the Christian *logos*), and as revelation is the opposite of mystery, there is no conflict between spiritual authority and reason. A revelation from an infinite mind may transcend the reason of a finite one, but does not contradict or humiliate it.

Human society, as Milton saw it, is conditioned by the inertia of original sin to seek the habitual and customary, to do things because they have been done before, to make an idol of tradition. The impact of revelation, coming through reason, is always subversive and revolutionary: it is bound to shake up the somnambulism of habit and confront it with the eternal opposition of God and fallen man. Such reason is also liberty, which man does not naturally want, but which God wants him to have. Purely social changes are, at best, gradual adjustments: genuine liberty is sudden and apocalyptic: "In state many things at first are crude and hard to digest, which only time and deliberation can supple and concoct. But in religion, wherein is no immaturity, nothing out of season, it goes far otherwise. The door of grace turns upon smooth hinges, wide opening to send out, but soon shutting to recall the precious offers of mercy to a nation" (*The Reason of Church Government*). Temporal authority, however essential, is also provisional, the result of the permanent emergency in human affairs caused by the Fall. It can never be accepted as an end in itself: the reason why it is there is stated in scripture, and all non-scriptural ways of trying to justify it are suspect. There is no inherent authority, in other words, in tradition or custom or precedent, on which temporal authority may rest as a basis. Hence no church which bases its claim to authority on tradition can be a genuine embodiment of revelation. Milton's regicide pamphlet, *The Tenure of Kings and Magistrates*, is a work of extraordinary originality of thought, outlining an early theory of contract and being one of the earliest efforts to try to give some functional place to revolution in history. But even this involves an appeal to precedent, and Milton embarks on an appeal to precedent with the greatest unwillingness: "But because it is the vulgar folly of men to desert their own reason, and shutting their eyes, to think they see best with other men's, I shall show, by such examples as ought to have most weight with us, what has been done in this case heretofore."

We have, then, in Milton, a spiritual authority with its roots in revelation and manifesting itself largely in reason, and a temporal authority which is to be acknowledged and obeyed in its own sphere, but should not be rationalized by arguments drawn from precedent or custom. Temporal authority is primarily something that is there, whether we like it or not. If we don't like it, we turn to a conception of spiritual authority and subordinate the temporal power to it as far as possible, if only in our own minds. If we do like it or want to defend it, on the other hand, we tend to see in tradition, custom, habit, in short the process by which temporal authority came to be, some kind of inherent right. We may note in passing that if social revolution is not, for Milton, organically related to precedents, it is not organically related to the future either. The rebellions of the Jews against their overlords, as recorded in the Old Testament, had varying degrees of success, but none were permanently successful. Hence the significance of such a rebellion is typological, manifesting the power of the true God for and at the moment. The extent to which Milton was able to reconcile himself with the failure of the revolution of his own day is perhaps indicated in *Samson Agonistes*, where the temporary victory of Samson in destroying the Philistine temple has this kind of significance.

In the eighteenth century the conception of the natural society in Bolingbroke and Rousseau brought a new kind of revolutionary dialectic into social argument. Rousseau thought of man in his context as a child of nature, and not, as Milton did, in his context as a child of God whose original state was civilized. It was reason and nature that were associated in his thought, not reason and revelation, and the original free and equal society of man was not something intended for man by God which man irrevocably lost, but something man still has the power to recapture. Rousseau's thought resembles Milton's only in associating reason and revolution, and in thinking of reason as essentially the vision in the light of which the free act is performed. It is with the counter-revolutionary thought that developed in Britain in opposition to Rousseau, particularly in Burke, that the problem of spiritual authority in the nineteenth century begins.

For Burke, in almost direct contrast to Milton, the first justification for temporal authority consists in the fact that it is there: the right underlying its might, therefore, is the process of tradition and precedent that has brought it into being. The social contract of any society "is collected from the form into which the particular society has been cast." Any developed society is found to consist of various classes, and the tendency of each class is to promote its own interest by acting "merely by their will." This creates tyranny, whether exerted by the king (who is historically a class in himself), by the nobility, or, as in France, by the "people," which means one class or group of people. The source of spiritual authority for Burke, therefore, is to be found, not so much in tradition as such, as in a kind of *telos*, a sense of belonging to a social organism whose health is preserved by maintaining a balance of power among the different organs. The health of the social structure is the end of all social action from any class, and the standard by which such action should be judged. Revolutionary action, which sets free an automatic and unconditioned will, is to society what the cancerous growth of tissue is in the individual. A social organism of this kind is the only genuine form of natural society, for nature is to be thought of as an order that preserves constancy in change by a process of continuous repair. "Thus, by preserving the method of nature in the conduct of the state, in what we improve, we are never wholly new; in what we retain, we are never wholly obsolete."

Two factors in Burke's thought are particularly relevant here. In Milton, the current of liberty, so to speak, normally flows in a deductive direction, from revelation to reason, and from reason to social action. For Burke, liberty can only be preserved by the inductive, empirical, even *ad hoc* procedures of the political action that operates on the basis of what is there: prudence is the greatest of political virtues, and prejudice the only valuable form of deductive thinking. It is the revolutionary action leading to tyranny which is deductive, like the "metaphysical" French Revolution which had begun with a set of major premises about the abstract rights of man, and had then attempted "a decomposition of the whole civil and political mass, for the purpose of originating a new civil order out of the first elements of society." Hence reason, given its full deductive and speculative head, is not an emancipating but a destructive and ultimately enslaving power in politics. Spiritual authority, at least, is something to which we owe loyalty, and loyalty is not primarily rational; hence society is held together by profounder forces than the reason can express or reach.

In the second place, most temporal authority is vested in the ascendant class: this class is faced with a strong revolutionary bid for power coming from further down in society: the maintenance of the health of the social organism, which means the maintenance of spiritual authority, is therefore bound up with preserving the existing rights and privileges of the ascendant class. "We must suppose [society] to be in that state of habitual social discipline, in which the wiser, the more expert, and the more opulent conduct, and by conducting enlighten and protect the weaker, the less knowing, and the less provided with the goods of fortune." Burke goes on to say that "the state of civil society, which necessarily generates this aristocracy, is a state of nature"—that is, once again, the genuine form of natural society. The ascendant class includes the church, as for Burke the church is a continuous social institution, and its spiritual authority is inconceivable without that continuity. Hence Burke says, in what from our present point of view is a key statement of his thought: "Nothing is more certain, than that our manners, our civilization, and all the good things which are connected with manners and with civilization, have, in this European world of ours, depended for ages upon two principles; and were indeed the result of both combined; I mean the spirit of a gentleman, and the spirit of religion."

The ascendant class, therefore, and more particularly the aristocracy, comes to represent an ideal authority, expressed in the term "gentleman," at the point in history at which its effective temporal authority had begun to decline (though of course its privileges and much of its prestige remained for another century). The social function of the aristocracy has always included the art of putting on a show, of dramatizing a way of life. It is natural that America, with no hereditary aristocracy as such, should have invented an *ad hoc* aristocracy out of its entertainers, who attract much the same kind of identification that royal figures do in British countries. In the thought of Carlyle, who has no interest in spiritual authority distinct from temporal authority, and wants only to identify the two, the reactivating of the aristocracy naturally occupies a central place. For Carlyle the "holiness" or radiance of the indwelling divinity in man, which is perceptible in the hero, is the source of an undifferentiated authority which is spiritual and temporal at once.

Yet even Carlyle distinguished the *de jure* authority of the aristocracy from the *de facto* authority of captains of industry and self-made heroes of the Napoleon and Cromwell category. The basis of the distinction seems to be that as *de facto* or temporal authority is essentially active, so *de jure* or spiritual authority has something about it associated with the contemplative. In his chapter on symbolism in *Sartor Resartus* Carlyle sees the heroic personality as an "intrinsic" symbol (that is, one that has value in itself, as distinct from the flag or the cross which are extrinsic and have value only as indicators). As a symbol, the hero is the focus of a community, and the purely *de jure* figure seems to have the most prestige as one. Crowds gather to see the Queen in order to see their own unity as a society reflected in her. Here again there is a link between the recognition of spiritual authority and the dramatic function of an ascendant class.

Samuel Butler also associates spiritual authority with the aristocracy, in a more speculative and paradoxical way. He is, of course, particularly fascinated by the working of the evolutionary process in human society, and his conception of education, traditional as it is in itself, reflects this interest. He points out in *Life and Habit* that no skill is learned thoroughly until it passes through consciousness into the unconscious. It follows that the most profoundly educated people are those who have been born to wealth, leisure, and privilege, and have never been troubled by a conscious idea, which includes a good many of the aristocracy. Thus in *The Way of All Flesh* the hero, Ernest Pontifex, at that time engaged in social work in East London, meets an old classmate named Towneley who is large, handsome, simple-minded, well to do, and altogether admirable. Ernest asks Towneley effusively if he doesn't love the poor: Towneley says no, and gets away as quickly as possible. It could hardly be a briefer encounter, but it is an epiphany for Ernest: spiritual authority has spoken, as unmistakably as it spoke from the burning bush. Ernest considers this situation carefully, and finally decides: "I see it all now. The people like Towneley are the only ones who know anything that is worth knowing, and like that of course I can never be. But to make Towneleys possible, there must be hewers of wood and drawers of water—men, in fact, through whom conscious knowledge must pass before it can reach those who can apply it gracefully and instinctively as the Towneleys can."

We are reminded of the respect paid in *Erewhon* to those who are handsome, healthy, and rich, and how Erewhon considers it a crime to be ill or unfortunate. In Huxley's terms, society's sympathies are with nature, rather than with ethics, even though society itself is an ethical creation. Yet Ernest's solution is still a trifle immature, and *Erewhon* brings us a little closer to Butler's real view of spiritual authority. Most of the Erewhonians, according to Butler, are unthinking, instinctive conservatives, whose values are determined entirely by habit and prejudice: worshippers, as he says, of the goddess Ydgrun. But there is also in Erewhon a small group of "high Ydgrunites," whom the narrator describes as the best people he met in Erewhon. Of them he says: "They were gentlemen in the full sense of the word; and what has one not said in saying this?" The high Ydgrunite would be something like Montaigne, presumably: able to live in and with society, able to see not only the power but the real significance of convention and prejudice, yet remaining intellectually detached from them. Such gentlemen are not only the natural aristocracy but the genuine apostles of society, correcting instinct by reason and reason by instinct, and never allowing the two to make that fatal alliance which is the mark of all bigots, whether reactionary or revolutionary.

The problem of spiritual authority, we see, has as its crucial point the problem of defining the community of such an authority. The writers we have been quoting, all of whom are deeply conservative, associate this community with the ideal aristocracy which the term "gentleman" conveys. For a revolutionary thinker, such as William Morris, spiritual authority would be isolated from society, confined to the small conspiratorial group of those who repudiate its values and are shut out from its benefits. It is perhaps worth noting that Morris's revolutionary ideal, as outlined in the future Utopia depicted in *News from Nowhere,* is the assimilating of the conception of a natural aristocracy to the whole of society. In *News from Nowhere* everybody has the creative versatility and the *sprezzatura* that are the marks of the ideally educated courtier in Castiglione, except that, of course, there is no court and no prince, and no one to serve except one another. They are at once producers and consumers, and as consumers they have the sharply limited and defined quality of a privileged class. "We know what we want," says one of them, "so we make no more than we want." This applies even to the production of human beings: the population has become stabilized, apparently, because people are no longer rutting out of nervous instability, as they do in societies based on exploitation. The curiously childlike quality of Morris's ideal citizens is also significant, for of course the real natural aristocracy, the society of those who are genuinely entitled to leisure and privilege and consuming the goods produced for them by others, are the children.

We have just traced a parabola from the counter-revolutionary polemic of the later Burke to the revolutionary polemic of Morris. The former places spiritual authority in the middle of the ascendant class, or at least its center of gravity is to be found there, and the *Appeal from the New to the Old Whigs* ends in contemptuous ridicule of John Ball, "that reverend patriarch of sedition," who could not find the conception of "gentleman" in the original producing society when Adam delved and Eve span. Morris, in contrast, places spiritual authority for his own time in the small alienated group who are possessed by the ambition of realizing the dream of John Ball. For Morris the Peasants' Revolt was the one brief moment when something like a proletariat appears in British history. In the thought of John Stuart Mill the problem of spiritual authority is located in a much less simplified view of society. For Mill, Burke's continuum of habit and prejudice is the way in which the majority of people live. Being a majority, they are not confined to a single class, and the progress of democracy involves making their will the source of *temporal* authority. As in Burke and Butler, their motivation is instinctive and empirical. Over against them are the smaller group of the liberal opposition, a much more highly individualized group, of whom Mill says that they initiate all wise and noble things.

Mill, somewhat unexpectedly, resembles Hegel in seeing the political opposition of Conservative and Liberal as the symbol of an ideal or intellectual opposition of conservative and liberal attitudes. As the liberal opposition is intellectually always a minority, it has the peculiar problem of getting enough mass support to be effective in a democratic election. Some of Mill's devices, such as a plurality of votes for the educated, are sufficiently desperate to indicate that this is a matter of some difficulty. To grasp the nature of the ideal opposition we have to grasp two principles. First, the majority is always right, for the majority is the source of temporal authority. Second, the majority is always wrong, for it is not the source of spiritual authority. The latter is to be found in the intellectual opposition, for "almost all the greatest men who ever lived have formed part of such an Opposition."

Authority in its two forms, therefore, rests on a paradoxical and illogical tension between majority rule and minority right. The minority are not a class but an elite, and no social epithet like "gentleman" will apply to them. In practice most of them may be gentlemen, but that is not why they belong there. The gentleman behaves according to a social convention, and for Mill the toleration of unconventional or eccentric behavior is the mark of a mature society. What holds this elite together is something intellectual, though it is certainly not intellectual agreement. To put the question in another way, what gives a minority a right? Criminals are a minority, but clearly have no right to be criminals. In the *Essay on Liberty* the right appears to be the ability to contribute something to the area of free thought and discussion which for Mill is the real parliament of man, the ideological debate that is close to being the source of spiritual authority because it supplies the vision for temporal power. To permit freedom of thought is to direct freedom of action, as unrestricted speculation is the best check so far discovered on premature, spasmodic, or panic-stricken action. Here again we run into a Hegelian element in Mill's thought: no idea contributed to this social debate has any real effectiveness unless it contains its own opposite: unless, therefore, the possibility of refuting it is also present. Mill draws our attention to the peculiar importance of Rousseau in challenging the validity of the structure of society itself.

Burke's counter-revolutionary argument was based on a completely inductive conception of political action; Mill's argument attempts to associate his liberal opposition with a more deductive point of view. He remarks for example that "the non-existence of an acknowledged first principle has made ethics not so much a guide as a consecration of men's actual sentiments." The Utilitarian philosophy held his loyalty because it provided a major premise for majority behavior. That people will seek what they consider pleasure and avoid what they consider pain is individually probable and statistically certain. But this purely descriptive principle supplies no standard or value, no way even of distinguishing reality from illusion in the conception of pleasure. In Milton, who in *Areopagitica* presents a similar conception of truth as something arrived at dynamically through the conflict of opinion, the major premises come from scripture. Milton never conceived the possibility of a free society trying to find truth without the aid of scripture. In Mill there is no clear source of the premises of debate of this kind, no set of standards and assumptions that can be taken as given. The absence of such a source may be one reason for his curious attraction toward the most uncongenial types of political dogmatists, including Carlyle and Comte (it would take us too far afield to apply this principle to Harriet Taylor), as though he felt that they held some missing piece he was looking for.

In Newman, on the other hand, the source of spiritual authority is the church catholic: his great strength as a nineteenth-century thinker lay in his unvarying acceptance of that view. At no time in his adult life was Newman ever anything that a Protestant would call a Protestant: his problem was only to decide whether the Anglican or the Roman communion was the genuinely catholic one. He takes our present argument a step further by finding the road to spiritual authority through education. Education for him is partly social and retains the social aim of producing the "gentleman" which we met in Burke and Butler. Even its intellectual characteristic, a disinterested or liberal quality in it which is "its own end," has an analogy with the social ideal which is detachable from the necessity of earning a living. On its intellectual side, liberal education is essentially a discipline of reason, as in Milton, and, as in Mill, it seems to have something to do with a "master view of things," a deductive or synoptic sense of intellectual form which gets one's head above the habit of living: "The principle of real dignity in Knowledge, its worth, its desirableness, considered irrespectively of its results, is this germ within it of a scientific or a philosophical process. This is how it comes to be an end in itself; this is why it admits of being called Liberal."

But the university turns out to be a function of the church, and the education it gives confronts the student with a dilemma: he must either attach himself along with his education to the church or keep his education as a private possession. Recurrently we have come to this point of having to define the community of spiritual authority. The individual can readily be seen to be capable of understanding more than society in general, and hence of possessing standards and values, with an authority superior in kind if not in power. But the conception "gentleman," however interpreted, defines the superior individual rather than the superior group, even granted that one may recognize the individual as one of a group. For Newman only the church provides this community, and of the gentlemen who cannot commit themselves to it he says: "When they do wrong, they feel, not contrition, of which God is the object, but remorse, and a sense of degradation. . . . They are victims of an intense self-contemplation."

In Newman's view of the church there is no place, as there would have to be in Protestant thinkers, including Milton, for a dialogue between scripture and church. The church for Newman is the definitive teacher of doctrine; hence it encloses scripture, and operates on ordinary society very much as the British constitution does in Burke. For Burke the conflict of classes and their interests, in a free society, is settled by a legal compromise which preserves the rights of both parties, and these compromises then form a series of precedents diffusing freedom through society, as the quarrels of king and barons produced Magna Carta and the quarrels of king and Parliament the Bill of Rights. Newman sees church doctrine as developing in a somewhat similar way, being evolved out of the crises of history, defining a dogma here, marking off a heresy there, in an endless pilgrimage toward the City of God. Thus spiritual authority in Newman is, as in Milton, a revelation, but a revelation that has no place for metamorphosis, for the revolutionary and apocalyptic transformation of society.

In Arnold, the conception "culture" is the basis from which we have to start. In using the phrase "spiritual authority" to describe a pervasive problem of nineteenth-century thought, I have been putting unfamiliar conceptions into the minds of some of my writers. For Mill, the problem is not exactly one of *spiritual* authority, and for Butler, it is not exactly a problem of authority. But Arnold is quite explicit about the authoritative nature of culture: "If we look at the world outside us we find a disquieting absence of sure authority. We discover that only in right reason can we get a source of sure authority; and culture brings us towards right reason." The traditional elements of gentleman and liberal education are both involved in Arnold's culture, but Arnold clears up a point about the social location of spiritual authority that has been confusing us so far. We noticed that the more conservative a writer is, the more inclined he is to locate spiritual authority in the middle of actual society, in the place of greatest prestige and prominence. The more radical he is, the more inclined he is to locate it in an opposition, an alien or even excluded group. Something in Arnold—possibly the Romantic poet in him— realizes that the center is the place of greatest isolation. The argument of *Culture and Anarchy* is to the effect that what is of greatest cultural value, such as a university or the established church, is central to society and demands to be placed at the center, in the position of Carlyle's intrinsic symbol. Society itself presents a conflict of class interests, and culture for Arnold operates like law in Burke or doctrine in Newman, as a harmonizing principle creating a new kind of order out of this conflict. Those who support it have to begin by isolating themselves from class conflict, which means isolating themselves from the present structure of society: "Within each of these classes there are a certain number of *aliens,* if we may so call them,—persons who are mainly led, not by their class spirit, but by a general *humane* spirit, by the love of human perfection."

Culture represents an evaluation—the *best* that has been thought and said—and the conception of "best" is bound up with permanence. Class conflict deals with temporary issues, and its arguments are rationalizations based on a temporary situation. Temporal power is based on the ascendancy of one class—here we come back to Milton's conception of temporal power as an interim power. The class qua class is always anticultural: the aristocracy, considered purely as a class, are only barbarians, the middle class only Philistines, the lower class only a populace. Hence it would be the wildest paradox to think of creating a new society through the dictatorship of one class. It is culture that is the genuinely revolutionary force in society, for culture "seeks to do away with classes," and tends to create out of actual society an ideal order of liberty, equality, and fraternity. Culture for Arnold is a whole of which the church forms part, but as culture is not, like church, the name of a specific community, the problem of defining the community of spiritual authority is still with us.

The question of the origin of spiritual authority, and of whether that origin is purely human, partly human, or wholly superhuman has come up at various times in this inquiry. Anyone working out this question in Christian terms, whether Catholic or Protestant, would be likely to say that its origin is out of human reach, though the fact that

Christ is at once God, Man, and Logos guarantees the validity of human reason as a means of receiving it, at least up to a point. For Burke and Butler, in different ways, spiritual authority, or whatever is homologous with it, comes to us as a process of nature, a datum or something given, which we may modify but must first of all accept. We have seen that spiritual authority begins in the recognition of truth, and truth usually has about it some quality of the objective, something presented to us. But for a liberal thinker, such as Mill, there can hardly be any real spiritual authority apart from what man himself creates. A revolutionary thinker would go a step further and see in truth itself a human creation which, as man continues to create it, he may also re-create. Marx's second thesis on Feuerbach makes this quite clear: "The question whether objective truth can be attributed to human thinking is not a question of theory, but is a practical question. In practice man must prove the truth, that is, the reality and power, the this-sidedness of his thinking." Arnold's "culture" unites these qualities of the datum and the continuous creation, being a human construct which, so far as it is rooted in the past, possesses an objective authority. This authority, we should note, is not exclusively intellectual, for "many things are not seen in their true nature and as they really are, unless they are seen as beautiful," and the imagination as well as the reason may recognize a monument of its own magnificence.

Wherever we turn in nineteenth-century thought we meet some version of a "drunken boat" construct, where the values of humanity, intelligence, or cultural and social tradition keep tossing precariously in a sort of Noah's ark on top of a menacing and potentially destructive force. This is the relation of the world as idea to the world as will in Schopenhauer, of ethics to evolution in Darwin and Huxley, of the ascendant class to the proletariat in Marx, and, later, of ego to libido and id in Freud. There are also many variants of a "saving remnant" theory, ranging from Coleridge's "clerisy" to various pleas for a new kind of monastic movement (one thinks of the symbolic function of the idealized monastery in the argument of Carlyle's *Past and Present*). Of other metaphors of spiritual authority, two are conspicuous. One is the metaphor of the social human body, whose seat of intelligence and authority ought to be somewhere on top, as it is in the individual body. The other is the thermostat or feedback metaphor which has organized so much social thinking in the last two centuries. In a sense the search for spiritual authority is really the search for a "governor" in the mechanical sense, something that distributes the rhythm of a mechanism without being involved in the mechanism itself. This figure appears in Huxley's *Evolution and Ethics:* "To this extent the general cosmic process begins to be checked by a rudimentary ethical process, which is, strictly speaking, part of the former, just as the 'governor' in a steamengine is part of the mechanism of the engine."

The problem dealt with in this paper could of course be extended over a far wider area of nineteenth-century thought than I am here able to cover. So far as I know, the twentieth century has not added much to the question, which may be one reason why the political axioms and assumptions of the twentieth century are still rooted in the nineteenth. It seems to me, however, appropriate for an audience celebrating a step in the progress of a university to consider whether the university itself may not have a peculiarly close relationship to the question. In particular, the university seems to me to come closer than any other human institution to defining the community of spiritual authority. Newman's view that the university is a function of the church, with theology occupying a central role as the queen of sciences, does not seem to be borne out by the development of universities in the last century. I have no doubt that religion indicates where the ultimate source of spiritual authority is, nor that the churches have an essential function as custodians and interpreters of its tradition. But in the present-day shape of society, so dominated by science and technology, they clearly have only a partial and peripheral role in embodying the spiritual authority of that society.

Arnold comes nearest to seeing the universities in this light, but universities in his day, and more particularly as he conceived them, made it necessary for him to distinguish them from "culture." A century later, we seem to be living our lives on two levels. One is the level of ordinary society, which is in so constant a state of revolution and metamorphosis that it cannot be accepted as the real form of human society at all, but only as the transient appearance of real society. Real society itself can only be the world revealed to us through the study of the arts and sciences, the total body of human achievement out of which the forces come that change ordinary society so rapidly. Of this world the universities are the social embodiment, and they represent what seems to me today the only visible direction in which our higher loyalties and obligations can go.

WILLARD THORP

The Literary Scholar as Chameleon

DURING THE FIFTY YEARS of Rice University's existence methods of literary study have undergone several transformations. To show the stages and results of this evolution may be illuminating, even startling, to economists or physicists whose disciplines have changed even more rapidly in this time. A rehearsal of these cycles of change will, I hope, be of interest to our oncoming professionals, the majors in literature and the graduate students. Younger students of literature who are scornful of literary history and of the biographical approach to a poem or a novel and whose working vocabulary derives largely from the essays of the New Critics may not be aware of where they stand in this half-century of change. They may also wonder, at times, why their professors talk about literary works in such varying ways; why in one classroom there is stress on the cultural context of the poem under consideration while in the room next door the talk is about the levels of meaning in the poem and its symbolic structure. Then why, in a third room down the hall, the sessions seem always to be in quest of an elusive archetype which must be found by the time the bell rings, or all's lost.

If, like Tiresias in T. S. Eliot's *The Waste Land*, I talk about how I "perceived the scene" (though I cannot, like him, foretell the rest), it is because any teacher of literature of my generation has either fought in the ranks of this revolution or has cheered or jeered the combatants in a safe retreat far from the struggle. He cannot fail to have noticed what went on.

What were the postures of the teaching and study of literature when as an eager graduate student I made my way from Hamilton College in New York State to Harvard in Massachusetts? It was evident at once that I must swallow a big dose of philology: the more courses in the older stages of the modern languages, the more certain the cure. So I went to work. I keep to this day my Wilhelm Braune's

WILLARD THORP is Holmes Professor of Belles-Lettres at Princeton University.

Gotische Grammatik to prove that I could once read all there is of Gothic—a small part of the New Testament—in the original. To bolster my ego, I also have up there on the shelves behind the books I consult rather more frequently, Klaeber's edition of *Beowulf* and Gaston Paris's *La Chanson de Roland.* Both contain interlinear glosses which were once of much value to me. When we were not busy at our philological chores, we were pursuing the classical echoes in Milton, the influence of Milton on Wordsworth, and of Wordsworth on Arnold. The study of literature after the Renaissance seemed to be largely a matter of influences and parallels. As I look back on this training in the light of what goes on now in many if not most graduate seminars in English, what I find remarkable is that we were always talking around and behind works of literature. We almost never went inside them. To have spent all of an hour on Keats's "Ode to Melancholy" would have seemed a wicked waste of time. The job was to "cover" all the Keats odes in one hour, so that the student could salt away some truisms about Keats and the Ode.

And so we went out to teach. In American higher education the idea of selective admission had only recently taken hold. Colleges admitted the best students they could get, of course, but too many athletes and preferred sons of alumni made the grade. English, we beginners discovered, was *the* cultural subject. The classics had dwindled away and though given injections constantly, never recovered health. The study of fine arts and music was in its infancy. The modern languages were too difficult for the lazy. Thus, partly by default, English was the favored department. But not only because its courses seemed to be easy. America was still a culture-hungry country, and the notion was about that some culture would rub off if the soon-to-be lawyer or engineer associated with Matthew Arnold or Ruskin for a semester. Undeniably, there was the added attraction of the snobbery of the subject. For most cultivated Americans, England was still, in Hawthorne's phrase, "our old home." A provincial American college boy or girl could learn urbanity from Lord Chesterfield, high seriousness from Milton, the ways of genius from Shakespeare, wit from Congreve, whimsy from Charles Lamb, and romantic melancholy from Keats.

Somewhat to our dismay, we new Ph.D.'s found that the professors of English who appealed to the lazy and the industrious alike were by and large the "appreciators," such men as Charles T. Copeland at Harvard, William Lyon Phelps at Yale, and Princeton's J. Duncan Spaeth. They were the cheerleaders who roused the lecture room to a frenzy as the team of poets ran onto the field. The Copeland magic was a combination of wit, a beautiful reading voice, and eccentricity.

With Phelps it was uplift, culture-transfer, and keeping ahead of the procession. He was always discovering some new writer or school of writers and sharing his discoveries with his listeners. Spaeth was a great hulking man with a booming voice and endless energy. For years Princeton's amateur coach of crew, he had no need of a megaphone when he shouted advice from the launch. Spaeth specialized in aphoristic generalizations such as these: "Each play of Shakespeare is built around one of two themes: the power of love or the love of power." "Browning," he declared, "touched only the major chords of life." To make certain this stuck, Spaeth would rush over to the piano on the platform and play all the chords in C major he could wham out of the instrument.

The "appreciators" were, of course, greatly beloved. There was a new "Copey" or Spaeth story every week. In his energetic reading of Falstaff's lines or Ophelia's (in falsetto) Spaeth often sprayed the front row with enthusiastic spit. One morning the whole front row arrived in raincoats. English courses were fun in the hands of the appreciators and relieved the monotony of the accounting lab and the rat-tending requirements of the psychologists. There was no doubt, too, that the appreciators genuinely loved literature. If a six-footer on the crew read Shelley rapturously because he admired Duncan Spaeth, that was a good reason, if not the best.

Two things were wrong: the "personalized" approach and the thinness of what was said. The appreciators often got in the way of the authors they lectured about. The student confused Billy Phelps with Browning or Copeland with Dickens and usually remembered the acting rather than the lines being acted out. We youngsters who listened to these elders of ours with mingled awe and embarrassment noted the lack of substance in what was said and the lack of any real engagement with the text.

I have dwelt this long on the appreciators—their tribe included critics and reviewers as well as professors of literature—because I think the revolution which was soon to follow constituted an effort to take the criticism of literature away from them and make it an exacting discipline.

To demonstrate for you how extensive the revolution has been, I wish to put two critical passages about Whitman side by side. The first is the conclusion of an essay by Professor Phelps, published in his *Howells, James, Bryant and Other Essays*. The other is a brief explication of Whitman's "When Lilacs Last in the Dooryard Bloom'd," written for this occasion by Professor Thorp in the present critical mode.

Here is Professor Phelps:

The art of poetry is an art of expression; we are all poets at heart. . . . But we are inarticulate; we cannot express ourselves; we love music, and we cannot sing. The great poets are the spokesmen for humanity. Whitman spoke out for us all. There are passages in such poems as *Columbus, When Lilacs Last, The Man-of-War Bird,* that rhythmically sing thoughts that are universal.

Furthermore, there is something healthy in his optimism. He was never petulant, never cynical, never despairing. To him Life was good. He belongs not among those who have despised the supreme gift of life, not among the deniers, but among the Affirmers. He was entirely free from the prevailing modern disease, the fear of life. He loved life, and welcomed experience; he was devoid of fear. . . .

In a certain sense, Whitman interpreted America to Europe; and to America he tried to interpret the universe.

What has Phelps said? That poets sing for us though we are inarticulate poets. Whitman is an Affirmer. He tried to interpret the universe to Americans.

I assure you that in the whole essay there is no passage that tells us anything about a particular poem of Whitman's except to say it is good, noble, true, healthy.

How differently we do things now! I'll admit that the concocted passage I am about to read uses as many critical concepts and terms as I could crowd in. But all of them are currently in high favor. Nor can I be blamed for the slight tone of burlesque which may have crept in. A passage of modern criticism sometimes reads like a travesty of itself.

Considered as a construct these sixteen stanzas constitute one of the most remarkable of Whitman's poems. It is also one of the first in the Whitman canon to indicate that he had escaped from the blind alley of the pseudo-poet. In no earlier poem were Whitman's necessary strategies so clear to himself. Though the poem suggests the rhetorical ambition of the neo-classical ode or the romantic elegy, its two principal structures borrow from neither tradition.

We note first a threefold symbolic structure, placed before us in the opening stanzas: the lilac, the powerful western star, and the song of the solitary thrush. We must always be wary, of course, of being betrayed into the intentional fallacy, but it is not going too far to say that the lilac, like Eliot's hyacinth of *The Waste Land,* is a symbol of resurrection; the western star, now fallen, is Lincoln in death; the song of the thrush tallies the poet's song. One may go farther with this third symbol and see in it Whitman's favorite persona, transmuted here into the archetype of the bard.

To this symbolic structure Whitman later joins two other shadowy but powerful symbols from which a magic *mana* emanates—the companions walking on each side of the speaker, "the knowledge of death" and "the thought of death." When the song ceases in stanza 16, these two companion-symbols are united with the lilac, star, and thrush symbols.

The second structuring device Whitman characteristically borrowed from grand opera, to which he was passionately addicted. The aria-like inner-poem "Come lovely and soothing death" is prepared for in much the way an aria is introduced on the operatic stage, by modulation into the key to be used and by language which is in effect gesture.

Thus the poem makes its way satisfactorily through its own inner contradictions, its *agon* (for example, the paradox of the movement of the black coffin through the smiling land) and is resolved in a higher synthesis of tragedy. Left far behind now is the polymorph perverse world of the child that Whitman in his honesty let us see in the early poems. Instead we have in the figure of the "Dark mother always gliding near with soft feet" an obvious use, however unconscious on Whitman's part, of the anima whose compelling power is due to her image being, in Jungian terms, the most immediate primordial archetype of the collective unconscious.

In conclusion we must note that this is phrasal poetry at its best and that it fulfils, in every respect, Ransom's definition of a poem as a logical structure having a local texture. If we agree with the late Professor Chase that the anthropologists' definition of myth will not serve us but that we must nevertheless appropriate this highly useful concept and remake it for our own ends, then this poem, in that it is "magic literature," is truly a mythical poem.

I hope my little passage of criticism in the modern mode has awed you and has convinced you that the literary scholar-critic now has something to talk about and an abundant vocabulary for his task. My job will be to try to explain where his vocabulary came from: how we got from there to here.

The first event which helped to transform the writing of literary criticism into a discipline was the invasion of Freudian concepts of human behavior. As it happened, Freud's earliest studies were the ones which proved to be most useful to creative writers and to critics: *Psychopathology of Everyday Life; The Interpretation of Dreams; Three Contributions to the Theory of Sex;* and *Wit and Its Relation to the Unconscious.* Translations of these works appeared in America during the 1910's, all undertaken by Freud's American disciple and propagandist Dr. A. A. Brill. Older members of the audience can remember how such Freudian concepts as repression, dream work, infantile sexuality, the psychogenesis of wit, and the Oedipus complex were batted about at parties during the 1920's. We laughed at "Freudian slips" in conversation and refused to tell our dreams or listened with knowing delight when the uninitiated told theirs.

Freud had accomplished a revolution in the understanding of human behavior. In spite of objections to his theories, which were repulsive to many, there was no denying the clinical evidence and the cures. Freud never succeeded in photographing the id but he produced other kinds of evidence that it exists. Inevitably the writers were impressed. Some, like Thomas Mann, and James Joyce in his later years at least, were avowed Freudians. D. H. Lawrence resisted, but wrote his own *Fantasia of the Unconscious*. Not many major writers in this country came over to Freud in the beginning, though Sherwood Anderson, Waldo Frank, Floyd Dell, Thomas Wolfe, and Ludwig Lewisohn did. One of our first Freudians, Conrad Aiken, has continuously made use of Freudian theory in his poems, stories, and criticism, and in his fascinating psychoanalytic autobiography, *Ushant*.

As contemporary writers increasingly turned to Freud for corroboration in their presentation of character, it was incumbent on their critics and biographers to understand the nature and extent of this influence. Eugene O'Neill is a good case in point. O'Neill often angrily denied *any* Freudian influence in his work, but it is there, to be seen by any critic who knows what to look for. One of the best studies of this playwright, Edwin A. Engel's *The Haunted Heroes of Eugene O'Neill*, could not have been written without the comprehension of the theories of Freud, and of Jung as well, which it displays.

Freud induced the writing of several psychoanalytical biographical studies through example as well as precept. His *Leonardo da Vinci: A Study in Psychosexuality* and *Dostoevsky and Parricide* are masterly in their penetration and remarkable in the restraint they show. I don't know why I say "remarkable," since Freud knew well enough how difficult it is to get at the traumas a patient has suffered. How much more difficult, therefore, is it to work, *post facto*, from such scraps of evidence as survive and from hints in the artist's own work. That there have not been more biographies cut to the Freudian pattern may be ascribed to this fact: if the Herr Doktor himself dared to take only a segment of an artist's life and put it on the couch, who wanted to go further? Among laymen who did attempt to write Freudian biographies the most successful were Katherine Anthony in her *Margaret Fuller: A Psychological Biography* (1920) and Joesph Wood Krutch with his *Edgar Allan Poe: A Study in Genius* (1926).

There is at least one other area in which psychoanalysis and criticism can unite—in the Freudian analysis of a work of literature. The best example of this union is a famous book by Freud's English disciple, Ernest Jones's *Hamlet and Oedipus*. In such a study the fictional character is treated as if he were a patient undergoing analysis. Jones's work might have set a fashion. That it has not I attribute to two reasons. Only a professional analyst can do this sort of thing. The amateur is certain to make a fool of himself. *Hamlet and Oedipus* is an important study. So is Dr. H. A. Murray's psychoanalytic study of Melville's *Pierre*. But Dr. Murray is a distinguished psychologist as well as a perceptive literary critic. The second reason why this sort of study has only infrequently been attempted is that the formalist trend of modern criticism has moved away from the treating of fictional characters as if they were living people. A. C. Bradley's *Shakespearean Tragedy*, with its "character" approach, was shot down in 1933 by a famous little book by L. C. Knights, *How Many Children Had Lady Macbeth?* Character analysis was out; or many thought it was.

The pervasiveness of Freudian concepts and terms in modern writing and in the criticism which deals with it leads to the inescapable conclusion, so it seems to me, that students of literature must know their Freud, at least as much of him as can be found in A. A. Brill's edition of the *Basic Writings* or in Freud's *A General Introduction to Psychoanalysis*. Students must know what the critics are talking about when Freudian concepts are used, even if they do not wish to plunge in themselves. Let me offer you one example out of scores I might adduce. A few years ago a lost notebook of Thoreau happily turned up. Professor Perry Miller was asked by the Morgan Library to edit it, which he delightedly did. He believed he had found evidence in it that would explain Thoreau's reclusiveness, his pride in his chastity, and his attitude toward the women in his life. Though Professor Miller uses few Freudian terms in his devastating chapter, "The Stratagems of Consciousness—Woman and Men," Freud dominates the argument. The student or critic who reads such a passage as this must make up his mind about it. Has Professor Miller got the right answer? He cannot make up his mind unless he is familiar with the Freudian premises from which Miller argues.

Thoreau could never have made a serious offer to Ellen Sewall. His concern was already defined: to avoid entanglement, either with professions or with women; to arrange experience so that both the labors of other men and the affections of women—mother, sister, friends—would minister to his egotism. Only by such exploitation could the Byron of Concord . . . become a major writer.

We have presently to consider the coming into literature and criticism of three important and closely related concepts: symbol, myth, and archetype. These are sacred words to many in my profession. If the student says myth at the right moment, he goes to the head of the class. If he hesitates and then says archetype when he should have said symbol, he flunks for the day.

At this point we must abandon chronology because everything was happening at the same time. Roughly by 1935 all of these concepts were in use and discussions of their relevance in one work after another were going on at a furious rate. Since references to the psychology of Carl Gustav Jung turn up constantly in these discussions, it will be useful to digress for a moment and consider, in a general way, Jung's influence.

First to be noted is the congeniality to writers of Jung's theories, as contrasted with Freud's. There is an inexorability in Freud's belief in the paramount importance of sexuality in human life. If there is any deviation from the normal progression from infantile oral eroticism to sexual adulthood, neurosis will show itself eventually. Jung soon rejected this fundamental dogma, deserted the master, and went his own way. Writers and artists naturally resented Freud's belief that the artist is neurotic and that he sublimates his frustrated sexual desires in his creations. Writers were not willing to admit that their poems and novels were produced out of sickness, thus resembling the pearl which the oyster secretes. Jung offered them a happier view of their occupation. Analysis might alleviate the sickness in the poet's personal life but it could not and should not try to explain the sacred mysteries of the creative process.

There were many other ideas attractive to the writer in the Jungian psychology. As I have said, Jung was soon repelled by the sexuality theory. He had grown up among peasants, so he tells us in his *Memories, Dreams, Reflections*, and had learned around the stables what Freud had patiently listened to from the couch—incest and the perversions and the rest. Jung wanted something, as he said "different and better" for humanity than what Freudian analysis leaves the patient with. Furthermore, Jung saw himself as a man with far more general cultivation than Freud. His early studies in art, anthropology, myth, and religion led him increasingly into theorizing about the relations between these areas of study and psychology.

To come to specifics, Jung invented or transformed several concepts which have been immensely appealing to writers and critics. They were much taken, for instance, with his concept of the persona, "the facet of personality which is turned to the world and by which a relationship with the environment is made." They were also pleased with the anima-animus concept—the normal feminine residue in man and the masculine in woman. Congenial, too, was the concept of the shadow, that inferior thing in ourselves, "the one who wants to do all the things that we do not allow ourselves to do"—the Mr. Hyde to our Dr. Jekyll.

We must now turn back and attempt to untangle the nexus of

symbol, myth, and archetype. Symbol is, of course, old in the language. Greek in origin, it came into English by way of the church and early meant a creed or confession of faith. By the end of the sixteenth century it had been given its modern signification as something that stands for (not by exact resemblance) something else. In mathematics it was an indispensable term by 1700. Since every word is a symbol, the symbolic nature of language itself was speculated about as early as the seventeenth century. The later interest in the operation of symbols on the part of men of letters can be seen in two famous works of the nineteenth century, Emerson's *Nature* (the fourth chapter is entitled "Language") and Carlyle's *Sartor Resartus*.

Because of the medium in which they work, writers have always, consciously or unconsciously, used symbols to convey meaning. It was in the nineteenth century, and particularly in France, that the poets began to explore knowingly the evocative possibilities of symbols. In France the important symbolist movement originated with Baudelaire, Verlaine, and Mallarmé and continued on down into this century with Rimbaud, Laforgue, and Corbière to Proust, Claudel, and Valéry. Since French writers like to form themselves into schools, it was inevitable that the symbolists should at some moment band together to defend and propagate their artistic principles. The occasion was an attack in *Le Temps* following the uproar caused by the publication of Huysmans's *À Rebours* in 1884. The writer of the article attempted to pin the word "decadents" on the symbolist poets. They struck back with a signed reply rejecting this nasty appellation and asserting their right to be called symbolists. In 1885 *symbolisme* came of age.

Symbolism and the study of it spread far beyond France. Looking back now, we can see that many nineteenth-century writers who may never have heard of *les symbolistes* were practicing symbolism and had some notion of what they were doing. Herman Melville is a good example. *Moby-Dick* is a plum-pudding of symbols, from the sealand bipolarities, the doubloon, and the try-works down to Ahab's pipe and Queequeg's idol Yojo. As you will imagine, one of the chief occupations of literary scholars in recent years has been symbol-hunting in works written in the dark ages before writers knew much about symbols. The game-bag is huge.

Both Freud and Jung gave sanction and impetus to the search. Freud had discovered that in dream-analysis symbols turned up constantly. Of course they were not what they seemed to be. A ladder was not a ladder or a spear a spear or a dish a dish. Almost every innocent object dreamed about masked and therefore symbolized sexual organs or sexual activities. Through these recurrent dream symbols

Freud could get at the disturbances, almost always sexual of course, in the lives of his patients. Jung, with his interest in archeology, myth, and religion, ranged far more widely than Freud in his exploration and interpretation of symbols. Besides his mandala, found first in Sanskrit and meaning "magic circle" but turning up today, so it seems, in the dreams of patients who have substituted the wholeness of man for deity, Freud's good old sexual rooms and portals, swords and plows are as simple as ABC.

When we consider the importance of myth in modern writing and criticism, we are dealing with a concept that is fairly modern. To the Greeks *mythos* first meant a speech or conversation. Later it came to mean to them a poetic or legendary tale as opposed to a historical account. Strangely enough, the current meaning of the word, as used by anthropologists or the students of literature, emerged only a little over a century ago. We can see at once how the new meaning came about. In the early years of the nineteenth century the discoveries of the folklorists and the students of comparative religion had made it evident that most legendary stories in any tribe or country had a deep-rooted significance. They were not merely exciting stories made up to delight the audience in the hall or around the fire. In them were concealed the efforts of the tribe to relate the human to the super-human. Myth was fairy tale on the way to becoming religious belief. Involved were magic, ritual, propitiation, initiation. Myths were, in the phrase of Susanne Langer, life-symbols, as she says in *Philosophy in a New Key:*

The great step from fairytale to myth is taken when not only social forces—persons, customs, laws, traditions—but also cosmic forces surrounding mankind, are expressed in the story; when not only relationships of an individual to society, but of mankind to nature, are conceived through the spontaneous metaphor of poetic fantasy.

When we come down to our own day we can understand without much scratching of the head why the relations between myth and literature have preoccupied so many. Jung adverted to myths constantly in his speculations. In his later years Freud gave his fancy rein, in this area, in such works as *Totem and Taboo* and *Moses and Monotheism.* Possibly the most powerful extra-literary persuasive came from Sir James Fraser's *The Golden Bough,* completed in twelve volumes in 1915. The one-volume condensation, issued in 1922, was one of the most influential works of the decade, all 752 pages of it.

You will notice that this condensed version of *The Golden Bough* appeared in the same year as T. S. Eliot's *The Waste Land,* one of the first modern works of literature to make extensive use of myth. As

Eliot admitted in his notes, it owed much to Jessie L. Weston's *From Ritual to Romance*, a work stemming from *The Golden Bough* and published only two years before *The Waste Land*. If we add one more work to this list of inductors, we shall have the whole story in outline. This is a review-essay by T. S. Eliot of another work which counterpoints ancient myth against modern life, James Joyce's *Ulysses*. Eliot's essay, published in 1923, is "Ulysses, Order and Myth." From a single sentence in this brief article sprang a new concept of the possible structure of a work of fiction and of the way to study a work so structured: "Instead of narrative method, we may now use the 'mythical' method."

Here we have the triad: a great collection of myths from which writers could help themselves; two important examples of the literary use of myth, one a poem and the other a novel; and an essay showing us how to use and study the mythical method. These important events happened forty years ago. The critics and literary theorists sharpened their pencils and went to work. And so the shelves filled up. Here are some of the books you will find on them: Joseph Campbell's *The Hero with a Thousand Faces*, the prologue to which is entitled "The Monomyth"; Henry Nash Smith's *Virgin Land: The American West as Symbol and Myth*; and R. W. B. Lewis's *The American Adam*, the first sentence in which reads: "This book has to do with the beginnings and the first tentative outlines of a native American mythology."

I confess to considerable bafflement in trying to discuss the emergence of the word "archetype" in contemporary literary criticism. Its use is increasing, of this I am certain, and one must take it into account. One of the most influential of contemporary literary theorists, Northrop Frye, of the University of Toronto, has invented what he calls archetypal criticism, and he already has disciples by the dozen.[1] Archetype is in the guest room and intends to stay for some time.

Jung brought the word, in its earlier meaning, into the language. He had discovered, so he believed, that certain symbolic figures recurring in the dreams of his patients were identical with certain traditional mythological figures scattered all over the world. What connection could there be between the figure in the dream and the figure in a myth of which the patient could not possibly have any knowledge? In a dream of his own, so Jung tells us in his *Memories, Dreams, Reflections*, the solution came: the collective unconscious, that "deeper stratum of the unconscious than the personal unconscious." Each

---

[1] An early and probably very influential work which moved in this direction is Maud Bodkin's *Archetypal Patterns of Poetry* (Oxford, 1934).

human being experiences life in a manner conditioned by and thus similar to the past history of mankind. The *forms* of apprehension are, so Jung declared, the archetypes. Some of the Jungian archetypes I have already mentioned: the animus, the anima, the shadow. In the late 1920's Jung began discovering new archetypes and expanding his descriptions of earlier ones at an alarming rate. I say "alarming" because one had to race in order to keep up with the additions and changes. For example, Jung's early image of the anima, the feminine in man, now advanced to the highest place, becoming "the most immediate primordial image, for she is in every way the nearest and most powerful experience." There was, then, perhaps, a hierarchy of archetypes? There were certainly several new ones: for example, the wise old man, the trickster, and the divine child.

All can play at this game, as long as there are more myths to investigate and new versions of old myths to be found in modern literature. In every myth there is at least one archetype. The more myths, ancient and modern, the more archetypes.

As I have said, it was left to Professor Frye to bring the word "archetype" into criticism and, by transforming its Jungian meaning, to use it as the basis of a theory of literaure. The first statement of his hypothesis was advanced in an article in the *Kenyon Review* in 1951: "The Archetypes of Literature." From this Frye proceeded in 1957 to his encyclopedic and synoptic *Anatomy of Criticism*, a work which has made an immense impression. I shall have to oversimplify his schema, but I think I can show what in essence he has done. Frye believes that the great central myth is that of the solar cycle of the day, the seasonal cycle of the year, and the organic cycle of human life. All narratives, old or new, are related to some phase of the cycle. There are four phases: the dawn, spring and birth phase; the zenith, summer and marriage or triumph phase; the sunset, autumn and death phase; the darkness, winter and dissolution phase.

At this moment: enter archetype. Frye believes that each phase of the universal myth requires and has evoked its own form or archetype. Thus, the archetype of the spring phase is the romance and "most dithyrambic and rhapsodic poetry"; the archetype of the winter phase is satire.[2] And so on.

Professor Frye was induced to work out this vast table, into which any literary work can be fitted, because he found modern criticism a chaos of conflicting terms and concepts. He has invented a unifying schema as perfect and complete as Mendeleev's table of the chemical

[2] These are the equations of phase and archetype as given in the article. In the *Anatomy of Criticism* Professor Frye makes alterations: comedy now belongs to the mythos of spring; romance to the mythos of summer.

elements. Every slot is filled or if one or two may still be vacant, we may expect to find neglected poems or novels which belong there. I can foresee the time when some ingenious popularizer will have provided, for every college freshman to use, a ready-reckoner based on Frye's *Anatomy of Criticism*. The freshman pushed for time will then be able to dispose of *Comus* and *The Confidence Man* without having read them.

Meanwhile a group of critics had emerged who paid scant attention to the connections between psychology and literature. They are known as the New Critics, though they did not so name themselves; nor did they form a school, in the French fashion. Nevertheless there were connections among them and they reinforced one another in many ways. Their collective influence has been so great that old-line scholars blame them chiefly for the mystagogic jargon which appears in the papers of their students.

The New Criticism arrived unostentatiously in a series of works published in the 1930's. Chronologically they are Kenneth Burke's *Counter-Statement* (1931), Richard Blackmur's *The Double Agent* (1935), Allen Tate's *Reactionary Essays on Poetry and Ideas* (1936), Yvor Winters's *Primitivism and Decadence* (1937), John Crowe Ransom's *The World's Body* (1938), and Cleanth Brooks's *Modern Poetry and the Tradition* (1939). Most of these works are collections of review articles: Blackmur on E. E. Cummings and Wallace Stevens; Tate on Donne and Robinson; Ransom on Milton and Eliot. Many of the essays would become classics of the New Criticism along with those in T. S. Eliot's first collection, *The Sacred Wood: Essays on Poetry and Criticism* (1920).

These early essays show us clearly the aims of the new critics. To them the literary work itself is paramount. The critic must stay with it until he has said all he can about what strategies the author has used in constructing it. There is no need to go outside the work for biographical facts. Because the poem or story is timeless, the critic has no business trying to place it in time. In a very real sense, so these critics believed, a work of literature is autonomous and has, so to speak, a life of its own. As soon as the poet prints his poem, it begins to lead its separate life. Consequently there is no point in asking the poet what his intentions were in writing it. He may have forgotten or he may never have known. Intention is beside the point, in any event. We need to know what is there, present and active—not what the poet hoped would be there.

In discussing individual works with this required minuteness, the new critics found the available critical vocabulary deficient. So they began inventing terms for what they observed about the poem's structure, diction, syntax, metaphors, and symbols. These terms have been pinned on their inventors rather like badges or medals: Tate's "tension in poetry"; Winters's "pseudo-reference"; Empson's "seven types of ambiguity"; Ransom's "ontological criticism"; I. A. Richards's "stock response"; Blackmur's "language as gesture"; Warren's "pure and impure poetry." T. S. Eliot wears the most ribbons. To name only a few: "objective correlative"; "the dissociation of sensibility"; "poetic assent"; the autotelic nature of a work of art. When William Elton prepared his "Glossary of the New Criticism" for *Poetry*, his article was so long that it had to be serialized in three issues, in December 1948 and January and February 1949. It contains 115 items which range alphabetically from "action, symbolic" to "wit."

The New Critics moved on from the explication of individual works to speculations about the nature of literature and the relations between literature and criticism. Either in a single essay or a full-length book each of them sooner or later stated his critical position and described his ideal critic. If the portrait was a self-portrait, this was natural enough. Taken together these expositions of critical methods and aims constitute the most impressive body of writing about the art of criticism to be found in any language.

You may have noticed that thus far my approach has been mainly expository. This was, if I may use the horrid word, my "intention." I wished to give you an idea of the bewildering rapidity with which critical concepts have been arriving over the past four decades. These shifts compelled the literary scholar to change color or risk being terribly exposed. Of course many scholars didn't in the least mind keeping their mauve coloration when the whole critical landscape turned, for the moment, moss green. But the chameleon is not compelled to change color and his change from mauve to green may depend on mood as well as a stimulus received from the conditions which surround him. There are still many moodily reluctant chameleons among my colleagues in the profession. They may have begun to lecture warily about symbols but they would go out the window if an archetype came in the door.

You have a right to ask what I think about the new colors in the critical landscape. In spite of some follies, I am glad we have moved from appreciation to technical criticism. I never found the role of exhorter very congenial, though I certainly want my students to enjoy what they read. Enjoyment comes first and should not be taken for granted by the critic or the teacher.

I do have some reservations. These theorists we have been talking about, like theorists in all fields, are sometimes too confident that they have found the truth and too ready to propagate their discoveries in the minds of the tender and the immature. The arguing and the testing should be kept out of the kindergarten, at least. How much more testing is needed I can demonstrate from two papers read at the English Institute in 1947. Professors Richard Chase and Donald Stauffer spoke, respectively, on "Myth as Literature" and "The Modern Myth of the Modern Myth." They were talking about quite different matters. It would be impossible to print the two papers together and say to a student: "Here you have it. Here is what we know about myth and literature."

As for that blessed word "archetype," the situation is still more confused. While Jung, the Zürich wise old man, continued to discover new archetypes, Professor Frye ran off with his word and built a critical system on it. Does Jung have the patent, or Frye?

So far as the use of the new theories in teaching is concerned, I am aware of two dangers. A teacher who becomes enamored of one or another of these theories is likely to praise his love to the exclusion of other possible favorites. This is why, as I said earlier, the stress in one classroom is on symbolic structure while next door the archetypes are being given a run-through. Students learn fast in such situations, as we know. I have a colleague who rides his novel theory of literature hard. He believes that writers, by and large, have to be adroit, covert even, in order to make their points. They must trap the reader into acceptance and belief. His students, as you will imagine, try to turn up a mouse trap on every page.

The second danger is—if I may invent a new-critical term myself—the reductive fallacy. If a poem has a symbolic structure, once you have said that, you have said all—or so the bemused student is inclined to believe. We have before us an autonomous, autotelic work of art which deserves a careful, thoughtful, loving, full-scale analysis. Yet, if the student knows which button to touch, it can be reduced to one of the seven types of ambiguity or to the quest for myth. Critical button-pushing can be as mindless as the warm glow of mere appreciation.

RENÉ WELLEK

The Literary Criticism of
Frank Raymond Leavis

Exactly a year ago, the name of F. R. Leavis appeared in many
American newspapers. The *New York Times* carried his picture and
a shocked report of a lecture at Downing College, Cambridge, delivered 28 February 1962, attacking Sir Charles Snow and his pamphlet
The Two Cultures and the Scientific Revolution.[1] The violent tone
of Leavis's criticism and the even more violently vituperative rash
of letters answering Leavis in the British press caused an enormous
sensation. Few commentators sided with Leavis: as far as I know
only Lionel Trilling in an article "Science, Literature and Culture:
The Leavis-Snow Controversy,"[2] though deploring Leavis's "unexampled ferocity," saw that Leavis was right in dismissing Sir Charles's
contrast between an old bad literary and a new good scientific culture.
Still, Leavis damaged his case not only by the acerbity of his tone
but by confusing the issue with a denunciation of the quality of
Snow's novels. It is, however, not true that Leavis did not argue the
case for literature at all. He not only denounced the emptiness of the
"social hope" held out by Snow, but he tried to show, though briefly
and obliquely, that men of letters such as Ruskin and Arnold came
to grips with the social question and that imaginative novelists such
as Conrad and Lawrence offered an ideal of life lived with self-
awareness, intelligence, and responsibility totally inaccessible to the

RENÉ WELLEK is Sterling Professor of Comparative Literature and Chairman
of the Department at Yale University.

[1] *New York Times*, 10 March 1962. Leavis's lecture was printed as "The Significance
of C. P. Snow," *Spectator*, 9 March 1962, pp. 297–303. Snow's pamphlet was his Rede
Lecture, Cambridge, 1959.

[2] *Commentary*, XXXIII (1962), 461–477. Leavis, in "A New Preface for the American Reader" to *Two Cultures? The Significance of C. P. Snow* (New York, 1963),
chides Trilling as "guilty of *la trahison des clercs*" (p. 16), surprisingly and perversely.

uncritical faith in hygienic and technological progress embraced by Sir Charles Snow. Unfortunately Leavis focused on the local English and even Cambridge issue of teaching literature and literary criticism, which he felt was endangered by the spread of scientific education and by the academic scholarship and criticism of the ruling professors of literature. Leavis was about to retire, at sixty-seven, from his lectureship, and he felt that his work and influence was being destroyed or discontinued. It was a parting shot, a bitter gesture of defiance.

Contrary to a widespread impression, Leavis did not and does not represent English teaching at Cambridge. Rather, he always struggled on the fringe of the university in opposition to the ruling group. For five years (1931–36) he was even denied a lectureship. In E. M. Tillyard's little book, *The Muse Unchained*, which professes to give "an intimate account of the revolution of English studies at Cambridge," Leavis is pointedly ignored, though his periodical, *Scrutiny*, is condemned for its dogmatism and authoritarian tone.[3] Leavis, in spite of official disapproval, succeeded in establishing a potent center of English studies at Downing College, which has carried his influence far and wide into English education through the agency of small but devoted groups of disciples. *Scrutiny*, which ran for twenty-one years, from 1932 to 1953, may not have been a financial success, but it became a widely noticed mouthpiece of the group. The Cambridge University Press will bring out a reprint of the complete run of the nineteen volumes of the magazine. An anthology from *Scrutiny*, *The Importance of Scrutiny*, edited by Eric Bentley (1948), first attracted attention to the group in this country; paperback editions of Leavis's writings are penetrating into the remotest college bookshops of the United States, and recently the seven-volume *Pelican Guide to English Literature* (1954–61), edited by one of Leavis's disciples, Boris Ford, has been selling at a tremendous rate. It is almost entirely written by former contributors to *Scrutiny* or personal pupils and represents his views most faithfully. A number of Leavis's closest associates have achieved academic status or at least reputation as critics: for example, L. C. Knights, now professor at Bristol University, is well known for his pamphlet *How Many Children Had Lady Macbeth?* (1933), and his book *Drama and Society in the Age of Jonson* (1937), a collection of essays, *Explorations* (1947), and the more recent *Some Shakespearean Themes* (1959) and *An Approach to Hamlet* (1960). Derek Traversi, a Welshman in spite of his Italian name, the author of two well-known books on Shakespeare,[4] is another Leavisite. Martin

---

3 (London, 1958), pp. 128–129.

4 *An Approach to Shakespeare* (London, 1938; new ed.; Garden City, N.Y., 1956) and *Shakespeare: The Last Phase* (London, 1955).

Turnell's books, *The Classical Moment* (1946), *The Novel in France* (1951), *Baudelaire* (1953), and *The Art of French Fiction* (1959), constitute a large body of comment on modern French literature. An American student of Leavis, Marius Bewley, has written two books, *The Complex Fate* (1952) and *The Eccentric Design* (1959), on the tradition of the American nineteenth-century novel. There is even a Frenchman, Henri Fluchère, the author of good books on Shakespeare and Laurence Sterne,[5] who has had early associations with Leavis and sympathizes with his general outlook.

I mention these facts, which could be easily added to, in order to suggest that Leavis's own view of his utter failure and isolation is a case of grossly misplaced self-pity. It is undoubtedly true that Leavis suffered persecution: he is still frequently treated with silent contempt or dismissed as a "cold intellectual." Leavis is, after all, reaping what he sowed. It would be childish to try to ascertain who, in each instance, began the fight. Leavis, no doubt, antagonized the older academic scholars and recently has emphasized his differences from Eliot and what in England is called the school of "Christian discrimination"; he always rejected Marxism and its allies; and he has shown only contempt for the mass media of literary information: the *Times Literary Supplement*, the Third Program of the BBC, the Sunday papers and the left-wing weeklies; and he has also, with some perversity, underlined his differences from the American New Critics and from F. W. Bateson, the editor of the rival journal, *Essays in Criticism*. Leavis is a man with a chip on his shoulder, a man of strong convictions, and even resentments, of harsh polemical manners, who has not practiced diplomacy and sometimes not even ordinary courtesy. He should be pleased that, with all these handicaps of temperament and situation, he has succeeded in establishing himself as the most influential English critic of this century after Eliot. There is a Leavis position, even an orthodoxy which can be described and criticized.

Leavis's initial views were a development of Eliot's insight and taste modified by some moral and generally cultural preoccupations reminiscent of Matthew Arnold. Leavis (as he is the first to acknowledge)[6] is deeply influenced by the early Eliot. His first major book, *New Bearings in English Poetry* (1932), can be described as an exposition, development, and application of Eliot's point of view: he

[5] *Shakespeare* (Paris, 1948), English translation with Preface by T. S. Eliot (London, 1953); *Laurence Sterne* (Paris, 1961).

[6] See Preface to *New Bearings* (for this and other books by Leavis mentioned in the notes see Bibliographical Note, below), p. ix; *Common Pursuit*, p. 280; and, more grudgingly, "T. S. Eliot's Stature as Critic," *Commentary*, XXVI (1958), 399.

starts with a sharp criticism of the Victorian and Georgian tradition, its conceptions of the "poetical," its escape into a dream world, its loss of touch with the intelligence of the age which led to the plight of poetry in the modern world as something inconsequential, as a polite amusement. In describing the situation at the end of the war, Leavis singles out for praise only the later Yeats, a few poems by Hardy, and something in Edward Thomas. He comes down hard on Rupert Brooke, on A. E. Housman, and Robert Bridges, and then launches into an exposition of T. S. Eliot, commenting on "Waste Land," "Gerontion," and "Ash-Wednesday" perceptively and sympathetically. The chapter on Pound is less favorable; but Leavis admires *Hugh Selwyn Mauberley* as a great poem, while he is—very properly—uneasy about the *Cantos*, which "appear to be little more than a game—a game serious with the seriousness of pedantry."[7] The chapter on Hopkins was one of the earliest highly laudatory criticisms, a piece which seems to me still thoroughly convincing in its emphasis on Hopkins's integrity and novelty, in its concern to dismiss the attempts to reconcile Hopkins with Victorianism and its lack of interest in Hopkins's metrical theory. He concludes, "A technique so much concerned with inner division, friction, and psychological complexities in general has a special bearing on the problems of contemporary poetry. He is likely to prove, for our time and the future, the only influential poet of the Victorian age, and he seems to me the greatest."[8] The love for Hopkins distinguishes Leavis from Eliot, and the last chapter shows Leavis's social concern—for the process of standardization, mass production, and leveling-down in literature, which became one of the major preoccupations of his periodical.

The second book of criticism, *Revaluation* (1936), can be described as an application of Eliot's methods and insights to the history of English poetry. It is, in a sketchy manner, the first consistent attempt I know of to rewrite the history of English poetry from a twentieth-century point of view. Spenser, Milton, Tennyson, the Pre-Raphaelites recede into the background; Donne, Pope, Wordsworth and Keats in part, Hopkins, the later Yeats, and T. S. Eliot move into the foreground. Leavis, more than Eliot, is concerned with establishing continuities: for example, on the seventeenth century he argues that the "line of wit" runs from Ben Jonson (and Donne) through Carew and Marvell to Pope. The chapter on Pope discovers his metaphysical descent; the chapter on Wordsworth makes much of the affinity with the eighteenth-century Georgic tradition. But the focus and tone of the chapters is rather various; the book, made up of articles, though

---

[7] *New Bearings*, p. 155.   [8] *Ibid.*, p. 193.

making a whole, shifts in its preoccupations: the chapter on Milton is an attack on his style and verse pursuing Eliot's suggestions, while the essay on Pope strikingly shows how Pope was inspired by an ideal of a civilization in which Art and Nature should be reconnected and humane culture be "kept appropriately aware of its derivation from and dependence on the culture of the soil."[9] Similarly, Wordsworth is discussed in terms of his "essential sanity and normality,"[10] and Keats in terms of moral maturity, of his "tragic experience, met by discipline."[11] The one chapter which is almost entirely negative is on Shelley, whose poetry is called "repetitive, vaporous, monotonously self-regarding, and often emotionally cheap."[12] The general agreement with Eliot both in implied standards and in taste is obvious. But Leavis does not share Eliot's interest in Dryden; he is much more sympathetic to Pope; and Eliot has little of Leavis's interest in Wordsworth and Keats.

The third book, *The Great Tradition* (1948), is devoted to the English novel. Actually, it contains only essays on George Eliot, Henry James, and Joseph Conrad. The introduction justifies and somewhat expands this choice of the tradition. Leavis disparages the eighteenth-century novelists Fielding and Sterne,[13] and sees Jane Austen as the wellhead of the English novel. No detailed consideration is given to her because Mrs. Leavis had written several long articles on her for *Scrutiny*,[14] which presumably would find Leavis's endorsement. But he traces Jane Austen's influence on George Eliot and hence to James, who went to school to George Eliot, and there is no need to argue that Conrad comes, in part, from James. Leavis has little use for Thackeray, a "greater Trollope." He dislikes Meredith; he cannot bring himself to consider Hardy a major novelist; and he dismisses Emily Brontë's *Wuthering Heights* as a "kind of sport."[15] Most astonishingly he excludes Dickens, who seems not to have "total significance of a profoundly serious kind." "That Dickens was a great genius and is permanently among the classics is certain. But the genius was that of a great entertainer."[16] Leavis somewhat perversely picks out *Hard Times* as a neglected book and gives it a sympathetic

---

[9] *Revaluation*, p. 80.

[10] *Ibid.*, p. 174.

[11] *Ibid.*, p. 272.

[12] *Importance of Scrutiny*, p. 39.

[13] *Great Tradition*, pp. 2–3: "Life isn't long enough to permit one's giving much time to Fielding." "Sterne's irresponsible (and nasty) trifling."

[14] Q. D. Leavis, "A Critical Theory of Jane Austen's Writings," *Scrutiny*, X (1941), 61–87, 114–142, 272–294; and XII (1944), 104–119 (on the Letters).

[15] *Great Tradition*, p. 27.

[16] *Ibid.*, p. 19. On *Hard Times*, Appendix, pp. 227–248.

reading that well isolates the wonderfully successful passages in a book which I cannot help feeling is, in general, a failure. The introduction also dismisses Joyce as a dead-end and praises, among recent novelists, only D. H. Lawrence, on whom Leavis had early written a sober little pamphlet (1930) and to whom he devoted his last book, *D. H. Lawrence: Novelist* (1955). Lawrence is to him "the great creative genius of our age, and one of the greatest figures in English literature," whom Leavis constantly and consistently defends for his fundamental intelligence and sanity, for his correct diagnosis of the ills of modern civilization. According to Leavis, "Lawrence belongs to the same ethical and religious tradition as George Eliot"[17]—the rural and nonconformist England. Leavis exalts *The Rainbow* and *Women in Love* as Lawrence's two greatest novels and keeps up a running fire against T. S. Eliot and other disparagers of Lawrence's creed or art. But Leavis's selection from Lawrence's other writings seems often extremely dubious: he extolls the dreary allegory, *St. Mawr*, or such a black-and-white fable as "The Daughters of the Vicar." He completely shirks discussing *The Man Who Died* and hardly comes to grips with Lawrence's politics or his peculiar "love ethic." *The Great Tradition* has its center in the essays on George Eliot, whom Leavis admires greatly and whom he helped to bring back from the comparative eclipse she had suffered. Leavis stresses George Eliot's later work: *Middlemarch*, parts of *Felix Holt*, and particularly *Daniel Deronda*, from which he would like to extricate the story of Gwendolen Harleth for separate publication and high appreciation.[18] The James essays emphasize the middle novels, in particular *The Portrait of a Lady*, and are sharply critical of the very late James. While in general it seems to me right to prefer the middle James, I find it impossible to dismiss *The Ambassadors* as brusquely as Leavis does and to give a reading to *The Wings of the Dove* and *The Golden Bowl* which not only sees James as losing his grip on reality but makes him morally obtuse and blind. The essays on Conrad extend the greatest admiration to *The Secret Agent* and *Nostromo* and disparage the early Malayan stories. *The Great Tradition* must be judged by the success of these essays, however much we may object to the harsh selectivity exercised among the books of Leavis's favorite writers; we must not be too put out by the sweeping dismissals of the first chapter.

The Common Pursuit (1952)—the title comes from Eliot's "Function of Criticism"—is a miscellaneous volume of essays. It reprints two

---

[17] *D. H. Lawrence*, pp. 18, 303, 204, 98, 104, 107.

[18] Recently Leavis withdrew the suggestion that the novel could or should be divided into two (see Introduction to G. Eliot, *Daniel Deronda* [New York, 1961], p. xiv; see *Commentary*, XXX [1960], 318).

widely noted but perverse essays: one on "The Irony of Swift" which makes Swift a purely destructive, though intense and powerful writer and ignores his implied religious and rationalist standards; and the piece on Othello, "Diabolic Intellect and the Noble Hero," which goes to the other extreme of Bradley's sentimental worship of the noble Moor. Othello appears as a brutal, obtuse egotist, sensual, stupid and jealous, who even in his last speech indulges only in rhetorical self-deception. Scattered essays can be found in Bentley's anthology, in *Commentary*, the *Sewanee Review*, and elsewhere. They become either more shrill and strident, as the polemical article against T. S. Eliot's criticism,[19] or show rather new interests or shifts of interest. The introduction to Marius Bewley's *Complex Fate* (1952) is Leavis's fullest pronouncement on the American novel and its great tradition, which he finds in Hawthorne and James and to which he would like to link Mark Twain. Leavis disparages the frontier tradition which "derives an illicit respectability from the aura of Mark Twain,"[20] and the whole attempt to exalt Whitman, Dreiser, and Scott Fitzgerald and their "Americanness" at the expense of what Leavis feels are the greatest and finest American writers: Hawthorne, James, and Mark Twain. It is only logical that Leavis also disparages Van Wyck Brooks for his uncritical nationalism and his interpretations of James and Mark Twain as defaulters from America.[21] Other new essays by Leavis are surprisingly mild and even conventional; thus an essay on *Dombey and Son*[22] is a quiet retraction (though not unreserved) of his earlier view of Dickens as a "great entertainer" outside the tradition of the English novel.

We come to better grips with Leavis's position if we abandon the attempt to describe his opinions and try to define his standards and methods. This is not quite easy, as Leavis himself constantly emphasizes his lack of interest in philosophical theory, in systematic defense and argument about principles, and recommends always a purely empirical textual approach to literary criticism.

I myself became the target of a piece, "Literary Criticism and Philosophy,"[23] in which I was selected as the occasion for Leavis's

[19] See n. 6 above.

[20] *The Complex Fate*, p. ix.

[21] "The Americanness of American Literature: A British Demurrer to Van Wyck Brooks," *Commentary*, XIV (1952), 466–474.

[22] *Sewanee Review*, LXX (1962), 177–201. See also the essay on Conrad's *Shadow Line*, *ibid.*, LXVI (1958), 179–200.

[23] Originally in *Scrutiny*, VI (1937), 59–70; reprinted with my original letter in *Importance of Scrutiny*, pp. 30–40, and without my piece in *The Common Pursuit*, pp. 211–222.

sharp discrimination between philosophy and literary criticism. I am several times called "a philosopher," presumably because I had written a book on *Immanuel Kant in England* and because I had tried to show that Leavis misunderstands the philosophy of the English Romantic poets. I became something of a straw man to knock down, a role I do not relish, as I did and do not hold the extreme intellectualist opinions he ascribes to me. I entirely agree with Leavis's general distinction between philosophy and poetry. It is not surprising, then, that my book *Theory of Literature* was reviewed in *Scrutiny* very unfavorably by an American follower of Leavis, Seymour Betsky.[24] He attempts to make me the propounder of a typically American, industrial, efficient, aridly theoretical ideal of scholarship. Leavis seems to have endorsed the review, as he chides F. W. Bateson for praising the book.[25] In the early piece, "Literary Criticism and Philosophy," Leavis emphasizes that they are two distinct and different kinds of discipline. The critic of poetry is the complete reader; the ideal critic is the ideal reader.

Words in poetry invite us, not to "think about" and judge, but to "feel into" or "become"—to realize a complex experience that is given in the words. . . . The critic's aim is, first, to realize as sensitively and completely as possible this or that which claims his attention, and a certain valuing is implicit in the realizing. As he matures in experience of the new thing he asks, explicitly and implicitly: "Where does this come? How does it stand in relation to . . . ? How relatively important does it seem?" And the organization into which it settles is . . . not a theoretical system or a system determined by abstract considerations.[26]

In a fairly recent discussion with L. A. Lerner,[27] Leavis seems to have shifted his ground slightly. He is puzzled by a pronouncement of one of his contributors quoted against him. Mr. Geoffrey Walton had said that "too great a concern with fundamentals, to repeat a *Scrutiny* platitude, is ruinous to literary criticism."[28] Leavis now recognizes more explicitly that a critic is concerned with critical principles, with fundamentals, but still insists that a discussion of fundamentals must not be philosophical. Criteria and grounds of criticism are now Leavis's concern, though they are defined only in the actual process of criticism.

[24] "The New Antiquarianism," *Scrutiny*, XVI (1949), 260–264.

[25] "The Responsible Critic," *Scrutiny*, XIX (1953), 182.

[26] *Importance of Scrutiny*, pp. 31–32.

[27] "Correspondence," *London Magazine*, II (1955), No. 3, pp. 77–83; a reply to L. D. Lerner's "The Life and Death of *Scrutiny*," *ibid.*, No. 1, pp. 68–77.

[28] Review of M. M. Mahood's *Poetry and Humanism*, *Scrutiny*, XVII (1951), 278. The context shows that Walton is thinking of religion. Leavis was unable to locate the passage.

His main concern is always with the concrete. "I hoped, by putting in front of them [the readers of poetry] in a criticism that should keep as close to the concrete as possible my own developed 'coherence of response,' to get them to agree . . . that the map, the essential order, of English poetry seen as a whole did, when they interrogated their experience, look like that to them also."[29] Leavis sees criticism very much in terms of pedagogy. "It trains, in a way no other discipline can, intelligence and sensibility together, cultivating a sensitiveness and precision of response and a delicate integrity of intelligence."[30] While it implies an "appreciative habituation to the subtleties of language,"[31] "everything must start from and be associated with the training of sensibility. It should, by continual insistence and varied exercise in analysis, be enforced that literature is made of words, and that everything worth saying in criticism of verse and prose can be related to judgments concerning particular arrangements of words on the page."[32]

This emphasis on the textual, even on the texture of the text in front of us, leads in Leavis to a complete dismissal of what is ordinarily called "literary history" or "scholarship." "There is no more futile study than that which ends with mere knowledge *about* literature. . . . The study of a literary text about which the student cannot say, or isn't concerned to be able to say, as a matter of first-hand perception and judgment—of intelligent realization—why it should be worth study is a self-stultifying occupation."[33] "Literary history" is called a "worthless acquisition; worthless for the student who cannot as a critic—that is, as an intelligent and discerning reader—make a personal approach to the essential data of the literary historian, the works of literature (an approach is personal or it is nothing: you cannot take over the appreciation of a poem, and unappreciated, the poem isn't 'there')."[34] Or similarly, "For the purposes of criticism, scholarship, unless directed by an intelligent interest in poetry . . . is useless."[35] In a very interesting exchange with F. W. Bateson, Leavis argues that the distinction between literary criticism and literary history made by Bateson, the difference between opinion and fact, is extraordinarily uncritical. "What is this 'fact' of the 'dependence of Dryden's poetry on Waller's'?" he asks.

I should like to see by what "sober evidence-weighing" Mr. Bateson would set out to establish it. The only evidence he specifies is "that provided by

29 *Importance*, p. 33.

30 *Education and the University*, p. 34.   33 *Ibid.*, pp. 67–68.

31 *Ibid.*, p. 38.   34 *Ibid.*, p. 68.

32 *Ibid.*, p. 120.   35 *Common Pursuit*, p. 9.

parallel passages"—by which, indeed, Dryden can be proved to have read Waller just as he can be proved to have read Cowley and Milton. But the most sober weighing can go no further, except in terms of critical judgements of a most complex and delicate order: "dependence" in any sense that can interest anyone interested in poetry . . . is still to be determined, estimated, defined, or pooh-poohed. . . . Mr. Bateson as literary historian can have access to the work he proposes to deal with—to his most essential facts—only if he is sufficiently a critic; only by an appropriate and discriminating response to them; a response that is, involving the kind of activity that produces value-judgements. And these judgements are not, in so far as they are real, expressions of opinion on facts that can be possessed and handled neutrally.[36]

Only very rarely does Leavis make some concessions to theory: he admits that a "critique of criticism" is needed[37] and he occasionally discusses other critics. Aristotle's *Poetics*, he thinks, does not itself provide the means of making one a better critic. One must take a critical apparatus to it, to derive any benefit from it.[38] Dryden's criticism he thinks much overrated: Dryden "showed strength and distinction in independent judgement, but I cannot believe that his discussion of any topic has much to offer us."[39] Leavis admires Dr. Johnson as a critic: he emphasizes his empiricism. "Johnson's recourse to experience is so constant and uncompromising and so subversive of Neo-classic authority that it is misleading to bring him under the Neo-classic head."[40] But he sees the defects of his sensibility,[41] for example, in his treatment of Shakespeare, in his preference for the comedies,[42] his bondage to the moralistic fallacy, his obtuseness to dramatic form. Leavis has hardly any use for Coleridge as a critic. He dismisses his aesthetics as a "nuisance" and comes to the conclusion that his "currency as an academic classic is something of a scandal,"[43] but he recognizes the value of some of his reflections on meter and imagery, and the novelty of his literary opinions. The student, he declares bluntly, "will have no use at all for Hazlitt or Lamb."[44]

Arnold appeals to him most of the older English critics. He admires his plea for critical intelligence and critical standards and the statement of the idea of "centrality"; he defends the phrase about "criticism of life." "Arnold's phrase is sufficiently explained—and, I think, vindicated—as expressing an intention directly counter to the tendency that finds its consummation in 'Art for Art's sake.'" Leavis, with his

---

36 *Importance of Scrutiny*, p. 21.

37 *Education*, p. 132.

38 *Ibid.*, p. 133.

39 *Importance*, p. 98.

40 *Ibid.*, p. 71.

41 *Ibid.*, p. 58.

42 *Common Pursuit*, p. 108.

43 *Importance*, p. 86.

44 *Education*, p. 133.

characteristic enmity toward theory, defends Arnold's lack of definition and explanation. His business was to evoke the criteria and not to define them. Similarly, he defends even the touchstones. "It is a tip for mobilizing our sensibility; for focussing our relevant experience in a sensitive point; for reminding us vividly what the best is like." Arnold may lack "the gift for consistency or for definition," but he has positive virtues: "tact and delicacy, a habit of keeping in sensitive touch with the concrete." Whatever his limitations, Arnold seems to him "decidedly more of a critic than the Sainte-Beuve to whom he so deferred."[45]

The defense of Arnold illuminates Leavis's central concern for the preservation of tradition. Leavis thinks of tradition primarily as literary and social, and he deplores Eliot's subordination of tradition to religion. Leavis's point of view is not antireligious; nor is it purely aesthetic. In discussing Arnold, he quickly abandons him as a theological thinker but defends his concern for culture. "Many who deplore Arnold's way with religion will agree that, as other traditions relax and social forms disintegrate, it becomes correspondingly more important to preserve the literary tradition."[46] This attempt of criticism to preserve the literary tradition is necessarily secular. "Literary criticism must, in this sense [separable from any particular religious frame or bias] always be humanist; whatever it may end in, it must be humanist in approach, in so far as it is literary criticism and not something else."[47] But this humanism is emphatically not aestheticism. "I don't think that for any critic who understands his job there are any 'unique literary values' or any 'realm of the exclusively aesthetic.' But there *is*, for a critic, a problem of relevance, . . . an understanding of the resources of language, the nature of conventions, a specially developed sensibility"[48] which always precede concern for more remote sociological or cultural surrounding circumstances. Bateson, for example, is severely criticized for his sociological criticism. "The poem is a determinate thing; it is *there*; but there is nothing to correspond— nothing answering to Mr. Bateson's 'social context' that can be set over against the poem, or induced to re-establish itself round it as a kind of framework or completion, and there never *was* anything."[49]

While Leavis rejects sociological or religious criteria, Marxist or Catholic, he constantly returns to the moral, social, and vital implications of literature. While he rejects ordinary didacticism, he emphasizes that the critical act implies "moral discrimination, and judge-

[45] *Importance*, pp. 89, 93, 95, 96, 98.   [47] *Education*, p. 19.

[46] *Ibid.*, p. 91.   [48] *Common Pursuit*, p. 114.

[49] "The Responsible Critic," *Scrutiny*, XIX (1952), 174.

ment of relative human value."[50] He even asserts that the critic will be compelled to become "explicitly a moralist."[51] The method is described when Leavis defends his devastating analysis of a poem by Shelley ("That time is dead for ever, child"). "In the examination of his poetry the literary critic finds himself passing, by inevitable transitions, from describing characteristics to making adverse judgements about emotional quality; and from these to judgements that are pretty directly moral; and so to a kind of discussion in which, by its proper methods and in pursuit of its proper ends, literary criticism becomes the diagnosis of what, looking for an inclusive term, we can only call spiritual malady."[52] But also the social meaning of literature is precisely in these implications of health and disease, in a sound tradition of a good society. Literary tradition is, he admits, "largely a development of the language,"[53] but this is involved in a cultural and social pattern. In a little book written with Denys Thompson, *Culture and Environment* (1934), and in Mrs. Q. D. Leavis's *Fiction and the Reading Public* (1932), this thesis is pursued in sociological terms. It is a concern for the effect of mass production, standardization, leveling-down, advertising and its effects, the whole development of modern urban and industrial civilization, which is contrasted with the organic community of the English countryside and the communal life of earlier ages.

Mrs. Leavis analyzes concretely the different strata of English taste —high-brow, middle-brow, and low-brow—and accumulates a great mass of evidence for the successive deterioration of standards. In contrasting modern conditions with the past—the Elizabethan period, the eighteenth century, the Romantic Age—she always concludes that standards used to be higher and taste better. But in her exclusive regard for the "high-brow" she overlooks the genuine social function of much modest art and genuine craft and overrates the blessings of older ages. Classes whose tastes were simply not satisfied in earlier ages have become vocal today. Even though we may think that their voices are pretty raucous, speech seems better than silence, or mere inert acceptance of upper-class standards. But, of course, the Leavises deplore precisely this present lack of a central authority in criticism— the anarchy of values of our time—and propose to combat it by creating, at least, a small critical minority.

Leavis does constantly use a criterion of integration in a healthy

---

[50] *Great Tradition*, p. 29.

[51] *Importance*, p. 39.

[52] "Thought and Emotional Quality," *Scrutiny*, XIII (1945), 60.

[53] *Education*, p. 118.

society. For example, he describes Pope's concern for the "positive bases" or "the basic moral values of his civilization"; he praises Johnson and Crabbe for "bearing a serious relation to the life of their time"[54] which is lacking in Gray and Thomson. He criticizes the Restoration for having no "serious relations to the moral bases of society."[55] With him, the poet has always an important social function. "The poet is at the most conscious point of the race in his time,"[56] and literature is the "consciousness of the age."[57] Thus Johnson's feeling for a literary order is inseparable from a profound moral sense,[58] but this feeling is criticized, surely in too unqualified terms, as being one for a merely literary order which has lost a sense for social order, for Good Form, for a social code which is still overwhelmingly present in Pope. Dr. Johnson's manners may have been, at times, deplorably coarse, but his concern for social order is surely as intense as his regard for literary tradition.

Some of Leavis's pronouncements on tradition, on old society, even a social code, on order, etc., sound very conservative. The term "centrality" which comes from Arnold underlines this "humanism," the concern for "civilization" in an eighteenth-century sense, while other favorite terms—"maturity," "sanity," "discipline"—circumscribe the same values. Just as, negatively, Leavis always disparages emotionalism, afflatus, rhetoric, he would say of some lines of Shelley that they are "distasteful, because there is strong feeling, and the feeling is false. It is false because it is forced."[59] "Shelley offers the emotion in itself, unattached, in the void, while Wordsworth's emotion seems to derive from what is presented."[60] It is in Eliot's term, attached to some "objective correlative."

But these standards are often modified in Leavis, and possibly contradicted by a concern for Life, for vitality. At times this merely means a proper concern for reality, a distaste for aestheticism, an emphasis on the empirical. The three great novelists Leavis admires most, George Eliot, Henry James, and Conrad, "are all distinguished by a vital capacity for experience, a kind of reverent openness before life, and a marked moral intensity."[61] In the Keats essay the emphasis on life is also, sometimes simply, anti-aesthetic. "Keats's aestheticism does not mean any such cutting off of the special valued order of experience from direct, vulgar living ('Live!—our servants will do that for us'), as is implied in the aesthetic antithesis of Art and Life."[62] But

54 *Revaluation*, pp. 77, 83, 105.

55 *Ibid.*, p. 113.

56 *New Bearings*, p. 13.

57 *Education*, p. 119.

58 *Revaluation*, p. 117.

59 *Ibid.*, p. 237.

60 *Ibid.*, p. 214.

61 *Great Tradition*, p. 9.

62 *Revaluation*, p. 257.

"life" assumes there the more doubtful role of a criterion of health. "The 'Ode to a Nightingale,' " Leavis says strangely, "moves outwards and upwards towards life as strongly as it moves downwards towards extinction."[63] Life, with Leavis, becomes a dynamic, vitalistic force. The praise of Lawrence even as a critic is thus justified. "He has an unfailingly sure sense of the difference between that which makes for life and that which tends away from health. It is this that makes him a so much better critic than Eliot."[64]

But it would be unjust to emphasize only these moral, social, and vitalistic criteria in Leavis. He does, after all, start usually with an examination of the text, with aesthetic observations. But there he always insists that all elements collaborate and are not really divorceable. In criticizing Pound's distinctions between melopoeia, phanopoeia, and logopoeia, Leavis makes the point that melopoeia is quite inseparable from meaning and from imagery, and that phanopoeia, imagery, is not merely visual, still less a matter of seeing little pictures. "It may range from incipient suggestion . . . to complete realization."[65] "Technique can be studied and judged only in terms of the sensibility it expresses." Otherwise it "is an unprofitable abstraction."[66] Still, Leavis, like Eliot, in practice constantly values sharply visualized poetry, sensuous particularity, the lack of which he feels in Milton especially strongly. Like Eliot, Leavis insists on language vitally related to common speech. Milton is criticized for "renouncing the English language,"[67] while Hopkins, "paradoxical as it may sound to say so, brought poetry much closer to living speech."[68] Poetry, however, must not flatter the singing voice, should not be merely mellifluous, should not, for example, give a mere general sense of motion. Incantatory poetry, remote from speech, is always disparaged. Milton treats language as "a kind of musical medium outside himself";[69] he "seems to be focussing rather upon words than upon perceptions, sensations or things." "He exhibits a feeling *for* words rather than a capacity for feeling *through* words."[70] Language, while considered the immediate surface of literature, is thus only a surface leading to things, to objects, to reality. The linguistic interest in Leavis is strictly subordinate to his interest in what he would call life. Thus the emphasis on the text is somewhat deceptive. Leavis's observations on linguistic points seem often vague and imprecise or concern

63 *Ibid.*, p. 246.

64 *D. H. Lawrence*, p. 311.

65 *Education*, p. 115.

66 *Ibid.*, p. 113.

67 *Revaluation*, p. 52.

68 *New Bearings*, p. 168.

69 *Ibid.*, p. 82.

70 *Revaluation*, pp. 49–50.

the effect of individual words or reflect on imagery;[71] he is not interested in stylistics or metrics and avoids all technical analysis of this kind. He is also quite uninterested in questions of the technique of the novel. He will often speak about the "pressure behind words"[72] or "the absence of controlling pressure from within,"[73] which seems a mere gesture toward some indistinct feeling. Actually, he quickly leaves the verbal surface in order to define the particular emotion or sentiment which an author conveys. Like Croce, he is primarily interested in "sentiment" and hence soon becomes a moral and social critic.

There seems to me a contradiction between this emphasis on words and their final dismissal as servants whom you can only feel *through*, as there is a contradiction, or at least a tension, between Leavis's emphasis on civilized tradition, on humanism, and his advocacy of life for life's sake. It seems strange that he is able to admire (and I mean not passively but ardently) Eliot and Lawrence, though in recent years he has more and more turned against Eliot and exalted Lawrence to the position of the greatest English writer of the twentieth century. Leavis cares for Henry James, G. M. Hopkins, and Jane Austen on the one hand, and for Bunyan, Blake, and Mark Twain on the other. He cares for Pope and the "line of wit" as well as for the groping irrationalism of Lawrence. The central value, Life, is an ambiguous term which shifts from meaning "reality" and "truth" to "sincerity" and even to a "sense of community" and "oneness." On occasion Life assumes even a religious coloring, either in the literal sense of "religion" meaning "relation, bond, allegiance," a sense with which "men and women know that they 'do not belong to themselves,' " but are "responsible to something that transcends love and sex too."[74] Elsewhere Life means a feeling of "belonging in the universe," which seems to approximate Albert Schweitzer's "reverence for life":[75] it means often simply courage, devotion, and finally op-

---

[71] George Watson (*The Literary Critics* [Harmondsworth, 1962], p. 209) goes too far when he denies that Leavis is "a verbal analyst." He knows only one analysis, that of Arnold's sonnet on Shakespeare (in *Education and the University*). But there are two substantial articles, "Thought and Emotional Quality: Notes on the Analysis of Poetry" (*Scrutiny*, XIII [1945], 53–76) and "Imagery and Movement: Notes on the Analysis of Poetry" (*ibid.*, XVI [1948], 119–134), which discuss words ("diurnal"), kinetic imagery, metrical effects, etc. See also "*Antony and Cleopatra* and *All for Love*," *Scrutiny*, V (1936), 158–169, for a comparison commenting on verbal and metrical effects.

[72] *Revaluation*, p. 56.

[73] *Common Pursuit*, p. 57.

[74] *D. H. Lawrence*, p. 111.

[75] *Revaluation*, pp. 161, 164. On reverence see *Lawrence*, pp. 75, 127–128, 235.

timism. In a curious paper on tragedy (which puzzles me for its ignorance of any theory of tragedy besides Aristotle's and Santayana's), Leavis rejects *catharsis* as purging of the passions, as the achieving of equilibrium, of "calm—all passion spent." Tragedy rather has an exalting, exhilarating effect: it enhances our sense of life, frees us from the limitations of ourselves, makes us recognize value as in some way defined and vindicated by death.[76] Art thus always "ministers" to Life, serves the spontaneous-creative fulness of being. Artists who "do dirt on life" are disparaged: Eliot, particularly in the *Cocktail Party*, shows attitudes of "disgust and fear and rejection" to Life;[77] Flaubert lacks compassion and trust in human dignity.[78]

I am, I fear, too much of a theorist not to feel strongly the ambiguity, shiftiness, and vagueness of Leavis's ultimate value criterion, Life. In its implications and rejections it brings out the limitations of Leavis's concept of literature and the narrow range of his sympathies. Life for Leavis is first of all simply realist art—not merely in a sense of copying or transcribing a social situation, a dramatic, objective rendering of life, of course, but as we find it in Shakespeare and the English novel of the nineteenth century. In practice, Leavis has no sympathy for stylized, conventionalized art, the art defined in Ortega's *Dehumanization of the Arts*. This serious ideal of Life makes Leavis also suspicious of art which is merely playful, rococo, ornamental, aesthetic, formalistic in a narrow sense, while his optimism makes him hostile to out-and-out pessimists such as Hardy or Flaubert. Leavis's taste is rooted in nineteenth-century critical realism, to which he manages to add the early poetry of T. S. Eliot and a selection from the novels of D. H. Lawrence: *The Rainbow* and *Women in Love* in particular. He is really deeply hostile to what could be called modernism or avant-garde: to Joyce, Wyndham Lewis, Auden, Dylan Thomas, to almost every author who has become prominent in the last thirty years. He clings, as I suppose we all do, to the discoveries of his youth: Conrad, Lawrence, Hopkins, the early Eliot.

The emphasis on life in the sense of the concrete and immediate is connected with Leavis's concern with the English provincial rural tradition which he apparently finds in Shakespeare, in Bunyan, in Jane Austen, George Eliot, and D. H. Lawrence, all countryfolk of a sort to which the Londoners, Spenser, Milton, Dryden, provide a foil of learned urban poetry. Life means also pedagogy, the concern

[76] "Tragedy and the 'Medium,'" in *Common Pursuit*, p. 132.

[77] Reply to Robert D. Wagner, *Scrutiny*, XVIII (1951), 142. See also *D. H. Lawrence*, pp. 25–26, 308.

[78] *Great Tradition*, p. 60. See also *D. H. Lawrence*, pp. 25–26, 75, 86.

for his students, for the controversies of his university. It accounts also for what I cannot help calling Leavis's provinciality and insularity. Besides English and American, he seems to have no interest whatever in another literature: I can recall only a few highly laudatory references to Tolstoy and some critical remarks on Flaubert.[79] In *Scrutiny* he may have left French and German literature to the specialists, Martin Turnell and D. H. Enright. Leavis's gravest failing seems to me his distrust and even hatred for theory: his resolute, complacent, nominalistic empiricism, his worship of the concrete and particular at any price. This allows him to leave his norms unexamined: the standards of life, common speech, centrality, firm grasp of the actual, impersonality, no afflatus, no emotionality, but sharp concrete realization, sensuous particularity, presentment—all terms of praise which I quote literally from Leavis's writings, though he would object (and did so) that, stated so baldly, they are "intolerably clumsy."[80] I recognize that they assume their proper meaning only in a context, but they do represent implicit norms, an underlying scheme or pattern which is discoverable in every critic and which it is the business of a historian of criticism to describe and judge. The refusal to theorize has a paralyzing effect on Leavis's practice; it makes him reject the tools and concepts of technical analysis and be content with impressions or dogmatically stated feelings. He refers to the "complex rhythm organizing" *The Rainbow* without even attempting to describe it, or gropes to find terms for metrical or metaphorical effects in Donne which he can only sense but not name, or indulges in open contradictions when his feelings run counter to his unexamined presuppositions. Thus, we are told that "Johnson's abstractness here [in *The Vanity of Human Wishes*] doesn't exclude concreteness," since the style has "body," "a generalizing weight." Johnson's abstractions and generalities "focus a wide range of profoundly representative experience—experience felt by the reader as movingly present."[81] The struggle for expression, the entanglement in favorite words is painfully obvious in many passages of Leavis's tortuous and tortured writing, which, in its fierce clinging to the immediate, seems often to deny the life and light of Reason. Empiricism, observation, sensitive submission to the object postulated as an ideal have been increasingly

[79] On Flaubert see preceding note. On Tolstoy see "Note on Being an Artist," in *D. H. Lawrence*, pp. 297–302, commenting on the episode in *Anna Karenina*, in Venice, with the painter Mikhaylov. See also "T. S. Eliot's Stature as Critic," *Commentary*, XXVI (1958), 401.

[80] *Common Pursuit*, p. 215.

[81] *D. H. Lawrence*, p. 122; "Imagery and Movement," *Scrutiny*, XIII (1945), 124; *Common Pursuit*, p. 102.

in conflict with the obscurantist vitalism preached by Lawrence and accepted by Leavis with uncritical adoration.

Still, whatever Leavis's limitations, he has succeeded in defining his taste, identifying the tradition he considers central, and imposing his judgment on his contemporaries. Leavis has accomplished what he set out to do: "A judgment," he tells us, "is a real judgment, or it is nothing. It must, that is, be a sincere personal judgment; but it aspires to be more than personal. Essentially it has the form: 'This is so, is it not?' "[82] A great many of our contemporaries have answered "It is so," and this is after all the success which every critic who is not merely a theorist, but a molder of taste, can hope for. Leavis has defined and given voice to a widespread taste and change of taste. I am convinced that he will preserve a position in the history of English criticism not far distant and even different from that of the much sweeter tempered Matthew Arnold.

BIBLIOGRAPHICAL NOTE

For Leavis's ideas I quote his books when possible and only when those fail do I refer to his articles in *Scrutiny*, *Commentary*, etc.

New Bearings in English Poetry. London, 1932.
Revaluation: Tradition and Development in English Poetry. London, 1936.
Education and the University. 2d ed. London, 1948.
The Great Tradition. London, 1948.
The Importance of Scrutiny, edited by Eric Bentley. New York, 1948.
The Common Pursuit. London, 1952.
D. H. Lawrence: Novelist. London, 1955.
Two Cultures? The Significance of C. P. Snow. New York, 1963.

Comment on Leavis is still scarce, but, besides Bentley's introduction to *The Importance of Scrutiny*, see:

René Wellek, "Literary Criticism and Philosophy," *Scrutiny*, V (1937), 375–383, reprinted in Bentley, pp. 23–30, and "Correspondence: Literary Criticism and Philosophy," *Scrutiny*, VI (1937), 195–196.

H. A. Mason, "F. R. Leavis and *Scrutiny*," *Critic*, I (1947), 21–34.

Martin Jarrett-Kerr, "The Literary Criticism of F. R. Leavis," *Essays in Criticism*, II (1952), 351–368.

Bernard C. Heyl, "The Absolutism of F. R. Leavis," *Journal of Aesthetics and Art Criticism*, XIII (1954), 249–255.

L. D. Lerner, "The Life and Death of *Scrutiny*," *London Magazine*, II (1955), 68–77.

Eliseo Vivas, "Mr. Leavis on D. H. Lawrence," *Sewanee Review*, LXV (1957), 123–136.

[82] "Mr. Pryce-Jones, the British Council and British Culture," *Scrutiny*, XVIII (1951), 227.

Vincent Buckley, two chapters (pp. 158–213) in *Poetry and Morality*. London, 1959.

Andor Gomme, "Criticism and the Reading Public," in *The Modern Age*, pp. 350–376. *Pelican Guide to English Literature*, edited by Boris Ford, Vol. VII. Harmondsworth, Middlesex, 1961.

George Steiner, "F. R. Leavis," *Encounter*, XVIII (May 1962), 37–45.

Lionel Trilling, "Science, Literature and Culture: The Leavis-Snow Controversy," *Commentary*, XXXIII (1962), 461–77.

George Watson, in *The Literary Critics*, pp. 208–215. Harmondsworth, Middlesex, 1962.

In December 1947 I read a mimeographed paper on Leavis by Seymour Betsky.